P9-CMY-782

THE RETURN TO JUDAISM

The Return
to Judaism

Descendants from the Inquisition
Discovering Their Jewish Roots

Sandra Cumings Malamed

2010 · FITHIAN PRESS, McKINLEYVILLE, CALIFORNIA

COVER ILLUSTRATIONS

Manasseh ben Israel, portrait by Rembrandt van Rijn.
Eighteenth-century print from the collection of Sandra and Kenneth Malamed.
Photographed for production by Laird M. Malamed.

Passover Haggadah, two-page spread, printed in Holland.
From the collection of Sandra and Kenneth Malamed.
Photographed for production by Laird M. Malamed.

Auto da fé or burning at the stake.
Illustration courtesy of the Department of Special Collections, University of Notre Dame.
Photographed for production by Laird M. Malamed.

Published by Fithian Press
A division of Daniel and Daniel, Publishers, Inc.
Post Office Box 2790
McKinleyville, CA 95519
www.danielpublishing.com

Distributed by SCB Distributors (800) 729-6423

LIBRARY OF CONGRESS CATALOGING-IN-PUBLICATION DATA
Malamed, Sandra Cumings, (date)
The return to Judaism : descendants from the Inquisition discovering their Jewish roots / by Sandra
Cumings Malamed.
p. cm.
ISBN 978-1-56474-504-0 (pbk. : alk. paper)
1. Marranos—History. 2 Marranos—Interviews. 3. Marranos—Social life and customs.
4. Jews—Spain—History. 5. Jews—Portugal—History. 6. Sephardim—History. I. Title.
DS135.S7M26 2010
909'.04924—dc22
2010015666

Contents

Kol Nidre

Kol Nidre—chant of ages,
Chant of Israel, chant of sorrow,
Measuring off the throbbing heartbeats
Of a people bowed in anguish,
Crushed by tyrants, thwarted, broken,
Wand'ring ever—homeless, weary.
Generations set your motif
Out of trials, hopes, and yearnings,
Added each its variations
To your theme and to your cadence.
Diverse lands and diverse periods
Poured their soul into your music.
When we hearken with our hearts tuned,
We can hear the lamentations
Through time's corridor resounding;
We can see revealed before us
Heroes, martyrs, saints, and scholars,
Loyal, steadfast sons of Israel
Sanctifying God, their Father.

Kol Nidre—chant of ages,
Chant of pain and chant of pathos,
Mingled with your notes of sorrow
Vibrant measures trill and quiver,
Rising to a great crescendo
With the Jew's undying spirit
As he raises 'loft his Torah,
Symbol of his faith and vigor.
Notes of joyous exultation
Crept into your dirgeful music
As with fortitude held most sacred.
While our hearts beat to your rhythm,
Stir us with new consecration
To our fathers' God, to serve Him
With our heart and soul and fervor.

Kol Nidre—chant of ages,
Chant of grief and chant of triumph,
Echoing, this night of mem'ries,
In the ears and hearts of Israel,
Once again you draw together
All dispersed and all God's faithful
To return and humbly seek Him—
Supplicants for His grace and pardon.
Faced by grim, appalling forces
In these days of woeful living,
Do we plead before God's mercy
For His strength, His help, His guidance.

With your plaintive chant, Kol Nidre,
Rise our prayers to heaven ascending,
For a surcease of man's sorrows,
For the dawn of peace and freedom,
When all hearts are purged of hatred,
Passions, lusts that will rend asunder.
Then all men will stand together
To acknowledge God, their Father.

This prayer is sung at the beginning of the evening service on Yom Kippur, the Jewish Day of Atonement.

Preface

THIS BOOK GREW OUT OF a series of interviews I conducted in the 1990s. At that time I was becoming increasingly aware that there were people of Spanish and Portuguese descent, now living all over the world, who considered themselves Christians, or members of other religions, or even non-believers, who nonetheless practiced various Jewish traditions—often without knowing what these traditions were or where they came from.

Coming from a strong Judaic background, both as a scholar and as a practicing Jew, I found myself compelled to contact as many of these people as I could, to collect information about their family histories and the ongoing presence of Jewish traditions in their daily lives, and to explain to them if they were interested—and they all were interested—what these traditions were all about. Consequently I put the word out that I was interested in interviewing people who thought Judaism might be part of their families' histories, and before long people from all around the country and beyond began to contact me.

The interviews I conducted consisted of three parts. First, I gathered facts about the interviewee's life, such as his or her place of birth, family name, occupation, etc. The second part consisted of questions about the presence of ongoing Jewish traditions in their lives, such as their death rites, their dietary habits, and their practices concerning cleanliness and personal hygiene. Many of the questions I asked were derived from questions the ancestors of these people very likely had been asked by the Church or the government officials during the Inquisition in Spain and Portugal that took their Judaic traditions away. These questions were translated into English during the 1990s. Other questions I asked dealt with more subjective aspects of life, such as feelings, suspicions, joy or unhappiness, and personal needs. I also wanted to know about the interviewees' experiences with Jewish neighbors, club members, school friends, and adult friendships. I asked them what they knew and how they felt about Jewish history and about the State of Israel. During this part of the interview, I often responded to their answers, telling them how their answers reflected similarity in behavior to the worldwide Jewish community, showing parallels in such traditions as dietary laws, circumcision, and recurring holidays and customs throughout the year.

Part three was made up of the responses of the interviewees and the way they felt emotionally about the questions I had asked in the first two parts of the interview. At this point, many of them started asking questions of me: How would I use their answers? How would my findings be presented? I told them there would be four parts to a book: a history of the Inquisition, my interviews with the descendants of Marranos, a survey of Sephardic Judaism worldwide, and the concept of "Baal Teshuva." The follow-up question, of course, was, "What does 'Baal Teshuva' mean?"

"Baal," I explained, is the Hebrew word for "mouth." "Teshuva" means "to return." That was what these interviews meant for me. As I heard about the traditions told to me by each family, I in turn told them just what those traditions mean in Jewish beliefs and lore; so I put the words into their mouths, to help them return, to help them understand that their behavior is from their original Jewish tradition.

Each person I interviewed was an interested and willing participant in the project, and many of them stayed in contact with me after the interviews were over, contacting me often to add new thoughts and information about their families, their memories, and their emotions. Several of them have become my personal friends. After all, when questions this personal are probed, they can't help but touch the hearts and minds, and especially the souls, of both the interviewer and the interviewee. These people were like sponges, soaking up everything I could possibly tell them about their traditions, history, and the likelihood of their Jewish roots. I told each of them at the beginning of the interview that this was not an exercise to convert them, but rather to give them a chance to know their own heritage and to be able to pass it on to their children. For although their Jewish identity may have been taken away from them more than 500 years ago, they still had a right to know their origins and their heritage.

Baal Teshuva. That is why I conducted these interviews and why I wrote this book: to give them that chance.

Acknowledgments

I WISH TO THANK THE many people who allowed me to enter into their families' histories, for their cooperation with the interview process and for answering my questions so patiently. I also want to express my gratitude to the translators and interpreters who helped me when foreign languages became a barrier.

This book could never have materialized without the hard work of Dr. Wendy Maduff and Dr. Daniel Karen, who put all of my work onto the computer. Thank you so much.

Most of the photographs in this book were taken or processed by Laird Malamed, whose sensitivity to the archival materials, to the photographs of others, and to the objects he photographed is much appreciated. I can't thank him enough.

Elizabeth Malamed accompanied me to the Portuguese-Israelite Synagogue and cemetery in Amsterdam and to the old synagogues in Spain. I thank her for her beautiful drawings of these buildings and headstones, and for her excellent photography of Bevis Marks Synagogue in London.

My thanks to Ken for everything, always. And to Dr. Rebecca Malamed and Mr. Justin Silverman, who journeyed through the sugar plantations of Recife, Brazil, my thanks for their loving support and encouragement. I also wish to thank Mr. Eric Biederman, for his helpful search to find the right literary tools for my projects, and my publishers for their loving care of the work.

For friendship and support throughout the journey that became this book, I owe much gratitude to many people. There have been too many to mention them all by name, but I especially must acknowledge my thanks to Mimi and Marvin Friedman, Dr. Frank Crystal and Genie Crystal, Cindy and Sheldon Bass, Natalie and Marvin Shapiro, Lerma Maluluan, Dr. Tamara Kaufman, Elisabete Vieria, Deborah Green, Nancy Wang, Dr. Norman Fischer and Adrienne Fischer, Rabbi Irvin Ungar, Dr. Robert Peck and Ruth Peck, Delia Fishman, Daniel Maya, Carole Sherick, Roy Fiddler, Rochelle Caper, Arny Kaplan, Marla Harkness, Toby and Brandt Wax, Milton and Sheila Hyman, Doris Nuamu, Rabbi David Wolpe, Rabbi Marc Angel, Joseph Benevides, Zina Sherman, David Maya, Andrea Nolan, Paige Crystal, and Cantor Joseph Gole.

I also thank the following institutions for their cooperation and support: The

Archives of the Portuguese-Israelite Synagogue, Amsterdam; The Archives of Bevis Marks Synagogue, London; The Spanish Embassy and Historical Society of Córdoba; The Department of Special Collections of the University of Notre Dame; Arquivo Historico Judaico de Pernambuco, Recife, Pernambuco, Brazil; Eseme at the American Sephardi Federation; Sephardic House; and the Archives of Congregation Shearith Israel in New York.

Introduction

IN 1492 C.E., A DATE most commonly associated with Christopher Columbus's first voyage across the Atlantic, King Ferdinand and Queen Isabella of Spain expelled the Jewish citizens from their country. To most people, that year marks the beginning and the end of the Spanish expulsion of the Jews, and the climax of the Spanish Inquisition as far as Jews were concerned. This book, which is in part a brief history of the Inquisition, will show that the roots of the Inquisition and the expulsion go far back into history, even predating the time of Jesus Christ and the beginning of what is often called the Christian Era. On the other side of that important date, the persecution connected to the Spanish Inquisition and expulsion continued long afterwards, not only in Spain, but also in her many colonies in South and Central America, Mexico, the Caribbean Islands, Gibraltar, Morocco, and the Philippines. Portugal also persecuted Jewish people, beginning in 1496, both at home and abroad in her colonies, particularly in Brazil, the Azores, Madeira, India, and Africa.

This book will help people understand just how long the Spanish and Portuguese Inquisitions lasted, and how far-reaching the expulsions were. It is especially meant to educate descendants of those who endured the Inquisition and suffered the expulsion, people of the Jewish faith who now live in countries all over the world, who might not even know what their ancestors went through.

The lives of Jews who endured the Inquisition in the Iberian Peninsula were greatly altered. Many of them were forcibly converted from Judaism to the Catholic faith. These "Conversos," as they were known, or "Nuevos Cristos" ("New Christians"), "anusim" (the Hebrew word for "the forced ones"), or "Marranos" (the Spanish word for "pigs"), were required to give up their Jewish identity, including their religion, their customs and traditions, and in some cases even their names. Remarkably, however, many of the families' customs and traditions were preserved through the generations over the last 500 years, even though the reasons or meanings behind the traditions have more often than not been lost.

Interviewing Spanish and Portuguese descendants of the Marranos, who now live all over the world, I have been able to identify certain recurring Jewish traditions and explain to these people—many of them unaware of their Jewish heritage—what those traditions mean and where they came from. In some cases this new insight into their Jewish roots has inspired people to return to practicing the Jewish faith, at least on a partial basis. In others, it has sparked an interest in their family history, encouraging them to look even further into old records in their families' possession and to ask questions of other family members, especially the older ones, who could have remembered the generations that preceded them.

The possibility now exists for people all over the world—people who feel they may be descended from Jews who were forced to give up their ethnic and religious identity 500 years ago—to learn about and reclaim their heritage.

PART ONE

The Inquisition and the Marranos

LE PORTRAIT DE LA VOISIN.
Source de tant de maux maudite creature
Qui, par mille poisons destruisois la Nature,

OVERLEAF: THE DOMINICANS PREDICT....
From their headquarters on Lake Como, Italy, the
Fraternal Order of the Dominicans announced that an
Inquisition with persecutions instituted by the Papacy
would eventually take place in Spain.

Throughout the history of mankind, for many reasons, whole civilizations of people have come into being, been successful, and eventually ceased to exist. For example, the Vikings, who thrived from 793 C.E. to 1066 C.E. with their navigational and mercantile strength and sea-faring capabilities, came, conquered, and then went. The Babylonians who destroyed the first Temple in Israel, Solomon's Temple, and then took thousands of Jews into slavery in what is today Iraq, no longer exist. The Roman Empire, which destroyed the second Temple in Israel, ruled many areas of the world over centuries, with military, intellectual, and political prowess; but eventually Rome too disappeared.

The Grand Inquisition of Spain and Portugal tortured and killed thousands of people from 1347 C.E. to late in the nineteenth century, simply because they had Jewish roots and were successful financially. In spite of far-reaching autos da fé (religious cleansings) in many parts of the world, used as a threat to convert Jewish people to Catholicism, the days of the Inquisition ceased to exist. That regime, as powerful as it was, with both the blessings from the mouth of the Pope and the Crowns of both Spain and Portugal, is gone.

And finally, during the rise of Naziism and World War II, from 1933 to 1945, six million Jewish people lost their lives, exterminated by the very organized, tyrannical Adolf Hitler war machine of Germany, referred to as "The Third Reich." In addition, many people other than those of Jewish origin also were exterminated, including cripples, homosexuals, Moslems, and Gypsies. Finally stopped by the Allies, led by the United States Armed Forces, the Third Reich and Hitler were defeated.

There is one group of people with Jewish roots who, although they were forced to abandon their society and the civilization they knew, remain today as more than a mere remnant of their glorious past. Not just in archaeological digs, museums, or stories that are told, these are living people who are scattered throughout the world now. These people were and are called by many names: Marranos (Spanish for "pigs"), Conversos, and Nuevos Cristos or New Christians. Forced during the Inquisition to convert to Catholicism or die, by order of the Catholic Church and the political arms of both the Spanish and the Portuguese governments, their descendants still today keep certain customs in their homes and in their lives that bring them back to the Judaism that their ancestors practiced openly 500 years ago. And today, these descendants are questioning their own "unusual" habits that they recognize aren't Catholic or Christian, to find the deeper ties to their families' original roots as people of the Jewish faith who once lived an observant life in the rich and beautiful lands of Spain and then Portugal and their colonies. This is their story and it is really they to whom this book is dedicated.

CHAPTER ONE

The Jews in the Iberian Peninsula

IT HAS LONG BEEN THOUGHT that Jewish people have lived in the Iberian Peninsula since the sixth century c.e., and had also come to the area as traders as early as 300 b.c.e. with ancient mariners. The Phoenicians, who considered these lands the farthest point of Western Europe, called the area Espania, or the Hidden Land. Since trade relations between the ancient mariners and Hebrews had existed since the time of King David and of King Solomon, it has been thought that the Hebrew traders often came along with the Phoenicians to Espania. Hebrew coins have been unearthed in the Iberian city of Tarragona, from long before the arrival of the first Romans and the Visigoths to that area.

The Jewish people who come from this area are referred to as Sephardim, which is a word derived from Sefarad, found in Verse 20 of the book of Obadiah, in the Old Testament. Sefarad was a body of land that the Aramaic language version called Aspania. The Latin for Aspania became Hispania, and today we refer to it as Spain.

When Jews settled into Spain, a part of the Iberian Peninsula, they became the people of Spain (Sefarad), or Sephardim (the plural). Eventually, when the Jewish Sephardim moved into the area next door, called Portugal, after their expulsion from Spain in 1492, to join the Jews already living there, they were still called Sephardim. Today those Jews whose ancestors came from Spain or Portugal, no matter where in the world they lived since then, are still known as Sephardic Jews, or Sephardim.

Jewish people, or Sephardim, have lived in the Iberian Peninsula during the times of the Roman, Visigoth, Moslem, and finally, Christian governing bodies.

Jews became active participants in each of these societies; and although there were often periods of anti-Semitic rules and difficult, even torturous and murderous activities that they had to contend with, nothing matched in horror their treatment during the time of the Catholic Inquisition.

For many of those years, Jewish people were permitted some religious freedom and were even allowed to participate in the agriculture, merchant trades, and even public offices of Espania. All went well until King Reccared came to the Visigothic throne. He decided that all of his Visigothic people should be of Catholic persuasion, when he announced his own conversion at the Third Council of Toledo in

THE IBERIAN PENINSULA. *This 1730 map of Spain and Portugal shows Granada, Toledo, Barcelona, Girona, Seville, and Córdoba, the main communities for Jewish population in Spain.*

589 C.E. Included in his new edict were not only old Visigoths, but Hebrews (Jews) as well. General violence and open civil wars began to happen, leaving Spain (Espania) open to the next group of conquerors, who came from the Arab or Moslem world, beginning in 711 C.E.

Known as the people of the book, the Jews became the administrators of the Moslems' newly conquered towns and cities, serving often as treasurers, trading merchants, doctors, and scientists. Now under Moslem rule began what is known as the Golden Age for the Jews in Spain. During this time, Spanish Jewish people developed their sciences, arts, mercantile skills, music, poetry, and commentaries by citizens like Moses Maimonides, who codified all Jewish Law. They even developed a language of their own, called Ladino.

In the year 1107, the Jews of Moslem Spain began to see new rules from a fanatical faction of Moslems who were called Almoravides. They demanded all Jews be converted to their faith, called Islam, or be exiled. At the same time Moslems called Almohades came down from the north, also demanding that the Jews be converted to Islam or be exiled.

However, a greater threat to Jewish freedom in Iberia occurred in the form of the Christian re-conquest of Spain.

MOSES BEN MAIMONIDES. *This statue of the doctor, teacher, scientist, and rabbi is now outside the Synagogue in Córdoba, Spain.*

MAIMONIDES'S LOGICA. *This title page is from the 1527 first edition of Rabbi Maimonides's* Logica, *written in both Hebrew and Latin. It was the first work on logic written by a Jew. Maimonides began it in 1158 while he wandered with his family in exile from Córdoba, Spain, before settling in Fez, Morocco. Originally written in Arabic and titled* Magāla, Fi-Sina at Al-Mantiq, *it is a treatise on the 175 most important logical, physical, metaphysical, and ethical terms used in a discussion of logical theory.*

Between the thirteenth century and 1492, the Jewish people and the Moslem people of Spain were subject to the whims of the ecclesiastical proclamations of the Christian Church ordering their conversion to the Christian faith. This happened even though the Jewish people had been an integral part of Spanish and Portuguese society for generations, making many important contributions as scholars, scientists, map makers, merchants, royal treasurers, physicians, and advisors to many of the kings and queens who ruled. Even though Jewish citizens had helped to produce revenues for the Kingdom of Spain by developing industries and commerce and by representing the kingdom in diplomatic circles to ensure the continuation of trade with other countries of the world, Jewish people became the targets of abuse by the Church and the political bodies of Spain's territories, including the cities of Toledo, Seville, Avila, Córdoba, Granada, Barcelona, Girona, and Saragossa. Jewish people at this time also lived in the towns of Lucena, Daroca, Salamanca, Segovia, Tarragona, Tortosa, Tudela, and Vitoria. In each of these places Jewish people had distinguished themselves by creating poetry, literature, and the most important work of spiritual writing in the Jewish tradition, called the Kabbalah.

Jews at the Court of Prince Henry. Jewish doctors, rabbis, and scientists served as consultants to Prince Henry, the Portuguese navigator, during the period of intense scrutiny of Jews by the Catholic Church.

For the Jewish people in the Iberian Peninsula, the date June 6, 1391, marked the beginning of the end of life that, in that part of the world, was known as the Golden Age of contributions and advances. The blood that was shed that day in Seville, Spain began the pattern that was to be repeated in the many cities and towns where Jewish people lived. The conversion of the Jews became compulsory and for those Jews who did not cooperate, humiliating and insulting names were assigned to them by the Spanish Church. For example, even for those Jewish people who converted to Christianity in the public sphere but continued to practice quietly some Judaism privately in their homes, the term "Marrano" was assigned. The word "Marrano" was a derogatory word meaning "pig," which also refers to the Jewish dietary laws, which prohibited Jews from eating pig. Often Marranos were also referred to as Nuevos Cristos, or New Christians, because they had not been baptized Christian from the beginning of their lives as the Old Christians had been. They were

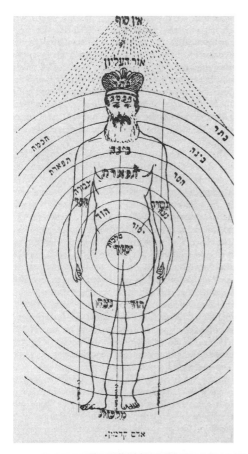

MAN FROM THE KABBALAH. *This page is from the Kabbalah, also known as the Zohar, which is a collection of mystical writings from Spain, originally. The Zohar teaches goodness to help one become closer to God's ideals.*

THE BARCELONA HAGGADAH. *This Haggadah was published in the eighteenth century in England in the Barcelona style. Used during the Passover meals, it brought to the Portuguese and Spanish Jews a sense of their historic roots from the Iberian Peninsula.*

also referred to as Conversos, or those who had been converted. Even Jewish New Christians who did not practice any form of Judaism were always suspected by Old Christians, the Crown, and the Catholic Church of not being true to the belief or doctrine of Christianity.

In order to seek out unfaithful or false Christians, at the request of Queen Isabella and other Spanish prelates, Pope Sixtus II issued a bull on September 17, 1480, instituting a holy tribunal called the Spanish Inquisition, made up of inquiring enforcers, who became the ones who judged the Jewish behavior, and established

ZACUTO'S ASTROLOGICAL CHART. *Abraham Zacuto was a scientist who produced this astrological chart and the astrolabe, both of which were used to help the first explorers from Spain and Portugal to seek new territories to colonize.*

the punishments that accompanied the Inquisitors' decisions. In 1483, under the first Inquisitor General, Frey Tomás de Torquemada, who supposedly had Jewish roots himself, the Inquisition developed a process, which included the Inquisition's rights to inquire about the purity of one's commitment to Christianity or the purity of one's blood. It was thought that investigating one's blood helped to cleanse the Catholic Church of false commitments and non-believing members of Christian society. Because of Torquemada, an important position in the Catholic Church was granted to a body of people called Inquisitors, not only by the Church but also by the political arm of the Spanish states and eventually by Portugal as well.

GRAND INQUISITOR TORQUEMADA. *Tomás de Torquemada was the Grand Inquisitor who made the rules other Spanish Inquisitors followed in investigating and questioning Jews for the purpose of accusing Jews of practicing their religion and to force them to convert to Catholicism.*

CHAPTER TWO

The Inquisition

THE INQUISITION HAD MANY LAWS and much power from the beginning. For example, one who was accused by the Inquisitors had a grace period to come forward and confess the sins of which they were accused and also to provide names of anyone else committing heretical practices (in the form of Jewish traditions) against the Church. Those who did not come forward to confess and pay fines were the ones who were investigated and who suffered the most.

The questioning of a person who was accused often included torture. If the accused person did not confess and the Inquisition found him or her guilty, then being burned at the stake or strangulation took place. If at the end, the person did confess, he or she was strangled to death to be spared the torture of then being burned alive. The public burnings were called autos da fé, or acts of faith, and were the Inquisition's way of getting rid of those who were thought to be the unfaithful in Spain who were not true to Christianity. The Church also called the killing of the unfaithful, and the autos da fé, the cleansing of the blood of Spain.

What the Inquisition looked for in identifying the false Christians, or Marranos, or Nuevos Cristos, included one's diet, death rites, birth rites, food preparation, religious rites, marriage rites, and holiday observations.

When one was suspected of observing Jewish practices, that person was accused of Judaizing, or practicing Judaism. Some of those practices included: wearing clean and fancy clothing from Friday night to Saturday night, cleaning house on Friday and lighting candles earlier than usual on that night, fasting a whole day until nightfall, and referring to Queen Esther (a biblical Jew in a foreign land who kept the truth of her religion secret from those around her and who became a heroine and inspiration to the Marranos). They also included eating unleavened bread and beginning their meals with celery and lettuce during Holy Week; saying prayers facing a wall while bowing back and forth; preparing meat in a special way, killing the animal by slitting its throat, draining its blood, and cutting away fat and gristle; not eating pork, rabbits, eels, or scale-less and fin-less fish; observing Sabbath on Saturday; covering mirrors during periods of mourning; practicing male circumcision; leaving small pebbles on the cemetery headstones of family members; playing with a gambling top with letters on four sides, called a *pon y saca* ("put in and

Las pragmaticas del reyno.

TANTO MOTA

✠Recopilació de algūas bu-
las de nuestro muy sancto padre: concedidas en fauor
dela jurisdicion real:con todas las Pragmaticas:τ al
gunas leyes:fechas para la buena gouernació del rey-
no:con algunas otras añadidas que fasta aqui no fue
ron impressas con las dichas Pragmaticas antiguas:
ḡ son muy prouechosas:las quales quié presto querra
hallar:vaya ala tabla alphabetica:nueuaméte assimis
mo añadida:dóde las fallara con esta señal ✠ al prin-
cipio puesta.

THE INQUISITION LOGO. *Designed to show the power of the Spanish royalty, and of God, and the goodness of the governing bodies, this was the logo of the Spanish Inquisition.*

TORTURES OF THE INQUISITION. *There were many types of torture of Jews used during the Inquisition to convince Jews of their need to renounce their religion and convert to the Catholic faith.*

AN INQUISITION COURT IN SPAIN. *At courts like this, the fate of Jews was decided, often resulting in incarceration and being burned at the stake.*

THE INQUISITION IN LISBON. *In Portugal, as in Spain, the autos da fé, or the burning of Jews at the stake, were witnessed by many citizens. Not only were they spectacular events, they also served as a warning to citizens to behave themselves for fear of being the next victims.*

take out"); sitting on the floor, eating eggs and olives, and throwing morsels of bread into the fire upon the death of a relative; naming their children after personages in the Old Testament; and never saying "Glory to the Trinity." Other signs of Judaism were eating meat during Lent; fasting on the Jewish Day of Atonement; washing hands before prayer; blessing a cup of wine before eating; having a charity box in the home; substituting a celebration feast of Esther for the celebration of the traditional Purim holiday; mistreating Christian images or speaking in a way to ridicule or speak with irony about Christianity, the Church, or the Inquisition; referring to themselves as anusim or "the forced ones"; using a special candelabra in winter; having gravestones without crosses

SAUSAGES OVER THE FIREPLACE.
The Jewish people would char their kosher chickens and kosher beef sausages over the fireplace so that the Inquisitors could not tell that they were not eating pork, which Jews, by kosher laws, are not allowed to eat.

for a family; cousins marrying cousins; speaking Ladino; having a day of rest each fall, Rosh Hashanah, and a day to repent called Yom Kippur; and having or possessing any amulet or symbol of Judaism, such as a Ten Commandments in silver or a Hebrew book or a menorah or a part of a circumcision set. Any of these practices were considered by the Inquisition to be evidence of Judaizing, or living like a Jew.

The word "Judaizing" also meant accusing a person of living like a Jew, so when the Inquisition suspected people of the practices listed above, the people were "Judaized"—accused, tried, and then imprisoned or humiliated publicly by either having to wear special clothes, called a Sanbenito, a sulfur yellow shirt with crosses, that came only to the waist (the lower part of the body was uncovered), or in some cases being paraded through the streets without any clothes, then tortured and finally facing an auto da fé, the religious cleansing rite that again included being killed by strangulation and hanging, or burning, or both.

Purity of blood became so important in preserving Christianity that anyone with any trace of Jewish ancestral traditions was Judaized.

Punishing the Jews was not only a religious event in Spain, for along with the religious persecutions came much pillaging of the wealth of the Jews, which added significantly to the financial resources for the King's and Queen's coffers. Spain was fighting wars that depleted her accounts, and eventually there were heavy financial burdens, because of exploration and colonization—to be able to have a foothold in the New World. In order to pay for all this, one of the Inquisition's processes was the collection of taxes, which was tantamount to robbery, as the Jews were also taxed to death more than any other Old Christian citizens.

Also the practice of "blood libel" became a way of accusing Jews and collect-

Jews with Sanbenito Hats. To both humiliate and punish Jews, they were forced at times to wear the short Sanbenito yellow costume and a pointed hat.

ing their money. An example of blood libel was when a Jew or group of Jews was charged with kidnapping a Christian baby and draining the blood in order to use the blood for Jewish rituals. One outrageous reason stated that Jews who suffered from hemorrhoids got them, the Christians thought, as a punishment for killing Jesus, and drinking the blood of Christians was the best cure for hemorrhoids. Christians also claimed all Jewish men menstruate and need a monthly blood transfusion; or Jewish men, when they are circumcised, lose so much blood because of the surgical procedure that they need to drink Christian babies' blood. Also they claimed human blood was the chief ingredient in matzah, and therefore prior to every Passover Jews would be requiring a large supply. Jews also need the blood, they claimed, to complete their rituals of sorcery and witchcraft.

If people were found guilty of these supposed blood-letting exercises, they usually met with death and all of their possessions were confiscated—again to provide more money for the King's coffers. One example of a blood libel was the Holy Child of La Guardia.

The Holy Child of La Guardia

The alleged martyrdom by Jews of the Infant La Guardia of Toledo in 1490 was a typical blood libel, which became a form of legal persecution which the Catholic Church had developed over centuries as a source of intense religious devotion, supposedly.

The Holy Child of La Guardia, the subject of this blood libel, became revered as a saint by the Spanish populace. Five Conversos and two Jews, inhabitants of La Guardia, Tembleque, and Zamora, were tried in connection with this libel in an irregular Inquisition trial which began on December 17, 1490. The trial was con-

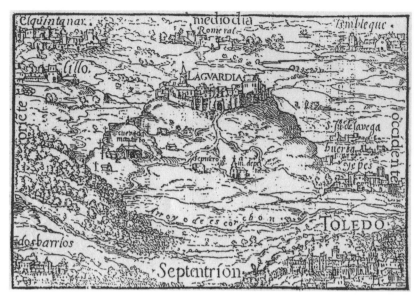

LA GUARDIA, SPAIN. *This map shows La Guardia, the supposed home of the "martyred child," who was supposedly killed by Jews for his blood. The allegation was false propaganda.*

cluded on November 14, 1491, when the accused were burned at the stake in the town of Avila. The Jews accused were Yuce Franco of Tembleque and Moses Abenamias of Zamora; the Conversos were Alonso, Juan, Benito Garcia, and Lope, all of the Franco family, and Juan de Orana, all inhabitants of La Guardia in the province of Toledo. The depositions and confessions extracted under torture reveal that they were accused of two things: first, the profanation of a Host, which the accused Conversos had purchased and which was found in the bag of Señor Benito Garcia, and second, that in order to perform acts of sorcery, the extraction of the heart of a Christian child murdered on Good Friday was supposedly performed by the accused. The beginnings of the trial have never been clarified, but during the proceedings its motivations became evident. Torquemada himself was to preside.

A special tribunal was thus set up, formed by carefully chosen judges. The judges and the investigators who assisted them resorted to provocative methods to extract evidence in prison and were even compelled, in order to reconcile the contradictions between the various "statements," to bring together the accused and force them to relate in each other's presence details of the "deed" so that a tale of at least some coherence could be contrived. The judges even sat on a special panel (*Consulta-de-fé*) in Salamanca, with the participation of the celebrated monk Antonio de la Peña, the associate of Fernando de Santo Domingo in his anti-Jewish activities. There is also no doubt that the Inquisition wanted to prepare public opinion for the expulsion of the Jews from Spain by creating a background of an alleged Jewish–Converso conspiracy to bring about the annihilation of both Christianity and the Inquisition. Even so, the recorded statements of these Conversos are a profound expression of their belief in the Law of Moses, their readiness to die as martyrs, and their contemptuous attitude toward Christianity and its way of life. Torquemada was referred to by one of the accused as the "arch-antichrist" (*antecristo mayor*).

The guilty verdict of the killing of the child was made public and circulated throughout Spain, and the worship of the "Holy Child" was rapidly instituted. For fear of riots, the Jews of Avila felt compelled to request a document of protestation (granted December 9, 1491). With time, details were added to the story until it assumed impressive proportions in both works and plays which were presented on the subject. In 1583, Fray Rodrigo de Yepes wrote a book entitled *Historia de la muerte y glorioso martirio del Sancto Innocente, que llaman de la Guardia*. In the seventeenth century, the story served as the basis of a play by Lope de Vega, *El Niño Inocente de la Guardia*. The tale was adapted again during the eighteenth century by José de Canizares under the title *La Viva Imagen de Cristo*.

However, the Child of La Guardia never existed. The crypt where he was said to have been buried has been opened and the supposed coffin containing the body was found to be empty. There is no DNA and there is also no record of the infant ever even having been born. However, the worship of the Child of La Guardia went on for hundreds of years in Spain, along with the hatred of all the Jewish population, not just the accused, who it seems never had any role other than to be tried and executed for this erroneous story. It has been stated that this trial was a way to explain to the Spanish citizenry the reason that Jews had to be eradicated from Spanish society. Again, this was done so that the expulsion of Jews in 1492 would be understood and justified in the eyes of the Spanish population.

MARTYR'S DEATH FRONTISPIECE.
A page from the blood libel about the burning at the stake of innocent Conversos and Jews accused of killing a child to use his blood in Jewish rituals. The child never existed, but the trial in Avila, Spain, was presided over by Torquemada, the Grand Inquisitor himself, to prove to Spain why the Jewish presence had to be removed from Spanish land.

Autos da Fé Celebrated in Spain, Portugal, and Their Colonies

Here is a list of documented autos da fé, including what statistics are known on the numbers of those victims punished and burned.

Autos da Fé Celebrated in Spain
Indicates that Jews were punished but numbers unknown

Date	Place	Punished	Burned	Date	Place	Punished	Burned
May 10, 1484	Saragossa	4	—	1578	Toledo	1	—
June 3, 1484	Saragossa	—	3	March 13, 1587	Saragossa	—	1
Dec. 20, 1485	Saragossa	—	2	1591	Toledo	—	24
Feb. 18, 1486	Saragossa	1	—	1598	Seville	1	—
Feb. 24, 1486	Saragossa	—	3	1598	Toledo	1	—
March 17, 1486	Saragossa	—	3	Nov. 7, 1610	Lograno	6	—
April 28, 1486	Saragossa	—	4	Oct. 15, 1619	Toledo	1	—
May 21, 1486	Saragossa	7	—	Nov. 30, 1624	Seville	*	—
June 25, 1486	Saragossa	5	—	Dec. 14, 1625	Seville	67	4
June 30, 1486	Saragossa	—	3	Dec. 21, 1627	Córdoba	71	—
July 28, 1486	Saragossa	—	3	July 22, 1628	Seville	2	—
Aug. 6, 1486	Saragossa	5	—	April 27, 1630	Toledo	1	—
Sept. 4, 1486	Saragossa	—	—	June 29, 1634	Cuenca	57	—
Oct. 21, 1486	Saragossa	—	6	June 22, 1636	Valladolid	28	—
Nov. 29, 1486	Saragossa	—	11	1641	Toledo	1	—
Dec. 15, 1486	Saragossa	—	1	April 17, 1644	Seville	1	—
Dec. 17, 1486	Saragossa	—	1	Aug. 2, 1644	Valladolid	1	—
Jan. 15, 1487	Toledo	700	—	Feb. 24, 1647	Córdoba	12	—
Jan. 21, 1487	Saragossa	—	5	March 29, 1648	Seville	—	29
Feb. 15, 1487	Saragossa	—	—	Dec. 28, 1649	Toledo	—	3
March 15, 1487	Toledo	1000	—	1649	Valladolid	—	1
May 7, 1487	Toledo	22	—	Jan. 1, 1651	Toledo	—	2
May 20, 1487	Saragossa	—	9	Jan. 1651	Toledo	—	63
Aug. 18, 1487	Saragossa	—	3	Nov. 30, 1651	Toledo	*	—
Aug. 20, 1487	Saragossa	—	3	April 28, 1652	Toledo	4	—
Dec. 8, 1487	Saragossa	—	—	Aug. 24, 1652	Toledo	4	—
Feb. 10, 1488	Saragossa	—	4	Nov. 3, 1652	Toledo	2	—
Feb. 15, 1488	Saragossa	—	1	Dec. 28, 1652	Toledo	*	—
July 30, 1488	Toledo	—	16	May 11, 1653	Toledo	*	—
March 2, 1510	Las Palmas	3	—	May 18, 1653	Toledo	*	—
March 2, 1511	Cuenca	—	—	Aug. 10, 1653	Toledo	*	—
Feb. 24, 1526	Las Palmas	5	—	Aug. 31, 1653	Toledo	3	—
May 21, 1559	Valladolid	—	2	March 15, 1654	Toledo	7	*
Dec. 22, 1560	Seville	—	1	June 29, 1654	Cuenca	47	10
Sept. 18, 1560	Madrid	—	29	Sept. 27, 1654	Toledo	*	—
March 15, 1562	Murcia	—	1	Dec. 12, 1654	Granada	*	12
March 20, 1562	Murcia	16	—	March 1655	Compostella	—	1
June 17, 1565	Toledo	1	—	May 3, 1655	Córdoba	78	—
Nov. 6, 1569	Las Palmas	*	—	Oct. 31, 1655	Toledo	7	—
June 18, 1570	Toledo	7	—	Jan. 30, 1656	Toledo	1	—

NUREMBERG CHRONICLE ACCOUNT OF PERSECUTION. This leaf from the fifteenth-century Nuremberg Chronicle shows both the horrors of the treatment of Jews by Spain during the Inquisition and the anger and disgust Germany felt towards Spain.

Date	Place	Punished	Burned
Sept. 10, 1656	Toledo	8	—
Sept. 17, 1656	Toledo	2	—
Oct. 8, 1656	Toledo	2	—
1657	Córdoba	—	1
1657	Córdoba	13	—
Feb. 11, 1657	Toledo	3	—
March 11, 1657	Toledo	3	—
May 6, 1657	Toledo	3	—
July 1, 1657	Toledo	8	—
Sept. 16, 1657	Toledo	6	—
Dec. 9, 1657	Toledo	17	—
Aug. 24, 1658	Toledo	7	—
May 9, 1659	Toledo	*	—
Sept. 7, 1659	Toledo	*	—
1660	Toledo	—	1
Jan. 11, 1660	Toledo	—	1
Feb. 9, 1660	Córdoba	13	—
March 19, 1660	Córdoba	*	—
April 11, 1660	Seville	80	7
June 13, 1660	Toledo	2	—
Sept. 26, 1660	Toledo	*	—
April 4, 1661	Toledo	*	—
Aug. 8, 1661	Toledo	*	—
Dec. 4, 1661	Toledo	6	—
Feb. 24, 1662	Córdoba	38	—
April 11, 1662	Toledo	*	—
May 6, 1663	Córdoba	19	—
Oct. 7, 1663	Toledo	*	—
Feb. 22, 1665	Toledo	*	—
June 29, 1665	Córdoba	96	—
1666	Toledo	—	1
June 7, 1666	Córdoba	23	—
June 15, 1666	Toledo	*	—
May 1, 1667	Toledo	3	—
Oct. 30, 1667	Toledo	3	—
1669	Córdoba	13	—
April 7, 1669	Toledo	*	—
Nov. 17, 1669	Toledo	*	—
May 18, 1670	Toledo	*	—
July 20, 1670	Córdoba	21	—
Oct. 19, 1670	Toledo	*	—
Sept. 6, 1671	Toledo	*	—
Sept. 11, 1672	Toledo	*	—
Feb. 11, 1674	Toledo	*	—
Oct. 14, 1674	Toledo	—	1
Feb. 14, 1679	Toledo	4	—
Dec. 17, 1679	Toledo	5	—
Oct. 6, 1680	Toledo	5	—
Dec. 21, 1680	Toledo	*	—
Sept. 29, 1681	Toledo	*	—
1683	Seville	—	1
April 25, 1683	Toledo	*	—
1684	Granada	—	—
May 22, 1684	Toledo	2	1
April 1, 1685	Toledo	1	—
Aug. 18, 1686	Toledo	3	—
Oct. 15, 1686	Toledo	1	—
April 18, 1687	Toledo	1	—
1689	Granada	—	—
July 2, 1691	Majorca	38	37
May 18, 1692	Seville	1	—
Nov. 9, 1692	Toledo	1	—
Feb. 7, 1694	Toledo	*	—
June 6, 1694	Toledo	3	—

Date	Place	Punished	Burned
May 8, 1695	Toledo	3	2
Sept. 22, 1695	Toledo	1	—
Oct. 23, 1695	Toledo	2	—
July 29, 1696	Toledo	1	—
Sept. 16, 1696	Toledo	2	—
March 17, 1697	Toledo	—	—
Nov. 29, 1699	Valladolid	many	*
1700	Seville	1	—
Sept. 26, 1700	Toledo	*	—
March 6, 1701	Toledo	*	—
Oct. 30, 1701	Toledo	3	—
May 21, 1702	Toledo	2	—
Nov. 12, 1702	Toledo	2	—
March 18, 1703	Toledo	2	—
Oct. 28, 1703	Seville	*	—
Sept. 8, 1704	Toledo	2	1
Nov. 22, 1705	Toledo	—	1
Dec. 31, 1706	Valladolid	*	—
Sept. 27, 1711	Toledo	1	—
June 30, 1716	Seville	—	1
April 4, 1718	Córdoba	5	—
June 29, 1718	Seville	1	—
July 25, 1720	Seville	—	1
March 19, 1721	Toledo	*	—
May 18, 1721	Madrid	*	—
Nov. 30, 1721	Granada	58	—
Dec. 14, 1721	Seville	38	—
Feb. 22, 1722	Madrid	10	—
Feb. 24, 1722	Seville	11	—
March 15, 1722	Toledo	—	—
March 15, 1722	Toledo	7	—
April 22, 1722	Córdoba	14	—
May 17, 1722	Murcia	36	—
June 19, 1722	Cuenca	18	—
July 5, 1722	Seville	43	—
Oct. 25, 1722	Toledo	12	—
Nov. 30, 1722	Seville	42	4
Nov. 30, 1722	Llerena	17	—
Jan. 31, 1723	Granada	54	—
Jan. 31, 1723	Barcelona	4	—
Jan. 31, 1723	Seville	54	12
June 6, 1723	Seville	31	2
June 6, 1723	Saragossa	21	—
June 18, 1723	Córdoba	23	15
June 20, 1723	Granada	25	—
Oct. 24, 1723	Granada	25	—
Oct. 28, 1723	Toledo	6	—
Feb. 20, 1724	Madrid	20	3
Feb. 24, 1724	Toledo	7	2
March 12, 1724	Valladolid	5	4

Date	Place	Punished	Burned
April 2, 1724	Valencia	5	—
April 23, 1724	Córdoba	26	14
June 11, 1724	Seville	33	1
June 25, 1724	Granada	39	5
July 2, 1724	Córdoba	6	—
July 23, 1724	Cuenca	8	—
Nov. 30, 1724	Murcia	8	2
Dec. 21, 1724	Seville	8	—
Jan. 14, 1725	Cuenca	9	2
Feb. 4, 1725	Llerena	4	—
March 4, 1725	Cuenca	1	—
May 18, 1725	Granada	20	7
July 1, 1725	Toledo	5	1
July 1, 1725	Valencia	2	—
July 8, 1725	Valladolid	5	—
Aug. 24, 1725	Granada	9	—
Aug. 26, 1725	Llerena	10	—
Sept. 9, 1725	Barcelona	2	—
Oct. 21, 1725	Murcia	6	—
Nov. 30, 1725	Seville	10	3
Dec. 16, 1725	Granada	10	1
March 31, 1726	Valladolid	2	—
March 31, 1726	Murcia	6	—
May 12, 1726	Córdoba	9	—
June 11, 1726	Toledo	2	—
Aug. 18, 1726	Granada	7	—
Aug. 18, 1726	Llerena	—	1
Sept. 1, 1726	Barcelona	1	1
Sept. 17, 1726	Valencia	*	—
Jan. 26, 1727	Valladolid	17	—
May 9, 1728	Granada	*	—
Oct. 10, 1728	Granada	5	—
May 3, 1730	Córdoba	14	—
March 4, 1731	Córdoba	6	—
March 20, 1738	Toledo	*	—
March 21, 1738	Toledo	12	1
Dec. 21, 1738	Toledo	1	—
June 13, 1745	Valladolid	3	1
Dec. 5, 1745	Córdoba	2	—
July 18, 1749	Córdoba	1	1
Dec. 13, 1753	Seville	1	—
Jan. 11, 1756	Toledo	1	—
Nov. 22, 1758	Seville	*	—
Dec. 1758	Seville	1	—
Dec. 1781	Seville	—	1
Aug. 11, 1799	Seville	*	—
Aug. 26, 1799	Seville	*	—
Feb. 27, 1817	Seville	—	—
Aug. 1, 1826	Valencia	—	1

Autos da Fé Celebrated in Portugal and Goa, India
Only such listed where Jews are known to have been punished or burned.

Date	Place	Date	Place
October 23, 1541	Lisbon	March 5, 1624	Lisbon
1541	Evora	April 1, 1629	Evora
1543	Porto	September 2, 1629	Lisbon
June 27, 1563	Goa	April 2, 1642	Lisbon
December 5, 1563	Goa	December 22, 1647	Lisbon
October 27, 1564	Goa	December 1, 1652	Lisbon
June 15, 1567	Goa	December 15, 1658	Porto
January 18, 1568	Goa	October 17, 1660	Lisbon
January 28, 1568	Goa	March 12, 1673	Coimbra
July 17, 1569	Goa	May 10, 1682	Lisbon
April 22, 1571	Goa	August 8, 1683	Lisbon
May 18, 1574	Goa	August, 1701	Lisbon
September 4, 1575	Goa	March 2, 1704	Coimbra
October 28, 1576	Goa	September 6, 1705	Lisbon
September 1, 1577	Goa	December 6, 1705	Lisbon
August 17, 1578	Goa	July 25, 1706	Evora
September 6, 1579	Goa	June 30, 1707	Lisbon
December 4, 1580	Goa	July 9, 1713	Lisbon
December 14, 1582	Goa	June 17, 1718	Coimbra
November 10, 1585	Goa	March 14, 1723	Coimbra
September 13, 1587	Goa	October 10, 1723	Lisbon
August 3, 1603	Lisbon	October 18, 1726	Lisbon
March 27, 1605	Evora	September 1, 1739	Lisbon
March 24, 1606	Evora	October 18, 1739	Lisbon
October 17, 1610	Evora		

Autos da Fé Celebrated in the Americas
Indicates where Jews are known to have been punished or burned.

Lima, Peru

November 15, 1573
April 1, 1578
October 29, 1581
November 30, 1587
April 5, 1592
December 17, 1595
December 10, 1600
March 13, 1605
June 1, 1608
June 17, 1612
December 21, 1625
February 27, 1631
August 11, 1635
August 17, 1635
January 23, 1639
November 17, 1641
January 23, 1664
February 16, 1666
June 28, 1667
October 8, 1667
March 16, 1693
November 28, 1719
December 21, 1720
1728
July 12, 1733
December 23, 1736
November 11, 1737
October 19, 1749
April 6, 1761
1776
February 18, 1800
August 27, 1803
September 10, 1805
July 17, 1806

Cartagena de las Indias, Colombia

February 2, 1614	April 4, 1677
July, 1618	October 23, 1678
March 13, 1622	November 12, 1679
January 17, 1626	December 21, 1681
August 6, 1627	October 28, 1682
June 25, 1628	July 29, 1683
March 7, 1632	August 29, 1683
March 26, 1634	February 11, 1685
June 1, 1636	September 9, 1685
March 25, 1638	May 30, 1688
July 22, 1642	December 11, 1689
May 24, 1648	April 29, 1691
November 28, 1649	March, 1695
December 21, 1650	April 27, 1697
April 25, 1653	April 29, 1699
July 22, 1653	January 10, 1700
April 28, 1654	June 20, 1700
May 8, 1655	February 24, 1707
June 6, 1655	March 18, 1708
October 1, 1656	May 21, 1708
September 16, 1657	May 26, 1711
May, 1669	July 9, 1713
March 2, 1670	July 29, 1714
August 4, 1671	June 11, 1715
September 4, 1671	November 30, 1715
September 4, 1672	June 20, 1717
February 17, 1675	February 5, 1782

Mexico

1524–26	1591	1652
1536	1592*	Oct. 29, 1656
1539*	1594	Nov. 19, 1659*
1549	1595	May 4, 1664
1555	Dec. 8, 1596*	Dec. 7, 1664
1558	March 26, 1601*	1690
1560	1603*	Jan. 15, 1696
1561	1606	March 20, 1697
1562	1608	1704
1569	1621	1708
Feb. 28, 1574	1625*	1712*
March 6, 1575	1626*	1722
Feb. 19, 1576	1630*	Sept. 6, 1767
Dec. 15, 1577*	1635*	March 13, 1768
1578*	1636*	August 9, 1795*
1579*	Jan. 12, 1639	Nov. 26, 1814
1579–90	1645–49*	1815
1590*		

CHAPTER THREE

The Expulsion of the Jews from Iberia

D ESPITE ALL OF THE PUNISHMENT by the Inquisition and the autos da fé and the blood libels, still some Judaism continued to be practiced at some level in Spain. Eventually the only recourse for Spain was to finally expel all of the Jews, and Spain's Queen Isabella and King Ferdinand tried to accomplish this in 1492.

As Queen, Isabella had her own story. Born in 1451, she was also the Queen of Castile from 1474 to 1504.

Against her father's wishes, she eloped with Ferdinand II of Aragon. The states of Castile and Aragon at that time kept separate laws, institutions, and governments until 1481, when all of Spain, except for Moorish Granada, was unified under both Ferdinand and Isabella, who became known as the Catholic Kings. They produced five children, Isabel, John, Joan, Maria, and Catherine.

On March 31, 1492, realizing that many Jewish citizens were really Marranos

QUEEN ISABELLA OF SPAIN. Queen Isabella (right) and her husband, King Ferdinand, were the Spanish royalty who issued the edict to have all Jewish rituals and all Jews banished from Spain.

THE ALHAMBRA, GRANADA, SPAIN. The Red Palace, known as the Alhambra, has among its treasures this fountain surrounded by lions, supposedly taken from a Jewish doctor's home after he was expelled from Spain. Spain took everything from the Jews, including the money from their coffers, their land, their artifacts, and their right to their religion.

who professed Christianity on the outside but secretly celebrated Judaism in the privacy of their homes, Ferdinand and Isabella issued their Edict of Expulsion, that stated, "[We] have decided to command all of the aforesaid Jews, men and women, to leave our kingdoms and never to return to them." The Jews were given until July 1, 1492, to leave the kingdoms. Any found within its borders after that would be killed. The edict was finally going to rid Spain, once and for all, of the insolent Jews.

The edict was issued from the Alhambra, a massive castle built in the thirteenth century by the then Moorish population. Built as a fortress, the Spanish called it "The Red One." It stands high on a mountain under the Spanish Sierra Nevada mountains in Granada. It was built in the Moorish style. But because this Moorish style was now used for another religion, that of Christianity, the style is referred to as Mudejar (Mudecha)—a term that describes any building in the Moorish architectural style which has a function other than for a Moorish purpose. The Alcazaba is the oldest building in the Alhambra.

The Expulsion Edict went public during the week of April 29, 1492. The charter declared that no Jews were permitted to remain within the Spanish kingdom, but a Jew who wished to convert was welcome to stay. The power of the wealthy Spanish Jewry, they said, was inconsequential. Whether a Jew was rich or poor did not matter, they all still had to convert or leave.

THE EDICT OF EXPULSION. In Spain's 1492 Expulsion Edict Queen Isabella and King Ferdinand gave Jews three choices: to leave in three months time, to convert, or to die.

Approximately 300,000 Jews left Spain prior to August 2, 1492, the day before Christopher Columbus sailed for the New World. That was also the ninth day of Av on the Jewish calendar, the traditional Day of Mourning for the destruction of the first and second Temples in Palestine (Israel). The first words in Columbus's log were "After you expelled the Jews your Majesties sent me with a fleet."

All those Jews who left in 1492 were forced to leave their possessions, including real property, jewels, gold, and bank accounts, behind, and that wealth added greatly to the coffers of the Spanish government that confiscated it. Spain needed the money to fight wars with her rivals, England, France, and Holland. At that time, Spain also wanted the money to help finance the exploration for new lands to acquire for her colonies and for world power.

Much of the human wealth in Spain left at that time when the Jews were expelled. Spain lost most of her Jewish scientists, map makers, merchants, and advisors, not to mention the taxes that would be paid by these people and their descendants in years to come. Spain also lost much of the intellectual and economic power that was generated by the Jewish community.

A FRIAR BORROWING MONEY FROM A JEW AFTER THE EXPULSION. One of the jobs Jewish people were forced to do before, during, and (as suspected Marranos) after the Inquisition, was usury, as moneylenders to Spanish citizens and to the clergy of the Catholic Church.

Looking back at the 1300s, Spain consisted of Castile, Aragon, and Navarre as individual states, and the general population for all was 5,500,000. The Jewish, or Sephardic, population then was 150,000. By 1490, Spain's Jewish population was 330,000 and the total population of Spain was 8,000,000. By 1497, there were supposed to be no more Jewish people or Sephardim openly left in Spain. About 60,000 Jews stayed and chose to completely convert to Christianity. Those who remained in Spain as "Secret Jews," or Marranos, if they didn't die at the hands of the Inquisition, left descendants today, who still have traditions that connect them to their Jewish roots.

But also, by the time of the expulsion, many Jews had already intermarried with members of the Christian population, and it is thought that more than thirty percent of the Spanish Christian population today has roots of Jewish ancestry.

The many Jews who were forced to leave Spain continued to see themselves

THE EXPULSION OF THE JEWS. *A page from the Barcelona Haggadah, published in England in the eighteenth century to remind the Portuguese and Spanish Jews of their Sephardic heritage and the reasons they were forced to leave Spain.*

as Spaniards in exile, still cultivating their traditions, including speaking their beloved Ladino language. For the Spanish Jews this became a tragic exodus from a land in which they had flourished and one that they had so passionately loved.

Into the Diaspora they went, to many lands, to reestablish Jewish communities and be able, they hoped, to live with the freedom to act as their consciences led them, to live openly as Jews, without someone looking over their shoulders with the kinds of threats they had experienced with the Spanish Inquisition. Many of the fleeing refugees went to the Ottoman Empire (Turkey) and to Greece. Others went to North Africa and to the Middle East. A group of Sephardim went to Portugal, right next door to Spain.

When the Kingdom of Portugal was formed in the twelfth century, Jewish people were already living on the land in specific areas of Portugal. During the reign of the first king, Dom Afonso Henriques (1139–1185 C.E.), the Jews were protected by the Crown. From 1279 C.E. onward, there were thirty-one places where Jewish people resided in Portugal.

But then, as Christians began to persecute the Jews who lived in Spain in 1391,

Portugal began to be the recipient of a new group of Jewish residents, and Jewish people now began residing in 135 different parts of Portugal. Jewish people lived in Lisbon, Castelo de Vide, Montanhas, Tomar, Costa de Prata, Belmonte, Oporto, Faro, Cavilla, Santarém, and Torre de Moncorvo. The Jewish religious life in Portugal included their being their own administrators and advisors for all legal decisions. When a Jewish person served one of the Portuguese kings as a doctor, or a treasurer, or advisor, he was given the title of Chief Rabbi by the Portuguese government there. As in Spain, even though there was some prejudice, there was a Golden Age in Portugal, when Jewish people, in addition to serving the Portuguese Crown, became contributors to many fields, including science, finance, mercantilism, navigation, map making, medicine, literature, astronomy, and other scholarly endeavors.

In 1492, after the Jewish expulsion from Spain, many more Jewish people moved into Portugal. All went well for them until 1497, when King Manuel was to marry the daughter of the Spanish monarchs, King Ferdinand and Queen Isabella, also called Isabella. The marriage contract stated there would be no Jews in Portugal, just as there were no Jews in Spain. On December 5, 1496, King Manuel issued an Edict of Expulsion to Jews, ordering them to leave Portugal by the end of October 1497. With the expulsion of the Jews, the marriage could take place between Manuel I and Isabella. However, King Manuel changed his mind and, instead of expelling the Jews, rounded up the Jews, took them to Lisbon, and forcibly converted them to Christianity. Then, after ordering them to leave, he refused to let them leave. He made them take new surnames. Most of the new names the Jews took fell into two categories; objects in nature such as Pinheiro ("pine tree"), or Figueredo ("fig tree"), or a state of being such as Henriques ("son of Henry"). There are hundreds of names which can identify the Jewish families of 1497, that are easily recognized today as they represent animals, plants, and trees, like Pinto (a spotted horse), Coelho (a rabbit), and Oliveira (an olive tree). King Manuel took children under the age of thirteen and forcibly baptized them. Many of them never saw their families again. Also, Isabella died while giving birth to King Manuel's first child, Miguel, in 1498.

Now, as baptized Christians with new surnames, the Jews of Portugal had to appear to be practicing Christianity. Many Jews wholeheartedly accepted being Christians, as a safe way to live in peace, but others continued to practice Judaism in secret. If they were caught, as in Spain, they were Judaized and arrested, and all of their property was seized. Called New Christians who were heretics, these Jews met the Church's Portuguese Inquisition, which was formally instituted by an edict in 1520 in Portugal. The Inquisition's procedures and punishments took the same forms in Portugal as those in Spain, including the wearing of the Sanbenito as penitence for being a Jew, trials, and autos da fé, which again included torture, imprisonment, or death by burning at the stake.

Many of the New Christians, who could, fled Portugal as they had fled Spain under the cruel punishments issued to them there. Jews went to states in southern

Europe, such as those in France in the cities of Montpellier, Avignon, Bayonne, and Bordeaux. Some went to the Italian republics of Ferrara, Venice, Livorno, Ancona, and Rome. Still others went to Amsterdam in Holland, or to Antwerp in Belgium, and eventually, many went to London. They also tried to live in the Islamic world of Fez, Tripoli, Smyrna, Salonika, and Constantinople. New Christians even tried to live on the Portuguese islands of Madeira and the Azores, where the language was still Portuguese, but the distance was great enough, they thought, to separate themselves from the seat of the Inquisition. Unfortunately, the Inquisition caught up with them there. When Brazil was colonized by the Portuguese, many New Christian Jews crossed the Atlantic to go to Brazil, because they thought that the tentacles of the Inquisition wouldn't be there either, and they could live in peace. Again, the Inquisition caught up with them in Brazil. (See the section on the Inquisition in the New World.)

New Christians traveled as far as India to colonize, to escape the Portuguese Inquisition. They thought and hoped, as Jewish congregations were organized in many new places in the world, that they could live as Jews in peace. Once again, the Inquisition moved right along with the Jewish Portuguese refugees, and life in their new homes was often as difficult as it had been in Portugal.

The Diaspora, which lasted from the fifteenth to the nineteenth century, played a major role in spreading the Jewish religion and values to other parts of the world. Jewish traditions of social responsibility, as well as literary, scientific, educational, political, mercantile, and artistic talents began to appear in every new community in which they traveled, always running from the Inquisition's rules.

By 1520, when the Portuguese Inquisition was instituted, for all practical purposes it was forbidden for Jewish people to live in Portuguese lands, as it had been forbidden for them to live in Spanish lands. Jewish life, at that time, seemed to cease to exist in the Iberian peninsula altogether. However, in the mountains in the village of Belmonte, Portugal, there was actually a Marrano community that, in secrecy, continued to exist. They had only one word left in Hebrew to use, "Adonai," the Hebrew word for God. They secretly baked unleavened bread for Passover (but not necessarily on the correct date) in the ovens of their kitchens with the windows shut tight so they would not be found. They celebrated Rosh Hashanah by going down to the sea to cleanse their dishes in the water, and they celebrated Yom Kippur by wearing only white clothes, and by baking flat breads (normally associated with matzah) at Passover. All traditions were slightly mixed up because there were no books or teachers to refer to. To keep the Christian community from suspecting the Jewish traditions that they were practicing, they put crucifixes on their gravestones and in their homes, and they attended the local Catholic Church.

The Jewish community of Belmonte exists to this day. As of 1997, Belmonte now has a synagogue, Portugal's first new synagogue in seventy years, and today they no longer have to hide, although remnants of anti-Semitism still exist in this small village, kept alive by only a few of its narrow-minded Christian citizens. The older

INQUISITION PROCESSION IN GOA. *Portugal's colonies were also included in the Inquisition's court activities, as shown in this procession by the court members in Goa, India.*

members of the Jewish community still practice Judaism in the convoluted form their families had followed for generations; but the younger generation has learned the proper traditions and the dates with which they are associated, as they practice traditional Judaism today. And in other Portuguese communities, especially in the mountains and in villages, some Jewish traditions were secretly being practiced for individual families, just not throughout for the whole community.

In 1834, the Spanish Inquisition's reign of terror finally ended, and in 1821 the Portuguese Inquisition ended. Throughout the long ordeal, however, Spanish and Portuguese Jews continued to play an important role by contributing to the explorations of new lands during the fifteenth and sixteenth centuries. Among their many contributions were the financing of the exploration fleets, working as cartographers, developing scientific instruments, working as mathematicians and as leaders in the field of medical research, and as interpreters and advisors to royalty, who were eager to plant their flags in new lands. Jews were paramount then, and present in helping to discover the New World.

Edict of the Expulsion of the Jews, 1492

Translated from the Castilian by Edward Peters

(1) King Ferdinand and Queen Isabella, by the grace of God, King and Queen of Castile, León, Aragon, Sicily, Granada, Toledo, Valencia, Galicia, the Balearic Islands, Seville, Sardinia, Córdoba, Corsica, Murcia, Jaen, of the Algarve, Algeciras, Gibraltar, and of the Canary Islands, count and countess of Barcelona and lords of Biscay and Molina, dukes of Athens and Neopatria, counts of Roussillon and Cerdana, marquises of Oristan and of Gociano, to the prince Lord Juan, our very dear and much loved son, and to the other royal children, prelates, dukes, marquees, counts, masters of military orders, priors, grandees, knight commanders, governors of castles and fortified places of our kingdoms and lordships, and to councils, magistrates, mayors, constables, district judges, knights, official squires, and all good men of the noble and loyal city of Burgos and other cities, towns, and villages of its bishopric and of other archbishoprics, bishoprics, dioceses of our kingdom and lordships, and to the residential quarters of the Jews of the said city of Burgos and of all the aforesaid cities, towns, and villages of its bishopric and of the other cities, towns, and villages of our aforementioned kingdoms and lordships, and to all Jews and to all individual Jews of those places, and to barons and women of whatever age they may be, and to all other persons of whatever law, estate, dignity, preeminence, and condition they may be, and to all to whom the matter contained in this charter pertains or may pertain. Salutations and grace.

(2) You know well or ought to know, that whereas we have been informed that in these our kingdoms there were some wicked Christians who Judaized and apostatized from our holy Catholic faith, the great cause of which was interaction between the Jews and these Christians, in the Cortes which we held in the city of Toledo in the past year of one thousand, four hundred and eighty, we ordered the separation of the said Jews in all the cities, towns and villages of our kingdoms and lordships and [commanded] that they be given Jewish quarters and separated places where they should live, hoping that by their separation the situation would remedy itself. Furthermore, we procured and gave orders that inquisition should be made in our aforementioned kingships and lordships, which as you know has for twelve years been made and is being made, and by many guilty persons have been discovered, as is very well known, and accordingly we are informed by the inquisitors and by other devout persons, ecclesiastical and secular, that great injury has resulted and still results, since the Christians have engaged in and continue to engage in social interaction and communication they have had means and ways they can to subvert and to steal faithful Christians from our holy Catholic faith and to separate them from it, and to draw them to themselves and subvert them to their own wicked belief and conviction, instructing them in the ceremonies and observances of their law, holding meetings at which they read and teach that which people must hold and believe according to their law, achieving that the Christians and their children be circumcised, and giving them books from which they may read their prayers and declaring to them the fasts that they must keep, and joining with them to read and teach them the history of their law, indicating to them the festivals before they occur, advising them of what in them they are to hold and observe, carrying to them and giving to them from their houses unleavened bread and meats ritually slaughtered, instructing them about the things from which they must refrain, as much in eating as in other things in order to observe their law, and persuading them as much as they can to hold

and observe the law of Moses, convincing them that there is no other law or truth except for that one. This proved by many statements and confessions, both from these same Jews and from those who have been perverted and enticed by them, which has redounded to the great injury, detriment, and opprobrium of our holy Catholic faith.

3) Notwithstanding that we were informed of the great part of this before now and we knew that the true remedy for all these injuries and inconveniences was to prohibit all interaction between the said Jews and Christians and banish them from all our kingdoms, we desired to content ourselves by commanding them to leave all cities, towns, and villages of Andalusia where it appears that they have done the greatest injury, believing that that would be sufficient so that those of other cities, towns, and villages of our kingdoms and lordships would cease to do and commit the aforesaid acts. And since we are informed that neither that step nor the passing of sentence [of condemnation] against the said Jews who have been most guilty of the said crimes and delicts against our holy Catholic faith have been sufficient as a complete remedy to obviate and correct so great an opprobrium and offense to the faith and the Christian religion, because every day it is found and appears that the said Jews increase in continuing their evil and wicked purpose wherever they live and congregate, and so that there will not be any place where they further offend our holy faith, and corrupt those whom God has until now most desired to preserve, as well as those who had fallen but amended and returned to Holy Mother Church, the which according to the weakness of our humanity and by diabolical astuteness and suggestion that continually wages war against us may easily occur unless the principal cause of it be removed, which is to banish the said Jews from our kingdoms. Because whenever any grave and detestable crime is committed by members of any organization or corporation, it is reasonable that such an organization or corporation should be dissolved and annihilated and that the lesser members as well as the greater and everyone for the others be punished, and that those who perturb the good and honest life of cities and towns and by contagion can injure others should be expelled from those places and even if for lighter causes, that may be injurious to the Republic, how much more for those greater and most dangerous and most contagious crimes such as this.

(4) Therefore, we, with the counsel and advice of prelates, great noblemen of our kingdoms, and other persons of learning and wisdom of our Council, having taken deliberation about this matter, resolve to order the said Jews and Jewesses of our kingdoms to depart and never to return or come back to them or to any of them. And concerning this we command this our charter to be given, by which we order all Jews and Jewesses of whatever age they may be, who live, reside, and exist in our said kingdoms and lordships, as much those who are natives as those who are not, who by whatever manner or whatever cause have come to live and reside therein, that by the end of the month of July next of the present year, they depart from all of these our said realms and lordships, along with their sons and daughters, man-servants and maidservants, Jewish familiars, those who are great as well as the lesser folk, of whatever age they may be, and they shall not dare to return to those places, nor to reside in them, nor to live in any part of them, neither temporarily on the way to somewhere else nor in any other manner, under pain that if they do not perform and comply with this command and should be found in our said kingdom and lordships and should in any manner live in them, they incur the penalty of death and the confiscation of all their possessions by our Chamber of Finance, incurring these penalties by the act itself, without further trial, sentence, or declaration. And we command and forbid that any person or persons of the said kingdoms, of whatever estate, condition, or dignity that they may be, shall dare to receive, protect, defend, nor hold publicly or secretly any Jew or Jewess beyond the date of the

end of July and from henceforth forever, in their lands, houses, or in other parts of any of our said kingdoms and lordships, under pain of losing all their possessions, vassals, fortified places, and other inheritances, and beyond this of losing whatever financial grants they hold from us by our Chamber of Finance.

(5) And so that the said Jews and Jewesses during the stated period of time until the end of the said month of July may be better able to dispose of themselves, and their possession, and their estates, for the present we take and receive them under our security, protection, and royal safeguard, and we secure to them and to their possessions that for the duration of the said time until the said last day of the said month of July they may travel and be safe, they may enter, sell, trade, and alienate all their movable and rooted possessions and dispose of them freely and at their will, and that during the said time, no one shall harm them, nor injure them, no wrong shall be done to them against justice, in their persons or in their possessions, under the penalty which falls on and is incurred by those who violate the royal safeguard. And we likewise give license and faculty to those said Jews and Jewesses that they be able to export their goods and estates out of these our said kingdoms and lordships by sea or land as long as they do not export gold or silver or coined money or other things prohibited by the laws of our kingdoms, excepting merchandise and things that are not prohibited.

(6) And we command all councils, justices, magistrates, knights, squires, officials, and all good men of the said city of Burgos and of the other cities, towns, and villages of our said kingdoms and lordships and all our new vassals, subjects, and natives that they preserve and comply with and cause to be preserved and complied with this our charter and all that is contained in it, and to give and to cause to be given all assistance and favor in its application under penalty of [being at] our mercy and the confiscation of all their possessions and offices by our Chamber of Finance. And because this must be brought to the notice of all, so that no one may pretend ignorance, we command that this our charter be posted in the customary plazas and places of the said city and of the principal cities, towns, and villages of its bishopric as an announcement and as a public document. And no one shall do any damage to it in any manner under penalty of being at our mercy and the deprivation of their offices and the confiscation of their possessions, which will happen to each one who might do this. Moreover, we command the [man] who shows them this our charter that he summon [those who act against the charter] to appear before us at our court wherever we may be, on the day that they are summoned during the fifteen days following the crime under the said penalty, under which we command whichever public scribe who would be called for the purpose of reading this our charter that the signed charter with its seal should be shown to you all so that we may know that our command is carried out.

(7) Given in our city of Granada, the XXXI day of the month of March, the year of the birth of our lord Jesus Christ one thousand four hundred and ninety-two years.

I, the King,   I the Queen,

I, Juan de Coloma, secretary of the king and queen our lords, have caused this to be written at their command.

Registered by Cabrera, Almacan chancellor.

CHAPTER FOUR

The Inquisition in the New World

T HE INQUISITION ALSO TOOK PLACE in the New World, in the area in and around the Americas. All of South America except for Brazil, all of Central America and Mexico, and some of the Caribbean islands belonged to Spain as late as 1820. The Spanish Caribbean islands were Santo Domingo, Puerto Rico, and Cuba. In the Far East, Spain's holdings included the Philippines; and in what was to become the United States, Spain controlled California, New Mexico, and parts of Arizona and Texas in the southwest, as well as Florida in the east, and for a long time Louisiana.

The history of the Inquisition continued for some of these Jews in other parts of the world long after the expulsion from Spain in 1492, and there are many stories of the Spanish Inquisition's rule in the New World, too. This is also true for Brazil, which was owned by Portugal. As in Spain and Portugal, the Catholic Church had the right to inquire as to the subject of faith and morality in the court of authority still called the Inquisition. Everywhere it was established, excommunication, torture, autos da fé, and the burnings at the stake were held in the New World, just as they had been in the Iberian peninsula.

The major Jewish Sephardic, or New Christian, population in the Spanish domain resided in New Spain (Mexico), Peru, Cartagena (Colombia), and Argentina. There were also New Christians in Costa Rica, Uruguay, and Venezuela. The major Sephardic Portuguese population was first in Brazil. They then migrated to other places they thought to be safe in South America, Central America, and Mexico.

INQUISITION PALACE IN MEXICO CITY. The Inquisition Palace in Mexico was where the Carvajal family and others suspected of Judaizing were tried.

In Mexico, during the colonial period, about 1,500 Jewish New Christians were convicted of Judaizing for their celebration of Jewish rituals and for adhering to the Laws of Moses. Just under one hundred people were burned at the stake and the same number of people died while in prison. In Cartagena, sixty-three Jewish people were brought to trial and nine were tortured.

Under King Philip of Spain, two tribunals were established in the New World, known as *"El Tribunal del Santo Oficio de la Inquisition."* One was for New Spain (Mexico), which serviced Guatemala, New Galicia, and the Philippines. The second tribunal at Cartagena was put into effect in 1610 and took charge of all trials for Panama, Santa Marta, Puerto Rico, Popayan, Venezuela, Santiago de Chile, as well as Cartagena. Before these tribunals were established, all prisoners who were south of New Mexico were sent to Lima, Peru. As for the trials in Brazil under Portugal's rule, there was never a tribunal established. All Brazilian prisoners were tried and punished in Portugal.

According to historian Seymour B. Liebman, generally speaking the Jews in the colonial New World got along with their Christian neighbors. However, the Catholic Church continued to relentlessly pursue heretics, including Jews, and the Inquisition had a strong presence in Spanish America, using sophisticated methods of torture to extract confessions and force conversions, punishing the guilty with death, and confiscating the property of the victims.

One example of the Inquisitors' cruelty is found in the incredible story of the Carvajal family. In 1580, the head of the family, Luis de Carvajal, was given the task and the honor of becoming the governor of the area in Mexico (New Spain) of the northeast, referred to as the New Kingdom of León, by King Philip II of Spain.

As it was considered to be a frontier society, the area of Nuevo León was thought to be a good place for Spain to allow New Christians, or Marranos, to populate, because they would bring their ability to serve as merchants with capital to the new settlement. Many New Christians came to New Spain because they thought there would be great opportunities in the New World, both economically and socially. Additionally, it was thought that they might even be able to recapture the practice of their Jewish traditions without the eyes of the Inquisition always on them.

Unfortunately, the Spanish sent representatives of the Inquisition Court and the Catholic Church to monitor the activities of the area.

Luis de Carvajal, for whatever reasons, decided to reveal his Jewish ancestry and roots by announcing to

THE GOVERNOR'S NIECE ON TRIAL. *The Carvajal family in Mexico was accused of practicing Jewish rituals. Although she was innocent, this woman, who was part of the family, became a victim of torture at the hands of the Inquisition.*

both the Church and the Inquisition that he was again going to practice his Jewish faith. He said that his family was also going to do the same. But even more than this, he began to openly encourage other New Christians to do the same. This did not please the Spanish powers, and one by one the members of the Carvajal family were arrested, tortured, and forced to confess. Many were not only jailed but burned at the stake, as were others who began to practice their Jewish traditions. Whatever tolerance had been given to New Christians in New Spain was shattered, and New Spain became a major seat of the Court of the Inquisition trials and its many punishments and deaths. As many New Christians as were able, about 250, left Mexico because the fears became so intolerable to live with, just as had been experienced in Spain.

By 1649, whatever population was left of New Christians became invisible as they stayed "under the radar" and passed on their traditions verbally only, father to son and mother to daughter. As a result, the autos da fé were eventually stopped officially. That is not to say, however, that when there were suspicions by Christians of New Christians, the prejudices didn't still continue. To this day, Jews in Mexico keep low profiles and still live quietly.

Another example of the Inquisitors' tentacles was that of Peru in South America.

In Peru, between the years 1570 and 1689, there were approximately 191 accused as New Christians, and brought before the Tribunal. Of those, more than half had to face an auto da fé and were burned at the stake. Many of these Jewish Nuevos Cristos were tried under *"La Complicidad Grande"* (The Great Conspiracy) of colonial Peru. By 1689, those New Christians who had escaped the Great Conspiracy left Peru for the West Indies or for North America, if they hadn't wholly accepted Christianity by that time.

After 1665, although there were still punishments of so-called Jewish heretics, the punishments became less severe. It was decided that some of the Inquisitors in the New World hadn't found any real reason for the punishments. As the goods seized by the Inquisition didn't amount to much money in value, so it was not profitable to

A MAN IS TORTURED IN MEXICO. Throughout both the Spanish and Portuguese colonies, anyone suspected of practicing Judaism was subject to the Inquisition's judgment, which could lead to torture and death.

spend the Inquisition's time to confiscate them. The sentences for the jailed accused became shorter, with the fines listed never now including all of their property.

Coming to North America

Many Sephardic Jews who fled to the New World came in secret, escaping to the Spanish and Portuguese colonies because of the persecutions that were taking place in the Old World. There were even Inquisitions in the Philippine Islands, in Lima, Peru, and in India (Goa). The Nuevos Cristos came, hoping to seek some sanctuary in the New World. The story of Brazil links both South and North America together in this need for a peaceful sanctuary away from the horrors.

Although Brazil was owned by Portugal, there was a brief period of time when the Dutch captured a piece of the northeast corner of Brazil, namely Recife, in the state of Pernambuco. Many Dutch settlers came to develop sugar plantations and live off the land in an attempt to be part of the New World. Among the Dutch were members of the Jewish community from Amsterdam. By 1636, they established a synagogue, Zur Israel, in Recife. As of 1637, Johan Maurits Van Nassau was the Governor General of Brazil for the Dutch, and Jews did well under his rule. Joining the Dutch Jewish community were those Nuevos Cristos or New Christians who had come originally to settle for the Portuguese. Here was a chance for them to take back their Jewish traditions in a safe environment in the Dutch colony of Recife, Pernambuco. All went well until 1654, when, under the Portuguese commander, Francisco Barreto, the Portuguese regained the state of Pernambuco from the Dutch. The Jews again were faced with the decision, as they had been in Spain and in Portugal, whether to convert to Christianity, leave, or face the Inquisition. They were given ninety days to decide.

Of those who left in 1654 on ships sent by the Dutch, one group on one of those ships was pirated, and the passengers left to die. Miraculously, a French ship, the *Sainte Catherine*, rescued the passengers and eventually brought them, penniless, to the Dutch colony of New Amsterdam in 1654. (Twenty years later the English took over the area and it subsequently became New York.) Among those passengers were twenty-three Jewish men, women, and children from Recife, Pernambuco, Brazil who were to form the first Jewish community in the North American colonies that would become the United States.

The newcomers were not welcomed into New Amsterdam. The governor of this Dutch colony, Peter Stuyvesant, objected to the presence of the Jewish people in his community, and he petitioned the Dutch West India Company in Amsterdam to have the Jews removed. The petition was denied, as the Jewish community by that time in Holland owned a large part of the Dutch West India Company and were not giving permission for the Jews to be removed. Also, the Dutch had trouble getting people to colonize their new lands, and these twenty-three Jewish people represented a willing body of people who would stay and make it their home. So Peter

MILL STREET SYNAGOGUE. *The Mill Street Synagogue in New York, originally called New Amsterdam, was the first Jewish synagogue in what are now the United States. It is still in existence today in its fifth location in New York at 70th Street and Central Park West.*

Stuyvesant had to accept that they could stay, and could trade freely, as long as the Jews took care of their own sick and poor.

Other communities would follow. Jews would eventually reside in Newport, Rhode Island; Charleston, South Carolina; Philadelphia, Pennsylvania; Savannah, Georgia; and Richmond, Virginia. Eventually, Baltimore, Maryland; Boston, Massachusetts; and Lancaster, Pennsylvania also became areas where Jews resided. Williamsburg, Charlottesville, and Norfolk, Virginia also each had one person or family of Jewish lineage.

Meanwhile, in Brazil, with no more obvious Jews, the Portuguese destroyed the synagogues and overturned the cemetery stones in 1654 in order to obliterate all signs of any Jewish presence in the Recife settlement. The Inquisition, like many dark times in Jewish history, was brought on by jealousy, prejudice, cruelty, and greed, and Jewish people became targets for all that the Inquisition's horrors once again represented. The large synagogue, Zur Israel, in Recife, Pernambuco, has been reconstructed on the foundations of both it and the mikveh or ritual bath and was opened to the public in the year 2002. The cemetery has also been found, but it is under a large group of buildings, and impossible to get to in downtown Recife. But the list of Jewish people buried there has been found and published. There are many thousands of Catholics and Christians today living in Brazil, who are descendants of those Jews who stayed and converted. Today many of them are beginning to recognize that they have Jewish roots.

In a better place, North America, the Constitution and the Bill of Rights of the United States gave the Sephardic people and all Jewish people a protection and freedom they had never before experienced. This freedom brought much opportunity for a life for the Jewish people that could be lived fully, without the possibility of an Inquisition happening there, and the Sephardic Jews could finally exist without fear, practice their beloved religion, and function as citizens for the most part in peace.

A Hidden Synagogue. In Brazil, the Señors Engenho were Marranos who observed Catholicism to the outside world, but secretly practiced Judaism in their home with a synagogue secreted away underneath this, their house near Recife, Pernambuco.

Spanish and Portuguese Jews Who Made a Difference

Here are just some of the names of those Jewish citizens of Spain and Portugal who made monumental contributions, many of them during the Inquisition period. There are many others that could be listed as well.

1055 **Samuel Hanagid** died having been successful as a court Jew to the Spanish Crown and a Torah scholar. He built a great library and synagogue in Granada. He was a Vizier of the Banaziri Dynasty in Granada.

1130 **Rabbi Yehuda Halezi** wrote a book of Torah based on the conversion of the seventh century Kuzari.

1135–1204 **Moses ben Maimon (Maimonides)** was a Jewish scholar, physician, and philosopher. He is often referred to as the Rambam. He organized Jewish oral law into what is called the *Mishnah Torah* (the Torah Revived) and is still used as a place to look for laws (halakah). He produced a work on logic, a treatise on the calendar, and medical books, including one on hygiene. He wrote *A Guide for the Perplexed* in Arabic, in which he explained the esoteric ideas in the Bible, speaking of God's existence and the principle of the creation and many metaphysical problems. Medicine, philosophy, ethics, and the law are the subjects on which he concentrated.

1400–1437 **Master Guedelha Negro** was a rabbi, astrologer, and physician to King Duarte and King Afonso V (1432–1481).

1437–1508 **Don Yitzhak (Isaac) Abrabanel**, scholar, philosopher, and statesman, spoke of the concepts of humanism and greatly influenced later Renaissance thought. He wrote the commentary on "The Ethics of the Fathers" ("Pirkei Avot"). Exiled from Spain, he wrote this work in Constantinople, Turkey, although it began in Spain in the middle of the Inquisition. He became the Royal Treasurer of the Count of King Afonso V of Portugal in Lisbon. He had contacts with the important non-Jewish Portuguese society. He ransomed many Jewish captives taken by Portuguese slave traders.

1439 **Gabriel de Vallsecha** did the first map of the Azores.

1480 **Ambrosio Fernandes Brandao** wrote one of the best books on Brazil, *Dialogos das Granadezas do Brasil.*

1491 **Gabriel Sanchez** was assistant to the Treasurer, Luis de Santangel, one of the Aragonese ministers of King Ferdinand.

1492 **Luis de Torres** was the only known Marrano to accompany Columbus's first voyage. He was baptized before sailing and he spoke Hebrew, Aramaic, and some Arabic as well as his native Spanish. He served as a translator. He set up an empire in Cuba and received acceptance as the independent ruler of a Spanish territory.

1496 **Abraham Zacuto** was an astronomer, and he provided astronomical instruments for explorers. He was a professor of science at Salamanca University, founded in 1230, and was the Court Astronomer to King Joao II. He developed a theory concerning the prediction of weather conditions, devised tables, and wrote the principal basis for Portuguese navigation. He wrote the *Almanach Perpetuum* in 1496.

1496 **José Vizinho** served as a doctor and astrologer to King Joao II. He took part in voyages as far as the Gulf of Guinea. His work was translated into Latin.

1500 **Abraham Cresques** was an astronomer and a master of world maps, atlases, and compasses. He brought the concept of printing to Palestine after he was expelled from Spain. He and his son, Jacobus Ribes, produced the Catalan Atlas. He worked in Spain for Prince John of Aragon as a cartographer and made the Majorcan Compass.

1500 **Gaspar de Gama**, forcibly baptized by the Portuguese in 1497, accompanied Pedro Alvares Gabral into what is now Brazil in 1500.

1500 **Master Jaime de Majorca** was the son of Abraham Cresques. He was a cartographer and constructor of the Majorcan Compass.

1501 **Vasco da Gama** was praised by King Manuel as Juan Cabral's interpreter, when he found Brazil. Da Gama was well known for his knowledge of languages and extensive travels to Asia. He was a cavalier of Manuel's household and was referred to by King Manuel as a Jew. He was granted a pension. He spoke Venetian and used Zacuto's quadrennial tables on his voyage to India.

1502 **Fernando de Noronha** led the Portuguese, with permission from King Manuel I, to colonize Brazil and to export Brazilian wood to Portugal for the dyeing of textiles.

1520 **Abraham de Beja** and **José Spateiro** both knew languages and went on a voyage to the East. They brought news of Prester John to Portugal with Pero da Covicha.

1534 **Garcia de Orta** (1501–1560) studied medical science as a professor in Lisbon until he left in 1534 as a doctor to Captain General Martin Afonso de Sousa in Goa. He wrote *Cologuios dos Somplese Grogas da India*, a comprehensive study of oriental flora applied to western medicine.

1535 **Rodrigo de Orgonos**, a Spanish officer, was a New Christian who accompanied Diego de Almagio when he discovered Chile in 1535. Diego Garcia de Caceres, of Plasincia, Spain, as a New Christian, also helped to colonize Chile for Spain.

1537 **Pedro Nunes** (1502–1578) was a mathematician and master cartographer who authored *Treatise on the Sphere* in Lisbon University. He was a teacher at Lisbon University. He organized the "Aula Daesfera," to teach navigators who were to follow the sea route to India. He worked on this at the University of Coimbra, Portugal.

1539–1591 **Luis de Carvajal de la Cueva**, comptroller of the Cape Verde Islands, was the Spanish fleet admiral in 1566, 1578, and 1579. He was appointed governor of the new kingdom of León, later called Monterrey.

1624 **Bento Teixeira Pinto** wrote "Prosopopda," the first Brazilian poem.

1627 **Francisco Maldonado de Silva** was a surgeon in Colombia in 1627. He was eventually arrested by the Inquisition and disappeared from view.

1642 **Rabbi Isaac Aboab da Fonseca** became the spiritual leader of the Jews in Refice, Pernambuco, and the first rabbi in the New World.

1720 **Daniel Israel Lopez Laguna**. Born of Marrano parents, he was a poet from Portugal who lived in France and Spain, where he was taken to prison by the Inquisition. After he was freed, he was naturalized in 1693 in Jamaica. By 1720 he had moved to London, where he published a paraphrase of the Psalms in various Spanish verse forms. It was called *Espejo Fiel de Vidas Que Contiene Los Psalmos de David in Verso*. He worked for twenty-three years on this project. His sponsor was Mordecai Nunes de Almeyda. As part of the book, he mentions both the Inquisition and the persecutions. He published it in Hebrew, Latin, Spanish, Portuguese, and English before returning to Jamaica, where he died.

PART TWO

Interviews with Descendants of the Marranos

OVERLEAF: LUCY WISDOM'S GARDEN.
The garden at the home of Lucy Wisdom's family in the Azore Islands,
which are owned by, but are a thousand miles from, Portugal.

The Dew of Mercy

Thy people, scorched by sun of hate,
Scourged by oppressors, Lord, compassionate!
Let healing mercy fall on fevered brow
And cruel wounds, as dew from heaven. For Thou
Art God who hears Thy faithful servants' plea,
Shield unto all that trust in Thee.

Thy quickening spirit on our flesh outpour,
Her pristine beauty to our land restore,
Thy saving grace bestow on us, as dew—
Return, O Lord, and make us live anew!

—Solomon Ibn Gabirol
Meditation from Evening Service, Yom Kippur

CHAPTER FIVE
The Interviews

THOSE AFFECTED BY THE WRATH of the Spanish and Portuguese Inquisitions ran, if they could, as far away from the Inquisition as possible. They kept running until they felt they were safe, or at least safer. The migration of Jews, Nuevos Cristos, and Marranos was vast, creating sometimes small and often large communities of people all over the world with the same roots. It's one reason today that in so many areas of the world it is not hard to find people with the same traditions of Judaism in their everyday actions and lives. It is most interesting to note that what the Inquisition most wanted to destroy in the world, Judaism, it instead helped to spread.

Unlike in Spain today, where the history of the Inquisition is not taught, the children in Portugal are taught about the Inquisition in classes where discussion is encouraged and feelings are respected. Many of the children express everything from horror to sadness, wondering just how the Catholic Church or the Inquisition Courts could gain such power in their country, causing such a negative impact on people who were of a different religion, but who made so many positive contributions to their country.

Some of these children are beginning to ask themselves if their ancestors might have been the Inquisition's victims too, and whether they are the descendants of those victims as well.

Hidden Sephardic Jews in many cities all over the world are also beginning to notice their own observance of their Jewish traditions, rituals, and customs that were once outlawed by the laws enforced by the Catholic Church and the Inquisition—first on their people, as Jews, and then on Jews as well who were called the New Christians—causing the many kinds of horror that their ancestors suffered.

It is amazing that in spite of all of the punishments, imprisonments, and confiscation of goods and the loss of life in the autos da fé, that legacy of Jewish traditions still quietly exists for these descendants today. Handed down from mother to daughter, father to son, most often with the meanings of why they are done lost, many of the Jewish traditions still impact the descendants of those persecuted generations of Spanish and Portuguese Jews.

How strong and determined the New Christian and Marrano families must have been for any of this to still be retained. Here, to be read, are interviews with some of the individuals who were interviewed by me, people who still keep some of their Jewish traditions alive, that lead them back to having Jewish roots from the period of the Inquisition.

It is indeed remarkable that so many people were willing—even eager—to be interviewed about their private lives. Most of the people I interviewed expressed the same basic reasons for wanting to share their stories:

1. They had never felt comfortable being Catholic but didn't know why.
2. They'd met people who were Jewish and felt they were like them in shared values and customs.
3. They had heard rumors in their families about possible Jewish roots.
4. They had found documents in family papers that contained Jewish references or words such as "Judea"—which is Portuguese for Jewish.
5. They had read something that touched them emotionally concerning Jewish traditions.
6. They had attended, as an invited guest, a Jewish celebration or ritual that felt right to them, as if it were also theirs.
7. They knew that their names were associated with being Jewish in Spain or Portugal.
8. They had recognized a name of an important Jewish person, such as Supreme Court Justice Benjamin Cardozo, as like their own name and had wondered if there was a family connection.
9. They, in seeking to find out their history, had asked Jewish people what made them different from other people in order to see if any patterns of Judaism fit with their traditions.
10. They had heard that their names, in Portuguese, meant something from the natural world, like animal (Coelho, which means "rabbit") or a plant (Da Silva, which means "of the blackberry plant") or a tree (Pereira, which means "pear tree") or that their name contained a hidden name, like Henriques (which means "son of Henry").

When some Portuguese and Spanish people heard of my interviews, they approached me and asked if I would take the time to question them. I always said yes—even if I had to do the interview on the telephone because of not being in the person's area. Often I had to use an interpreter to help to conduct the interview, in which case I had to make sure the question I was asking was the one being understood and answered.

These interviewees were generous with their time; the interviews lasted one and a half to two hours. Also, they often happened early, before their work day began, or after a long, hard day, or sometimes even during a lunch break, or on a weekend.

The joy of being interviewed for this project was so contagious that often upon hearing of their experience, their friends and family also wanted to be interviewed.

For myself, to be able to see the delight in their eyes when I explained to them just what their practiced traditions meant, and to see the deep searching in their hearts and souls to give me information about their traditions and to remember what elders used to do and what they had been told as descendants was so gratifying. I was glad to have the chance to help them understand the history behind those traditions. That is what these interviews were all about.

Finally, because I am on many websites with my work—including my own—it wasn't hard for people who wanted to be interviewed to contact me—and many people did, and I eventually spoke to all of them—many of whom are the people who are represented in this book.

Barbara Nancy Abreau (Clark)

Personal Information
FULL NAME: Barbara Nancy Abreau Clark
GRANDFATHER: John Germano Abreau
MOTHER'S NAME: Elsie Leandro
AGE WHEN INTERVIEWED: 63
PLACE OF BIRTH: Honolulu, Hawaii
DATE OF BIRTH: November 3, 1943
OCCUPATION: office manager
EMPLOYER: car rental
SURNAMES IN THE FAMILY: Abreau, Pimental, Freitas, Da Silva, Pereira
SURNAMES AMONG FRIENDS: Farias, Souza, Bento, Sylva, Coderio, Correa

Family History and Traditions
Barbara's family came from Madeira, off the coast of Spain, to Hawaii in 1850.

Her family came to Hawaii because they were recruited to run the fields of sugar cane and pineapple on plantations.

They came to Kauai and worked for the Robinson family that owned the island of Niihau. They then moved to Honolulu, where her grandfather owned two dairies and got vines from Madeira to start a ranch vineyard. Still on Kauai, her uncle owns pineapple, macadamia, and cattle and horse farms on over 100 acres. Some of her relatives moved to Hayward, California, as did many other Portuguese with roots from Madeira and the Azores.

The family has always been very clean in the house.

Barbara was raised without eating any shellfish.

The women, including her mom, clean the house thoroughly on Friday. The dirt is not swept out, but swept into a paper bag. The grandmother said it was bad luck to throw it out on Friday, so they kept it and threw it out Monday.

Meatloaf was made with a hard-boiled egg in the middle.

All of the men in the family are circumcised as part of their family tradition.

Her family has said there is no need to pray to Jesus Christ, that we don't need a middleman, and so we should just pray to God.

From Friday evening to Saturday evening, the family doesn't do any work—they think of Saturday as the Sabbath. Sunday is the first day of the week.

Religion is discussed on Friday night.

The blood is drained from animal meat after the animal is slaughtered. The family puts salt and water on the meat to drain it.

All fat is always carefully cut off all meat.

The family eats a lot of almond cookies, sweet honey cakes, eggs with onions, sardines, meatballs, meat pies, olives, and radishes.

There are never crosses on the walls of the home.

Her grandparents said she must marry only a Portuguese of her own type.

When someone in the family dies, the body is put in the living room, and the family sits with the body and it is buried within twenty-four hours, the next day.

Individuals shovel dirt onto the coffin.

When someone died, her grandparents would tear a part of their clothes to show their being torn away from a loved one.

On Friday night, the family relaxes, and there is no cooking. The family members eat what has already been prepared.

The family talks about the Old Testament to learn of the morals and values there.

Grandparents put their hands on the children's heads to bless them.

Although the family is Catholic, they never make the sign of the cross.

The family prays to God, not to Jesus or to the Son or to the Holy Ghost.

As a child, Barbara learned about Queen Esther.

The family gives to charity always—they give to people, but only anonymously.

Her mother is involved with astrology.

The mother and aunts believe in the Evil Eye—don't look at the cursed.

Upon death, there are no Last Rites asked for the person.

Barbara and her family are good at accounting and at business.

Thoughts and Feelings

Barbara has a menorah for Chanukah.

Barbara cooks potato pancakes and brisket for Chanukah.

Barbara buys chocolate covered with gold foil for Chanukah money for the family.

Barbara feels that she is Jewish and talks to her family, including her sisters, brothers, and children, about being Jewish.

Barbara reads books on Judaism.

She has always been drawn to Jewish customs and beliefs, even when she was much younger. The strong women in Jewish history are just like the women in her family, who can run the family, make firm decisions, and feel the most important thing for them is family.

She says Judaism has acquired strengths through all the hardships it has had to endure, and she sees that strength emulated and referred to in her family.

Her feeling is that she was never supposed to be Catholic—she never felt it was who she was. She didn't know Jewish people growing up. It is just in her soul, her instinct.

Delia Attias (Massias) (Fishman)

Personal Information

FULL NAME: Delia Miriam Attias Massias Fishman

AGE WHEN INTERVIEWED: 51

MOTHER'S NAME: Esther Massias Attias

FATHER'S NAME: Joseph Levi Attias

HOME ADDRESS: London, Middlesex, England

SURNAMES IN THE FAMILY: Sequira, BenOliel, Bensusan, Benzimbra

CHILDREN: A son, Laurence, and a daughter, Danielle.

Family History and Traditions

The family never converted to Christianity under the pressure from the Catholic Church and the Spanish government. They chose instead to leave Spain before the expulsion.

Between 1490 and 1500 Delia's mother's family went to Morocco in North Africa. There they were merchants and traders and had connections with merchants in Manchester, England.

Between 1490 and 1500, Delia's father's family went to Livorno, Italy.

Delia's family had lived in Spain and Portugal.

Between 1680 and 1690, the families returned to Gibraltar, which became British in 1713.

One of their relatives, Sol Hatchwell (Solika), remained in Morocco. The Moslem king, Abdrahaman, fell in love with her. She was only fourteen years old. He wanted her to convert to Islam. She said, "I'm Jewish, and I will die Jewish." The local rabbi, Rafael Haserfaty, visited her when she was imprisoned and smuggled kosher food to her. She was later executed, and her body was then burned. She was buried in the old Jewish cemetery in Morocco.

Until recently the family maintained their original "merchant palace" in Gibraltar.

After World War II, Delia's father went to college in Barcelona, where he met fellow students who had never before met a Jew. These students believed that all Jews had horns. As a result of these beliefs, he isolated himself in order to keep kosher and his religious beliefs. He realized that once people got to know him and understood his beliefs they would accept and respect him.

During World War II, Delia's family were evacuated by the British from Gibraltar. Her father's family went to England and landed at Swansea in South Wales and was greeted by Reverend Freeman, the leader of the Jewish community, who was the grandfather of Delia's husband.

Her mother's family went to Tangiers, Morocco, as they owned property there. They spent the war years there.

Delia's family loaned their beautiful family home to the Jewish forces to use as a canteen and meeting place. All the furniture was placed in government storage for the duration of the war.

The family, as Sephardim, from Spanish and Portuguese traditions, keep kosher, observe the Sabbath, and circumcise their males.

Thoughts and Feelings

Delia now lives in Middlesex, England. Her parents and brother still live in Gibraltar. Delia has one brother in New York, one brother in Israel, and two sisters in England.

Delia is a very proud Jewish person, who likes her parents, keeps a kosher home, and is *shomer shabbos*, keeps the Sabbath holy by not working or driving.

Delia wears a Jewish star around her neck and displays it openly.

Delia is close to her parents and siblings, and is very proud of her continuing Jewish heritage.

Joe Benevides

Personal Information

FULL NAME: José Bernard Carreiro Benevides
AGE WHEN INTERVIEWED: 47
PLACE OF BIRTH: San Miguel, Azores, Portugal
WIFE'S MOTHER'S MAIDEN NAME: Martins
WIFE'S MAIDEN NAME: Varao
MOTHER'S MAIDEN NAME: Carreiro
PATERNAL GRANDMOTHER'S NAME: Silva
HOME ADDRESS: Warwick, Bermuda
SURNAMES OF PARENTS' FRIENDS: Furtada, Dias, Silva
SURNAMES OF HIS FRIENDS: D'Acosta, Raposo

Family History and Traditions

Joe's father died when he was fourteen. His mother died when he was fifteen. His brother, sixteen, died of leukemia before them.

Joe's sister brought him to Bermuda to be with her.

It was said that his dad's mom came from Brazil. His mom had a church in her home that the family used to pray in after the brother's passing.

He has two daughters and is married.

When the brother died, he was brought home to his own bed for twenty-four hours. Family watched over the body, then it was buried in a wooden box.

His mom had separate pots for milk and for meat.

The whole family—including aunts, uncles, etc.—do not mix milk and meat together in the same pot or on the table.

The meat in the Azores was salted and left one day before it was cooked.

The veins are removed before cooking.

The women are fastidious housekeepers.

There was always a crucifix at home and on gravestones.

The headstone is put up thirty days after burial.

The family read the Old Testament together, and Joe's dad told him all about Moses, Isaac, Jacob, Abraham, and David.

The women wore a black ribbon for one year after a death.

The men wore a black ribbon on their arms after a death.

They put flowers on gravestones.

Joe's father-in-law is buried in New Bedford, Massachusetts, where one daughter lives; he died when he came from the Azores to visit.

If someone is dying, the person apologizes to anyone that he or she has hurt or had a disagreement with.

The family does not take Last Rites.

Joe was president of the Portuguese Cultural Association of Bermuda, and he organized a time for me to give a lecture to his group about a year in the life of a Jew.

He is a member of the Vasco da Gama Society, which runs schools where Portuguese children and adults learn history and language.

Joe goes to the Azores every year to pay respects to his parents.

The family stressed personal hygiene.

The family prayed at night together.

The father would put his hands on his children's heads and say a prayer for them.

The priest was Father Domingoes.

The Evil Eye was discussed.

When a family member died, the family washed the body of the deceased.

After the body was removed from the house, the bed linens from the deceased's bed were burned.

Often contributions were made to the deceased's memory.

God was prayed to, and Mary was prominent.

Joe did not know that Mary, Joseph, and Jesus were of Jewish lineage.

Joe only recently learned, from a Jehovah's Witness friend, that Jesus had two brothers.

All excess fat on meat is trimmed away before cooking.

Joe believes, as did his dad, in a common salvation.

The family ate eggs and onions, chickpeas, and foods fried in oil.

He was told to marry only within his community, to keep their traditions alive—and to keep their roots from disappearing.

The parents used the phrase "May God bless you" to the kids, as well as "Oh my God."

Education was stressed.

When family members marry outside their own community, it is considered a tragedy and a big loss.

Joe was told that it is fine for a widow to marry her deceased husband's single brother. This was encouraged.

Thoughts and Feelings

Joe was surprised at the meanings of his family's traditions.

He was eager to learn more.

He has no doubt at all about having Jewish roots, because so many traditions are there to enforce that opinion.

When Joe first heard about the lecture I have, he said he wanted to talk about his own family's traditions.

He will talk about the interview with his wife and children and his community.

Joe will send the family tree, with pictures and photos of the Society, by e-mail.

Helen Silva Bettencourt

Personal Information

FULL NAME: Helen Silva Bettencourt
AGE WHEN INTERVIEWED: 83
HOME ADDRESS: Campbell, California
MOTHER'S NAME: Olympia Enos
HUSBAND'S NAME: William (deceased)
SURNAMES IN THE FAMILY: Mello, Bettencourt, Silva
SURNAMES AMONG FRIENDS: Cabral, Rodrigues

Family History and Traditions

The family is from the Azores, Portugal.
Her mother came at age twelve, and her father came at age sixteen, from St. George's
   Island.
Her parents owned a dairy farm in Livingston, California.
Helen and her husband also owned a dairy farm.
She is Catholic. She is not religious, but she does go to church on Sundays.
She prays to God, Jesus, and Mary.
She has five children: four daughters and one son.
She went two and a half years ago to the Azores to find her roots.
Cleanliness was always stressed.
She prays for good health.
When her uncle died, the aunt kept the body at home one day.
People in mourning wear black and stay at home about one week.
When someone dies, friends bring food to the mourners.
The family prays together in the evening.
Helen went to school in the San Joaquin Valley, where a majority of kids were Por-
   tuguese.
Her mom, during the Depression, made plates of food to give to the poor who came
   to her door.
At Helen's wedding, the priest's name was Porto.
Her family never mixed milk and meat at the same time, either in a pot or on the
   table.
The family was very charitable, even though they had very little. They felt it was
   their responsibility always to help others.

Thoughts and Feelings

Helen asked many questions. She also asked me if, because she didn't answer "yes"
   to the traditions of which I spoke, did that mean she didn't have Jewish roots.
   I talked about all the names in the family tree, all with meanings in nature,

and also about circumcision being important in her family. She wanted me to tell Jennifer, her granddaughter, about the interview. She was very interested and said she came from a hard-working, poor farming family. They had left the Azores because of hardships for people in dairy farming and agriculture. She said she would like to know officially if her roots are Jewish.

Pedro Cardoso

Personal Information

FULL NAME: Pedro Rodrigues Cardoso

FATHER'S NAME: Edelvirio Pereira Cardoso

MOTHER'S NAME: Leonor Rodrigues Cardoso

AGE WHEN INTERVIEWED: 42

PLACE OF BIRTH: Maringa Parana, Brazil

OCCUPATION: runs a computer firm

EMPLOYER: self-employed

HOME ADDRESS: Atlanta, Georgia

SURNAMES OF PARENTS' FRIENDS: Elavio, Dos Santos, Sampaio, Benavides, Oliveira, Marques

NAMES IN THE FAMILY: Antonio Rodrigues da Silva, Darcy Teodoro da Silva, Ney Isaac Almodovar

NAMES OF HIS FRIENDS: Tatiana de Oliveira, Wagner Nunes, Ruselia Silva, Avelina Figueiredo, Marli Fraga

Family History and Traditions

He comes from very smart people, like Isaac, who is a government representative in Brazil.

When someone dies, a family member stays with the body for twenty-four hours and then the body is buried in a plain white box (*urna*).

The family mourns for thirty days, during which time the family has no music or partying.

Friends bring food and drink during mourning.

A candle is lit for the deceased.

A charitable gift is given in memory of the deceased.

Education was stressed in his family.

The whole family gives service to the community.

All the boys are circumcised.

Coins are given to the parents when a boy is born.

The mirrors are covered when someone dies.

Pedro's mom doesn't sweep dirt out of the house, because she believes it unlucky. She puts it in a pack and throws it out the back door. Pedro's great-grandmother said one should never sweep dirt out on Friday, because to do so is bad luck.

Saturdays were special because the family didn't work, but read the Bible instead.

The family never mixes milk with meat, and Grandma has separate milk pots and meat pots.

The family enjoys honey cakes, sardines, and hard-boiled eggs.

The family, including Grandma, made a special egg bread that she twisted and baked.

CARDOSA WEDDING PICTURE. Pedro Cardoso came from Brazil to work in America. He has successfully opened several businesses and recently married Maria.

The family made donuts cooked in oil in April.

The family used up flour before Lent, and during Lent the family baked and ate flat (unleavened) breads.

The family read both the Old and the New Testament.

Pedro is going to tell his mother about this interview.

His mother remarried a man named Oliveira.

He has been told he has to marry within his own neighborhood.

Thoughts and Feelings

Pedro is seventy-five percent certain that he has Jewish roots, because he knows he follows a lot of Jewish traditions.

He recently got married to Maria de Jesús Vargas, and his wife has the same traditions. They think they have Jewish roots also.

Beulah Carvahal

Personal Information

FULL NAME: Beulah (Vi) Moreno Carvahal

AGE WHEN INTERVIEWED: 63

DATE OF BIRTH: December 20, 1942, Agua Prieta (Dark Waters), Mexico

HUSBAND: David Bustamonte Carvalho

MOTHER'S MAIDEN NAME: Armedaiz

GRANDMOTHER'S MAIDEN NAME: Bonilla

PATERNAL GRANDMOTHER'S MAIDEN NAME: Gudino

HOME ADDRESS: San Dimas, California

Family History and Traditions

Her father left the family when she was two; he found her when she was thirteen
Her mom died when she was sixteen. Her grandmother on her mother's side
died when she was twelve.

She has one brother, Juan Pedro, in Los Angeles.

She has three children and three grandchildren.

She lived both in Agua Prieta, Sonora, Mexico, and in Douglas, Arizona, right
across the border, where her parents got her a green card when she was three
months old.

She married at age fourteen in Douglas. Her husband left her two years ago, after
forty-seven years.

Vi was raised by her maternal grandma, who lit two small gold candles on Friday
night and had a scroll of parchment with wooden handles that she would read.
Then Vi noticed these objects at a home she was invited to visit, and was told
that they were Jewish rituals and at that point she realized that she, too, had
Jewish roots.

Her grandma told her that her own grandmother's family had owned a *hacienda* in
Spain, but because they were suspects, in 1500 they took their family to Mexico
from Spain and then kept running north to the border between Mexico and the
United States.

Her grandma prayed only to God, even though she said she was raised Catholic.

There were never crucifixes in the houses of her relatives.

All the boys in her family were circumcised, because her grandmother said that
they must be.

There was never pork or shellfish in the house, because her grandmother said those
foods were dirty.

There were separate pots for milk and meat.

The meat is still boiled in salt water to get rid of the blood. Grandma said, "Never
touch the blood."

All women in the family were fastidious cleaners.

Saturday was a special day to pray.

On Friday she cooked stew with vegetables and potatoes.

Grandma read the Old Testament and told Vi about Moses, David, and Abraham as men of valor and integrity.

When Vi's four-year-old sister died, Grandma cleaned her and wrapped her in a white cloth and kept her at home for one day, then buried her. The family watched over the body before she was buried.

There were no Last Rites.

People brought food to the house during the mourning period.

After one month, the stone was placed on the grave and Vi was told to put pebbles on it.

At her mother's funeral, she was told to put handfuls of dirt on the casket.

Grandma wore a black ribbon for a month, in mourning.

In April, Grandma made *pan sim levadura* (unleavened bread).

Grandma used to kiss the doorpost of the house and bless it.

Grandma had a bucket to wash hands after a funeral.

Children were always blessed with hands on their heads.

Vi always cuts away excess fat from meat.

Grandma said the family couldn't eat tamales or sausages because they were made from pork.

Vi never takes Communion or goes to the Catholic Church.

Grandma used to braid bread.

Grandma spoke a strange language that sounded a little like Spanish.

The family ate figs and chickpeas.

Grandma made three-cornered cakes filled with pumpkin.

In December the family fried donuts in olive oil

The family never used lard.

Vi was told that Queen Esther won the king's love by healing him.

Vi was told to become educated.

The family read the Old Testament, and Grandma prayed by rocking back and forth with a shawl.

Grandma said that she was a "different kind of Catholic," with other ideas.

Thoughts and Feelings

Vi has had spiritual visions since she was a small child. So has her brother, and now so do her daughter and grandchildren. God and Jesus have come to her to tell her what to write and do.

After her mom's and grandma's passing, she lived on the streets until her dad found her again. Her husband was cruel.

She has a gift of being able to heal people, because God has told her how.

She works with people from all over the world, including Asia and Egypt, as a minister.

She works to help gangs in Southgate stay off drugs.

She is going to a conference in Jerusalem, where she will speak to the nations about her work.

She knows she is a Sephardic Jew.

She will discuss with her family all of the clues about her roots.

She wants to learn more.

She writes what the Father (a little white light) and Jesus (a dark-bearded man) tell her to write, in both English and Spanish.

She destroyed her husband's idols of Mary and Christ.

Her role is to tell people that God is everywhere and is alive, and that people should help others.

She has three children and three grandchildren.

Her grandson, Jacob, now has a tallis and a yarmulke, given to him by a rabbi.

God told her to watch the Day of the Horn and to start repenting in September, leading up to the Day of Atonement.

She believes that her grandma said, "If God created the cosmos, why would not one believe he would take care of her and everyone else?"

Vi never learned to read or write English or Spanish very well, but God and Jesus help her to read and write her thoughts, the scriptures, and the Psalms.

She knew that Jesus was Jewish, also.

Delaria Carvalho

Personal Information

FULL NAME: Delaria Carvalho Heito

AGE WHEN INTERVIEWED: 97

NATIONALITY: Brazilian

Family History and Traditions

Delaria was raised on a sugar plantation that her family owned for 300 years, and also in Recife's finest neighborhood.

The family, whose roots come from Spain, Portugal, and Holland, supplied sugar, and still does, to Europe, Asia, and North America.

Delaria speaks eight languages, including English.

She was married to a journalist and traveled all over Europe and Asia.

Although her family had slaves, they were very kind to them. The built a long house like the houses in Africa to house the slaves and make them feel more at home.

When slavery ended in Brazil, most of the slaves stayed on as hired help. She remembers some of these people from her own childhood.

The family was very charitable.

All of the boys in the family, including Delaria's three sons, were circumcised.

The family read the Old Testament.

They have a small church on the *fazenda* (plantation).

Delaria knew that there were neighbors who had hidden rooms and baths in their homes.

The family home still houses the largest library in Brazil in a private setting.

Thoughts and Feelings

Delaria knew she had to visit one country she'd not been to, Israel. She did visit Israel.

She brought back a Chanukah lamp and knew about the history and how to use it—which she does.

She now understands the reason for the washing station in terms of Judaism's traditions.

She brought back two small brass candlesticks, which she lights for Shabbat on Friday. She knows to hide her eyes to say the prayer.

She was wearing a large silver cross when I interviewed her. When I told her I was "Judio," she placed her hand on her heart and she hugged me. I asked her why she wore a cross, and she answered that it was for protection.

She said she's come to realize that the family has Jewish roots.

David Ulises Castro

Personal Information
FULL NAME: David Ulises Castro
FATHER'S MOTHER: Carmen Ramirez
MOTHER'S NAME: Maria de Jesús Herrera
AGE WHEN INTERVIEWED: 44
DATE OF BIRTH: December 19, 1960
PLACE OF BIRTH: San Salvador, El Salvador
SPOUSE: Vilma Guadalupe
SPOUSE'S MOTHER: Christina Molina
FAMILY HOME: Colina, Mexico
SURNAMES IN THE FAMILY: Dineda, Peno, Riveira
FAMILY ROOTS: Spain

Family History and Traditions
The family has a charity box in the house.

When a family member dies, the body stays at the house and is buried the next day. The family and friends watch over the body before the burial.

People bring food to the house during the mourning period. They pray each night for eight days.

The family wore black during mourning.

A year after the burial, the gravestone is put up, ending the mourning period. The family go to church, Cabo de Anno, and pray for the dead.

The men in the family are not circumcised.

Women in the family were taught never to sweep dirt out the front door, which would bring bad luck. They could sweep dirt out the back door, but not on Friday or Saturday.

They do not celebrate Easter.

They eat *pan de semita* every morning.

The women drain the blood out of the meat by cooking it with salt water.

When David's grandmother died at the age of ninety-three, there were no Last Rites, and no priest was present.

The family gives to charity in honor of a deceased person.

When someone dies, there is black drapery on the front door.

The family discussed the new moon.

The family is religious.

They clean their hands spiritually, as well as for cleanliness.

They cook pork, and other meat, in salt water to cook it.

They hang their sausages.

David's father was a carpenter, and his grandfather worked as a laborer on a farm.

They killed their animals for meat, and they cut the necks of their chickens.
They always trimmed the fat from the meat.
They believed in whole world salvation.
Education was stressed. David's uncle graduated from college.
The family removes the sciatic vein from their meat.
Personal cleanliness is stressed.
Each member of the family puts a scoop of dirt on the grave.
The family eats sardines, figs, almond cookies, honey cakes, meat pies, eggs, and onions.
David believes Christ was circumcised.
On the basket for the baby a red ribbon is placed to keep the baby safe.
His mother makes the bed quickly after arising.
No pork is served on Friday or Saturday.
The family mourns nine days, including the day of the death.
Family members cry and beat their breasts when a family member dies.
On Saturday, the family is together, and they pray before dinner on Saturday night.
The family thanks God before and after the meal.

Thoughts and Feelings

David thinks his roots are Jewish because his family acts and thinks a lot like Jewish people he knows.
He will talk to his children, to his uncle, and to his father in El Salvador.
There is much similarity between his life and Jewish customs.

Rose Cardoso (Cato)

Personal Information

FULL NAME: Rose Cato

AGE WHEN INTERVIEWED: 48

JOB: consultant for the Evora Tourist Bureau

PACE OF BIRTH: Evora, Portugal

Family History and Traditions

Both of Rose's parents' families came from Evora, where her family has lived since the sixteenth century.

Rose said that she, like most of the older inhabitants of Evora, has Jewish roots, and most families have lived there for hundreds of years.

She said that most people don't talk about that in Evora, because the Catholic Church is very strong, and the monsignor walks around daily, watching.

She gave me a map and pointed out the Jewish area where there was the Jewish synagogue, a center, and Jewish houses before the Inquisition.

She told me the addresses of houses where I could still see indentations where mezuzahs used to be, and some where I could see that the indentations were filled in.

She pointed out the Court of the Inquisition and the Inquisitor's Palace, neither of which were identified with signs or marks to tell the story of the horrors that took place in those buildings. The trials took place in the Court in Evora, and the accused Jews were then taken to Lisbon for the sentences (autos da fé) to be carried out. The goods and money confiscated from the Jewish community were kept at the Inquisitor's Palace.

She said there are still pillars to be seen from the synagogue that was demolished in 1506. She said there was a school and other civil buildings used by the Jews before the Inquisition, as Evora was one of the largest Jewish communities in Portugal.

She said that the coat of arms of the Inquisition—a cross flanked by a sword and an olive branch—still makes people shudder.

She said that in the Evora library there is a copy of the first edition (1496) of the *Almanach Perpetuum*, by the Jewish scholar Abraham Zacuto.

She told me about the palace of King Manuel, who in 1497 ordered all the Jews to be rounded up in Lisbon to be converted to Christianity, en masse. At that time all children under the age of fourteen were taken from their parents and forcibly baptized, many of them never to see their families again.

She said that the Court of the Inquisition was formally opened on October 22, 1536, and the work began. The first person to be tried was David Reuben, in 1542.

Rose told me that the blue and white tiles in the court and at the palaces are some of the most beautiful in Portugal.

The Jewish streets in Evora are called "Rua da Judiaria."

Thoughts and Feelings

Rose said the people with Jewish roots have names of mountains, plants, flowers, and other things in nature, and all those people know each other.

She said her family, like the others with Jewish roots, stick closely together and help each other.

The families with Jewish roots all marry within each other's families and thereby keep the traditions and roots together as much as possible.

The first names in the community are often names from the Bible, like Abrado, Merriam, Jacob, Isaac, and Deborah.

Rose is happy to have Jewish roots, to know about those Jewish roots, and is thankful her family somehow survived.

Rose was happy to speak with me, to help me, and to know that all of her information was going to be a part of a book to tell the Jewish story of Evora.

Maxine Chism

Personal Information

FULL NAME: Maxine Chism

AGE WHEN INTERVIEWED: 67

PLACE OF BIRTH: Maui, Hawaii

GREAT-GRANDFATHER'S NAME: John D'Abreau

UNCLE'S NAME: Da Silva (in Brazil)

Family History and Traditions

The family was originally from Madeira, off the coast of Spain.

They arrived in Hawaii in 1850.

The family in Hawaii was in agriculture and cattle on Kauai, where part of the family still lives.

When a child is baptized, coins are given.

Maxine was told that the Portuguese people are the smartest people in Hawaii.

The family stressed education.

The family prayed to God, never to Jesus.

The family doesn't believe in Jesus.

All boys in the family are circumcised.

The family and their friends are all buried together, just as they stayed together because they were alike.

Maxine has attended a Bar Mitzvah and felt totally comfortable with the ceremony and the reasons for it.

They are all buried together in Madeira, Portugal.

Maxine learned that she should never sweep dirt out the door on Friday when she cleans, because it is bad luck.

She gets rid of the flour before Lent by making donuts called *malassadas*.

There is a Malassadas Day before Lent. *Malassadas* means bad dough, or dough that isn't good, or doesn't rise; a holiday is made of this.

She cleans before Lent, in her kitchen.

She makes meatloaf with a hard-boiled egg in the center.

She believes one should cover one's head to pray.

Thoughts and Feelings

She doesn't know why, but she has always been fascinated by Judaism, especially as she has gotten older.

She thinks it is possible there are Jewish roots in her background.

She feels comfortable with Jewish concepts.

Emma Alvarez de Clavijo

Personal Information

FULL NAME: Emma Alvarez de Clavijo

AGE WHEN INTERVIEWED: 56

DATE OF BIRTH: August, 1949

PLACE OF BIRTH: Bucaramanga, Colombia

FAMILY ORIGIN: Spain (at least four generations ago)

MOTHER'S FAMILY: Estevez

SURNAMES OF RELATIVES: Soledad, Luzamerica, Gilberto, Mario

Family History and Traditions

Children in her family are baptized quickly after birth.

Emma's mother boils meat in salt water before cooking it.

Emma's mother is a fastidious cleaner of the house, and so is Emma.

The family reads both the New and the Old Testaments.

When a family member dies, the body is kept at home one day.

Mourners put handfuls of dirt on the coffin to help bury the deceased.

The family members wear black armbands during mourning.

CLAVIJO GRAVESITE. Julio Clavijo, shown here, lives in Pittsburgh, Pennsylvania. His mother, pictured with him, still lives in his native home of Colombia, South America. Julio and his wife, Giselle, are both physicians. She helped me do this interview in Colombia.

The family mourns for seven days.

Personal hygiene is stressed in the family.

The family participates in a benevolent society and therefore gives to charity.

The family washes the body of a deceased member. Family members take turns washing the body.

A memorial candle is lit for a week after the funeral.

Contributions are made in memory of the deceased.

The family uses the expressions "May the Lord bless…," "Oh my God," and "Please God."

Emma remembers that the family discussed Noah, and Jonah and the whale.

Emma trims the excess fat from the meat before cooking.

The family bakes and shares bread with their priest.

The family eats sugar cakes, eggs with onions, radishes, and meatballs, as well as figs, chickpeas, and macaroons.

The family believes in superstitions.

Emma braids the bread.

The women in the family pray with a shawl.

The family lights candles on December 7.

Emma knows that *"Judio"* means Jewish in Spanish.

When they cook a turkey, they first drain the blood.

She has played the game *pon y saca*.

The family eats pork and shellfish, but not eels or rabbits.

The family dips vegetables.

Dirt is taken outside the back of the house.

Thoughts and Feelings

Emma feels that this is a new subject for her to explore. There are so many Jewish parts of her traditions.

Adella Cordeiro

Personal Information

FULL NAME: Adella Cordeiro

DATE OF BIRTH: 1985

PLACE OF BIRTH: San Miguel, Azores, Portugal

MOTHER'S MAIDEN NAME: Ferreira

HOME ADDRESS: Toronto, Ontario, Canada

SURNAMES IN THE FAMILY: Costa, Banuelas

Family History and Traditions

Adella is a student, and she works in a Portuguese bookstore.

Most of her friends are Portuguese, with names like her family's.

As a child she played the game *pon y saca*.

The family mourns for seven days after the death of a family member.

The official mourning ends at the end of one year.

The family wears black for one year of mourning.

Her family eats *banuelos*, donuts fried in oil, every December.

The family eats codfish in December.

For seven weeks, from April to June, the family cleans the house thoroughly.

Education is stressed to ensure a better future.

The family lived in Providence, Rhode Island, before they moved to Toronto. There are still family members in Providence.

The family stays very close with Grandma, who tells them of the family traditions.

Cousins were encouraged to marry cousins to keep traditions and family close.

The house is thoroughly and always cleaned on Friday.

Family members still have shops in the Azores.

Thoughts and Feelings

Adella has heard about Portuguese with Jewish roots.

She says she has friends who are Jewish, and she relates to them and to their way of life.

She is interested in finding out more about her family's roots.

Bette Costa (O'Sullivan)

Personal Information

FULL NAME: Elizabeth (Bette) Costa O'Sullivan
AGE WHEN INTERVIEWED: 69
DATE OF BIRTH: September 15, 1937
PLACE OF BIRTH: Hanford, California
MOTHER'S MAIDEN NAME: Cardoso (Lena Cardoso Costa)
MATERNAL GRANDMOTHER: Georgina de Melo
MATERNAL GREAT-GRANDFATHER: Antonio José de Melo
MATERNAL GREAT-GRANDMOTHER: Eugenia Salvador de Melo
PATERNAL GRANDMOTHER: Anna Simones Texeira
PATERNAL GRANDFATHER: Joao Vaz da Costa
SURNAMES IN THE FAMILY: Costa, Miranda, De Melo (Melo and Mello), Texeira, Simones, Jaques, Ferreira, Machado

Family History and Traditions

All four of Bette's grandparents emigrated from Terceira, the second-largest of the Portuguese Azores Islands.

Bette was born and raised in California, and currently lives in New Jersey.

Her brother, Jim Costa, is a U.S. Congressman from Fresno, California.

The family story is that the real surname of her great-great-grandfather (Avo José Cardoso's father) was Jacques. According to the family story, he was falsely accused of murder and languished in a prison for years in the mid-1800s. The real murderer made a deathbed confession to a priest, declaring that Jacques was innocent. Though he was subsequently released, he died shortly thereafter of an illness (possibly tuberculosis) contracted in prison. The disgrace (*verguena*) attached to this incident and to the family name was such that his widow took Cardoso (also a family name) as her own and her son's surname. When she remarried, her son took his stepfather's name, Miranda. The Jacques surname could have roots in the early Flemish and Burgundian settlers to the Azores, as the Cardoso/Miranda sons of her grandfather's generation had fair complexions and many had light-colored eyes.

Bette's grandfather, José Cardoso, came to the U.S.A. in 1900, went back to Terceira about 1910, met and married Georgina de Melo, and returned with her to California in 1912.

Bette's maternal great-grandfather was Antonio José de Melo. He was from the village of Rebeirinha and was, Bette was told, the superintendent of schools for Terceira. In tracing the Melo family back to 1784, it was found that all the Melos had married within the village except one, who had married a woman from the neighboring village of Santa Barbara.

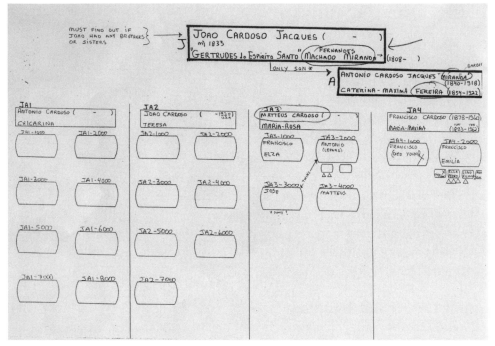

A FAMILY TREE. The biographical chart for the family of Betty Costa O'Sullivan, which came originally from the Azores. Her family settled in the Fresno, California, area, where they owned a ranch. Betty's brother, Jim Costa, has served as a member of the United States House of Representatives.

There were eight Cardozo brothers, of which five emigrated to the U.S.A. in the early 1900s. Three went back to the Azores and were then prevented from returning, because of changes in emigration law. Some of the remaining brothers went from the Azores to Brazil. Bette's grandfather was one of the two who remained in the U.S.A. and raised their families there.

Bette was told as a child that Cardoso was a Jewish name, and that they "probably" had Jewish roots. They referred to Benjamin Cardozo, the first Jewish Supreme Court Justice, as being Portuguese, and her grandmother reported this with some pride. That they might have Jewish roots was a familiar family story.

In 1971, Bette made her first trip to the Azores and spent some time in the archives tracing the Melo side of the family.

The second-largest town on the island of Terceira is called Porto Judeu (Port of the Jews). There is an old Jewish cemetery there. During her 1971 visit, Bette asked if there was a Jewish community, and was told it no longer existed. However, there still is one on the island of San Miguel.

Bette completed eight years of elementary schooling in a two-room school on her parents' ranch, then went to a Catholic high school in Fresno and was a history major at Fresno State College.

During high school, she lived with her maternal grandmother, Georgina Cardoso, who told her many stories of the "old country." In high school the nuns taught her that the Jews were the "chosen people" of the Bible, who did not recognize the Messiah, and that Da Vinci's "The Last Supper" was a depiction of a Passover Seder.

In the Cardoso/Costa families, they referred to "the Lord," "Our Lord," and "God" in many respectful and prayerful instances. They also commonly used phrases like "if God wishes," "if Our Lord permits," etc., mostly in Portuguese but also in English.

Cleanliness was a passion in the family, and poverty was not an excuse for not being clean.

Saturday was not a workday as such, but on a dairy the cows must be milked twice a day, every day. Soup that was made ahead of time was served for meals.

Friday was the big cleaning day.

When there is a death, the family mourns formally after the funeral for at least three days. They receive visits from family and friends at home as well as at the funeral home. When Bette was a child there were more formal rules about what was to be worn during mourning, and what activities could be engaged in for a certain time following the death.

Charity is given in the name of the deceased, and there is a custom, possibly Azorean, called *uma vesta da alma*, "clothes for/from the soul." A poor person is outfitted from the skin out, including shoes, socks, suit, shirt, etc., in memory of the deceased.

Like both of her grandmothers, her mother, and her aunts, Bette washes chicken and turkey, salts it in and out, and puts salt inside the skin prior to following a recipe or other preparation. Her mother told her this was done to make sure the food was clean.

Bette's mother stressed education for her and her brother, and from early in her life she knew she would go to college. This was not common for the community in which she was raised.

When she was a child, the children were blessed with hands on their heads. She can remember her father kissing his own hand when greeting an elder and saying, "Your blessing, Uncle," or "Bless me, Aunt." The response was "God blesses you," spoken with a hand on his head.

The Blessed Mary was respected and revered.

The boys in the second generation of the family are all circumcised.

The Evil Eye or Bad Eye was talked of as wishing someone ill, but it was regarded as superstition by Bette's maternal grandmother; her paternal grandparents seemed to give it more credence.

The traditional Easter bread was made every year, a sweet eggy bread with a hard-boiled egg baked inside of it.

Fat is trimmed away from meat before cooking.

All members of the family are enrolled in a benevolent society at birth, to provide insurance in case of death. This has continued to Bette's own children, whom Bette has enrolled.

Charity means taking care of one's own first, which is considered the decent thing to do.

When baking bread, a pinch is taken off and thrown away.

The family eats eggs and onions, sardines, almond cookies, sweet yellow sugar cakes, eggplant, and meatballs, among other food.

Sometimes Bette eats honey on apples.

Thoughts and Feelings

Bette thinks her roots are Jewish.

At various times, she feels Jewish guilt, but also the positive side of being Jewish: the importance of charity, of family, of togetherness, being supportive, and believing strongly in education.

Feeling connected with a larger community is a wonderful thing, and being included in this tradition feels right to her.

Lucy Leal Couto Wisdom

Personal Information

FULL NAME: Lucia (Leal) Couto Wisdom

AGE WHEN INTERVIEWED: 48

PLACE OF BIRTH: Terceira, Azores, Portugal

FATHER'S NAME: Manuel Eduardo Couto

GRANDMOTHER'S MAIDEN NAME: Maria Rozario Couto

PATERNAL GRANDMOTHER: Zelia Carmen Couto

HOME ADDRESS: Las Vegas, Nevada

SURNAMES IN THE FAMILY: Couto, Carmo, Da Silva, Silveira, Leal, Castrellon

SURNAME OF HER AUNT'S FRIENDS: Da Silva, Gracia

SURNAMES OF PEOPLE LUCY HAS KNOWN DURING HER LIFE: Fonseca, Mendes, Oliveira, Cardoso, Soares, Fontes, Segurado, Souza

MOTHER'S FAMILY: Da Silva

CHILDREN: A son, Travis, and a daughter, Jessica

Family History and Traditions

Lucy came to America at age eight, with an aunt and uncle.

She changed her name when she became a citizen, dropping the Portuguese name.

She first lived in Artesia and Cerritos, California.

Her parents came to America but didn't stay, and went back to the Azores.

Her mother has disappeared.

THE AZORES. *The Azores Islands, originally owned by Portugal, are 1,000 miles from the mainland. They were home to Lucy Couto's ancestors before they came to America.*

Lucy Leal (Lucia) Couto Wisdom's Family

Father's Side (from San Miguel, Azores)
FATHER'S NAME: Manuel Eduardo Couto
FATHER'S FATHER: Manuel Couto
FATHER'S MOTHER: Maria Rozario Couto
FATHER'S SISTERS: Maria-Jesús Couto (4 children), Evangelina Couto (11), Maria-Conceieao Couto (2)

Mother's Side (from Terceira, Azores)
MOTHER'S NAME: Zelia Carmo Leal Couto
MOTHER'S FATHER: Antino Joaquín Leal
MOTHER'S MOTHER: Cecilia Leal
MOTHER'S SIBLINGS: Leonel Leal (1 child), Mascelino Leal (8)
MOTHER'S AUNTS AND UNCLES: Jorenal Silva (4 children), Celtiberia Silva (3), Numancia Silva (0), Gavibalde Silva (2)

Her aunt married Manuel Borges, also from Terceira.

Her father, a fisherman, is from San Miguel, Azores.

All the boys in the family have always been circumcised. Lucy was told that it was one of the family's traditions.

In the Azores, there was always a crucifix in the house.

The family prays to God and to Jesus.

Her aunt always separated milk and meat, and used separate pots for each.

The meat was always salted to drain blood out before it was cooked.

Lucy remembers her aunt talking about removing the sciatic vein from meat.

Her family are fastidious cleaners, and they clean on Friday or Saturday.

In the Azores, a deceased family member is kept at home for one or two days, then buried.

A rosary is said prior to the funeral.

When someone in the family dies, the mirrors are covered.

No music or television is allowed for one week during mourning.

The men wear black armbands during mourning.

Visitors bring food to the house during the week of mourning.

In April, the family makes *malassadas*, a sweet bread.

The family uses expressions like "Oh my God" and "Please God."

The women always trim excess fat from the meat before cooking.

At funerals, both hard-boiled eggs and lentils are served.

Lucy believes in common salvation.

Her aunt often braided the bread.

Lucy was encouraged to marry a Portuguese from her own community in order to keep traditions alive.

Education was encouraged, so one could improve oneself.

At funerals, the men and women shrieked and beat their chests.

At weddings, the bride and groom drink from the same cup.

Lucy did not know that Mary, Joseph, and Jesus and his brothers were Jewish.

Thoughts and Feelings

Lucy never thought that she, or any other person of Portuguese descent, could be Jewish.

She has Jewish friends.

She now feels there is a real possibility of Jewish roots.

She will discuss what she has learned with her children, and she will ask her older sister, who still lives in the Azores, about the answers to the questions that she didn't know.

Tiaga Figueredo

Personal Information
FULL NAME: Tiaga Figueredo
AGE WHEN INTERVIEWED: 23
MOTHER'S NAME: Virela Simones
FATHER'S MOTHER'S MAIDEN NAME: Goncalves
PLACE OF BIRTH: Covilha, Portugal
OCCUPATION: junior management
EMPLOYER: Four Seasons Hotels
HOME ADDRESS: London, England
SURNAMES IN THE FAMILY: Da Silva, Oliveira, Pereira, Pinel, Pires

Family History and Traditions
Tiaga's mother is from Porto Alegre, Portugal.

Tiaga's birthplace, Covilha, is a mountain city on a plateau, twenty kilometers from Belmonte.

There is a feeling of this city having a Jewish population from long ago.

There is a business in his city that exports kosher wine.

After meeting people who are Jewish in London, he figured out that he has Jewish roots.

His mother cleans the house on Friday.

Meat and milk are never put on the table at the same time.

His mother has separate pots for milk and meat.

The family eats sardines, figs, olives, stews, and codfish cakes.

When someone in the family dies, the body stays overnight in the house, is washed, and then buried in a pine coffin.

The family prays to God and the Virgin Mary, but not to Jesus.

The family thanks God, not the Church.

Saturday is a special day, on which people are happy and very positive.

Tiaga's grandmother cooks lamb on Friday to serve on Saturday, when the whole family comes together. She does not cook on Saturday.

Covilha is an intellectual small community where almost all the children go to school and then to university. Parents there expect and support the children to be educated. Education is paramount.

The family supports the group that takes care of orphans, the poor, and the elderly.

In April, the family bakes and eats flat breads.

At Christmas, the family eats bread that is deep-fried in egg and oil and coated with sugar and cinnamon.

In January, the family members go to Oporto for a ritual bath in the ocean. Oporto is north, near the Spanish side. Tiaga assumes this custom is for the New Year.

The family discusses the presence of evil, and one has to be careful always not to
come up against a person or a situation that forebodes evil.

When a child is born, the *padrinho*, or godfather, has to buy gold or silver for the
baby.

Thoughts and Feelings

Tiaga believes there is a connection between the 500-year-old Jewish community of
Belmonte, Portugal, and his own community of Covilha.

He thinks he has roots that go back to Judaism. He feels like a Jew.

He will talk to his family about these feelings.

Jules Freitas

Personal Information

FULL NAME: Jules Freitas

AGE WHEN INTERVIEWED: 89

FAMILY ORIGIN: The Portuguese island of Funchal, Madeira.

Family History and Traditions

Jules's ancestors included Antonio José da Silva Foundlina, who was baptized in Funchal, Madeira, June 13, 1846. His godfather was José Gonsaloes.

In 1873, Antonio married Beatris de Camara, age 20.

Their children were Manuel, born July 28, 1876, and baptized 1876; and Lionidia, born February 1879 and baptized 1879.

Antonio applied for a passport on April 17, 1879, to go to the Sandwich Islands (Hawaii). In Hawaii, Antonio said that his real name was Ladeira, but in Madeira he was also known as Antonio José de Lyra, and also as Antonio da Carara Lyra.

Mary Julia Freitas Vidinhar, born June 2, 1905, on Madeira, Portugal, was the daughter of Alfred Charles Freitas and Aolinda Silva Freitas.

Jules says that his sister's marriage certificate has the word *"Judeo"* written at the bottom and that his sister was told that her roots are originally Jewish.

Jules says that there is an old family trunk with a secret hiding place that contains a Bible with births and deaths of his family going back to Portugal in the sixteenth century.

BAPTISMAL CERTIFICATE OF JULES FREITAS. Jules Freitas's family, from Madeira, Portugal, his family came to work in the sugar fields in Hawaii.

Jules was taken, as a young child, into the fields by his father, who told him that
the family's roots are Jewish, not Christian. His father said he should never tell
anyone in the community about this, because there would be punishment by the
priest and by the community.

Jules said that when a son is born, the father gives silver coins to poor people.

Education was stressed in his family.

The family does not eat pork.

The family watches over the deceased family member for twenty-four hours, and
then the deceased is buried.

The deceased is buried in the Portuguese part of the Catholic cemetery, so that all
the Portuguese are kept together in death, as they are in life.

Thoughts and Feelings

There is no question in Jules's mind that he comes from roots that are Jewish.

He is, and always has been, most eager to learn about Jewish traditions and customs.

He thinks it is special to come from Jews who have suffered for so long and are still
here to be and live as Jews.

Paula Martins de Freitas

Personal Information

FULL NAME: Paula Martins de Freitas
MOTHER'S NAME: Oliveira
FATHER'S NAME: Ramos de Freitas
PLACE OF BIRTH: São Paulo, Brazil
DATE OF BIRTH: February 28, 1978
OCCUPATION: student
EDUCATION: food safety Ph.D. candidate at University of California, Davis
GOOD FRIENDS: Wendy Maduff, Daniel Karen
SURNAMES OF FRIENDS: Machado, Carvalho, Pinto, Carneido, Coelho, Olmeida, Henriques
SURNAMES IN THE FAMILY: Martinez (which became Martins), Ramos, Da Silva, Ferreira, Mello, Pimental, Comargo.

Family History and Traditions

One of Paula's grandmothers comes from Saudi Arabia. Her maternal grandfather is from Holland.

Paula's brother, in Brazil, was circumcised.

The family prays to God and to Jesus Christ.

The children's heads are touched with the hands to be blessed.

When someone dies, the body stays in the house for one day, and the family stays with the body. There are flowers and sheer fabrics and candles. All the family says prayers.

After seven days, the family gathers and says prayers again.

Charity is given for the deceased.

Friends bring food for seven days after the funeral.

Some houses in the family have a ritual bath.

Some houses in the family have washing basins in the dining room.

There is a lucky ring as an amulet for protection. It has a red stone with pearls and gold, and it has been in the family for generations.

Saturday is a day of rest for the family.

The family reads the Old and the New Testaments.

Abraham was discussed as a father.

Mary was considered a good human woman, not a saint.

There are family crystals that get washed with salt water if someone is trying to hurt them. This is done for protection.

When something bad happens, they emphasize that it could have been worse.

They don't wear a cross because you could have a crucified life.

The family likes to read the Psalms of David.

The sciatic vein is removed from chicken and meat.

All fat is trimmed from chicken and meat.

The family eats almond cakes, sugar cookies, eggplant, eggs with onions, meatballs, stews, and figs.

Paula's mother makes meatloaf with a hardboiled egg in the middle.

The family gives time and money to charity, and family members are involved in the benevolent society.

On Friday, clean sheets are put on the bed and clean pajamas are worn.

Moses is discussed in the family.

Paula's mom's nails are done at the salon on Friday.

The family doesn't believe in the process of Confession.

Family members put dirt over the coffin before burial.

Around Christmas, the family plays a gambling game with a top that has numbers.

On Paula's mother's side, family members covered the mirrors with black fabric when someone died.

When they returned from the cemetery, they washed their hands.

The men wear a piece of black fabric on their suits when there is a death in the family. Women wear black outfits.

Part of Paula's family, the Buenes family, came from Spain, when Brazil was owned by Portugal and Spain.

The family on Paula's father's side came to northeastern Brazil and then moved to Minas Gerais.

Usually when they come in from outside the home, they wash their hands before they do anything else.

Thoughts and Feelings

Paula thinks that her origins are mixed, and that part of her roots may be Jewish.

She is going to ask her family the questions she was unable to answer during the interview.

José Constantino Teixara Goncalves

Personal Information

FULL NAME: José Constantino Teixara Goncalves

AGE WHEN INTERVIEWED: 31

DATE OF BIRTH: October 7, 1974

PLACE OF BIRTH: Funchal, Madeira

FATHER'S FATHER: Goncalves

FATHER'S MOTHER: Maria Goncalves

MOTHER'S FATHER: Teixeira Gonsalves

MOTHER'S MAIDEN NAME: Aguyar Teixara

HOME ADDRESS: London, England

OCCUPATION: works at Tristar Worldwide

SURNAMES IN THE FAMILY: Almeida, Presto, Aruajo, Silveira, Veiria, Goveia, Miranda, Colerais, Nunes

FRIEND'S SURNAME: Lopes

Family History and Traditions

The family came to Porto Santo, Madeira, in 1491, having been given permission by King Don Enriques of Portugal.

The family all lived on the islands. José's mother's father moved to Curaçao and was a carpenter who built coffins.

There are baptism records going back to the sixteenth century, and more in 1764.

The family are Catholic.

They put crucifixes on tombstones.

They pray to God.

They hang their sausages over the fireplace.

They boil their pork in salt water before cooking it.

They had separate pots for milk and meat.

They read the Old and New Testaments, and discussed Abraham, Isaac, Jacob, Moses, and the Psalms.

José knew that President Sampaio has Jewish roots, and that other Portuguese do also.

When someone in the family dies, the body is kept in a coffin in the house. Flowers are put in the coffin.

The family members put handfuls of dirt on the coffin at the funeral.

The family wears black for one month of mourning.

They mourn for one week, with prayers said each night

They give charity for the deceased.

For eleven weeks, from Easter to June, they celebrate Camacia Esperito Santo by baking bread and giving it to the church for distribution to the poor.

Personal hygiene was stressed.

The moon and stars were discussed.

Pregnant women hope for a full moon to deliver.

They worry about the Evil Eye.

When a family member dies, they watch over it for twenty-four hours, even if it goes to a funeral home.

The family knows that Christ was Jewish.

Foods eaten include eggs with onions, sardines, radishes, eggplant, and stews with chickpeas.

Vegetables are cooked in salt water or dipped in salt brine called *cozibo*.

The family played *pon y saca*.

Education was stressed.

The children were taught to make the bed quickly when awakened.

All boys in the family are circumcised.

José's grandfather called the family "People of the Race" and "the Nation of the Race."

Their neighbor, Nunes, a widow, married her husband's single brother.

Thoughts and Feelings

José believes he has Jewish roots.

He will talk to his grandparents about the questions and about his roots.

He now knows that names are often linked to Jewish roots.

He believes in a common salvation, not individual salvation.

Elizabeth Gonzales (Jaskulah)

Personal Information
FULL NAME: Elizabeth Gonzales Jaskulah
MOTHER'S MAIDEN NAME: Banuelos
AGE WHEN INTERVIEWED: 31
PLACE OF BIRTH: Santa Monica, California
SURNAMES IN THE FAMILY: Lopes, Luna, Rojas, Zuniga, Tello

Family History and Traditions
Elizabeth's grandmother, originally from Galicia, Spain, lived in Mexico (Jalisco, Zacatecas).

Her grandfather came from Zacatecas.

The family has separate pots for milk and meat, both in Mexico and in the U.S.

Their houses are cleaned thoroughly on Friday.

She was told there's a difference between being a Catholic and being a Jew.

The mother's and father's customs were the same in their neighboring towns.

Elizabeth was told that Jews don't believe in Jesus or in saints, implying that their family is different from typical Mexicans.

They eat a lot of figs and dates, and she was told this was typical food commonly eaten by Jews.

The family only socialized with other families who ate the same foods and shared the same ideas.

The family believed in being ambitious and hard-working.

The family is analytical, filled with educated people, and education is stressed in the home.

Creativity was also encouraged.

The family has many scholars, professors, and doctors.

Other people in the community thought they were weird.

The family knew they were different from people who lived around them.

The family were not religious Catholics. They struggled with Catholic rites of passage. They are uncomfortable about Communion and Confessions.

Jewish friends in America commented that that Gonzales family shared the same issues as Jewish families, according to Elizabeth's brother, Miguel.

Babies were given coins for good luck.

When Elizabeth's grandmother died in Mexico, the family stayed up all night with the body, in the home, and lit candles for twenty-four hours. Then the body was washed and buried. No embalming was done. The body was put in a plain pine box.

Friends and family bring food and drink to the house during mourning.

The family throws dirt on the coffin.

The family values charity and is very charitable.

They eat sardines, olives, codfish, aged cheese, dark butter and sugar over bread, which Elizabeth says is a Marrano dish.

Her father is very clean.

They do not practice Communion or Confessions in their family.

There are no crucifixes in the house.

The family members wear a black ribbon and also put a black ribbon on the house when one of them dies.

The Evil Eye is discussed, and horoscopes and astrology are referred to.

Elizabeth's great-aunt's husband was a Spanish person from Holland who had similar values to those of the Gonzales family.

The family lights candles, purposely facing east.

Certain family members think highly of a professor named Israel, whom they think is Jewish.

Expressions used in the family include, "Thanks be to God" and "Oh God."

On Passover, the family bakes a bread called a *sema*, which is flat, unleavened, and made with honey and sugar. It is called Sephardic bread baked for Lent. It is not sold anywhere, only home-baked.

Elizabeth's father's family pray to the Virgin Mary, not to Jesus.

They have a ritual every July called St. Santiago, in which people react as if being beaten by a sword during the Inquisition.

Many Sephardic communities exist in northern Mexico.

There is a taboo in her town against looking to any other religion, lest you be ostracized and rejected by the community.

Women salt their meat before cooking it.

They don't mix milk and meat because they say it can make you sick. They consider mixing meat and milk to be disgusting.

In Zacatecas there is a social club that does fundraising for the elderly, for burials, teaching, and helping others.

The Gonzales family values education for both men and women.

In her family, sons and daughters are considered equal.

Part of the family is called Henriques.

Thoughts and Feelings

Elizabeth feels that her family looks deep into discussions of life, both socially and psychologically, as Jewish people do.

In Jalisco, there are customs and values shared by some people, including Elizabeth's family, that set them apart from other people there.

The Gonzales family is very independent, and wants nothing from the Mexican government. They remind themselves of the times they had to be cautious, as during the Inquisition.

Elizabeth has questioned and feels unconnected to the Catholic Church.

She feels Jewish.

The homes of Elizabeth's grandmother, aunts, and cousins are clean, orderly, and spotless. As a psychologist, Elizabeth feels this trait in her family is not typical of people in Mexico and Latin America.

Hortensia Marcos (Bodker)

Personal Information

FULL NAME: Hortensia Marcos-Bodker

AGE WHEN INTERVIEWED: 50

DATE OF BIRTH: February 25, 1955

PLACE OF BIRTH: Havana, Cuba

MOTHER'S MAIDEN NAME: Jimenez

PATERNAL GRANDMOTHER'S SURNAME: Rodriguez

HOME ADDRESS: Leawood, Kansas

SURNAME OF FATHER'S RELATIVES: Acosta

SURNAMES OF MOTHER'S RELATIVES: Victorero, Mendez, Rodriguez, Jimenez

Family History and Traditions

The family on Hortensia's father's side came from Jovellanos, Cuba, and from
Matanzas, just outside Havana.

On her mother's side, the family was originally from North Asturias, Spain, and
from Caibarien, Cuba.

One member of the family fought in the Spanish–American War.

Although the family thought that Fidel Castro was good for Cuba when he first
came to office, compared to Batista, they later decided that Castro was ruthless.

Hortensia's father was a doctor with clinics. When Castro nationalized the clinics,
he forced her family to sign loyalty papers, or be imprisoned or killed. The clinics were forcibly closed.

Hortensia's grandfather was a pharmacist.

When the family left Cuba, they were searched at the airport, because they were
allowed to take with them only a small amount of clothes and other possessions.

They left Cuba in 1962; Hortensia's mother's family had been in Cuba since 1800.

Hortensia's mother is 82 and is Catholic. She prays to God and to saints, including
Santa Barbara; but rarely goes to church. She wears medals of saints.

There are no crucifixes in the home.

There are no bibles in the family's house.

The boys in the family were circumcised.

One of Hortensia's two sisters married someone Jewish and converted to Judaism.

Hortensia (Tensy) also converted to Judaism when she married someone Jewish.

When someone in the family dies, the body is kept at home for twenty-four hours.

A family member sits with the body.

Hortensia's mother and others wash the body.

Her mother fasts when a person has died.

The family gives to charity.

Hortensia's grandfather on her mother's side was a Mason.

Her mother is superstitious and believes stories about the Evil Eye.

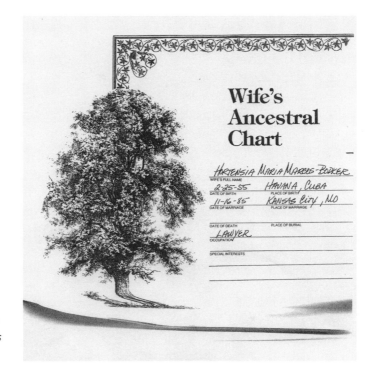

Wife's Ancestral Chart

HORTENSIA MARIA MARCOS-BODKER
WIFE'S FULL NAME
2-25-55   HAVANA, CUBA
DATE OF BIRTH   PLACE OF BIRTH
11-16-85   KANSAS CITY, MO
DATE OF MARRIAGE   PLACE OF MARRIAGE

DATE OF DEATH   PLACE OF BURIAL
LAWYER
OCCUPATION

SPECIAL INTERESTS

BODKER ANCESTRAL CHART. The ancestral chart for the family of Hortensia Maria Marcos Bodker, who came to America from Cuba after Fidel Castro nationalized her father's pharmacy.

Tensy has three children, all raised Jewish.

Education was always considered important in her family.

The family, led by the father, who was well-read, discussed social issues and concepts with the children.

Tensy always gravitated to the Jewish boys in the fraternity to date, as did her sister

Her mother knows about the Inquisition.

Her sister, Grace, loves the Ladino language and she sings in it.

Her sister is interested in family genealogy.

Thoughts and Feelings

Hortensia would like to find a family genealogy to formally connect the family's roots to Judaism.

When she studied Judaism and became Jewish, she felt it was like finally finding a pair of gloves that fit.

She feels totally comfortable about giving up salvation and Jesus Christ.

She and her sister share values in Judaism, not only religiously, but also culturally and ethnically.

Natalie Medina

Personal Information
FULL NAME: Natalie Medina

AGE WHEN INTERVIEWED: 48

DATE OF BIRTH: April 14, 1958

PLACE OF BIRTH: Brooklyn, New York

MOTHER: Margarita Lopez Gonzalez

MATERNAL GRANDMOTHER: Natalia Lopez Gonzalez

PATERNAL GRANDMOTHER: Monserrate Andujar

HUSBAND: Alberto Zarza-Lopez, from Paraguay

SURNAMES IN THE FAMILY: Freytes, Muhlach, from Puerto Rico. Her mother's mother is from Catalonia, Spain.

SURNAMES OF FRIENDS: Ruthenberg, Rey, Rivera (cousin), Ferrer, Colon, DeLeon, Henriques

Family History and Traditions
The family came from Puerto Rico, and Natalie's family on her mother's side came originally from Catalonia, Spain. Her father's family came originally from an area near Córdoba and Seville in Spain.

Now some of the family is in Chicago, some are in Puerto Rico, and some are in Los Angeles.

They pray to God.

There is no crucifix in the home.

Godparents give a wooden box with gold coins to a child at baptism. They give out pouches with nickels to guests.

Milk and meat are never on the table at the same time.

There are separate pots for milk and meat, as well as separate silverware and separate dishes.

They soak meat in salt water, then spice it and cook it.

They do the same with pork, which is a long process.

The sciatic vein is removed.

The family are fastidious housekeepers.

Sheets and clothes are cleaned on Friday.

No work is done on Saturday, which is a family time.

Stew is cooked on Friday, and the uncle also makes stew and soup to eat on Saturday.

Natalie's grandmother read the Bible, including the New Testament, but mostly the Old Testament.

Natalie's mother keeps both Testaments in her bedroom.

The Psalms were read by Natalie's cousin, Elias.

The family fasted during Lent, always hiding their behavior.

They made fried donuts using cornmeal during winter holidays.

The family belongs to a benevolent society, and the grandmother gave food to senior citizens.

Prayers were said to God in thanks for food, for the day before going to bed, and upon rising.

A word of blessing is said as they enter the house.

There is an amulet in the family to protect them from the Evil Eye; it is a blue or gold eye.

The father puts a hand on the heads of children when he blesses them.

Hard-boiled eggs were served at her grandmother's funeral.

The body was kept at home for twenty-four hours, and family members stayed with the body.

The body was in a simple white shroud.

People brought food to the family for nine days, including the day of death.

A memorial lamp was lit for nine days.

Contributions were made for the deceased.

Natalie was told to wear black for thirty days of mourning.

Wine was served and blessed with meals.

The family sometimes made the sign of the cross.

Familiar expressions in the family were "Please God," "Oh my God," and "May the Lord keep us."

The family prayed to God and to Mary, but not to Jesus.

They trim fat from all meat.

When they bake bread they throw away a pinch of dough.

They eat eggplant, eggs with onions, meatloaf with an egg in the center, radishes, and meat pies. Natalie's mother favors Jewish foods.

The family doesn't tell secrets and is unusually quiet about the past.

They bake egg breads, always braided.

Natalie believes in a common salvation.

The family members apologize to people who are close to dying.

Natalie knew Christ was Jewish.

Her grandmother stressed with pride that Christ was Jewish.

It is considered good when a child is born with a star over his head.

Neither the mother nor the grandmother takes Communion.

Honey and sweets are served at weddings.

They eat figs and olives.

They eat lamb in early spring.

Natalie's mother, grandmother, and son keep a charity box in the home.

No crosses are placed on family gravestones.

There are some marriages between cousins in the family.

The grandmother encouraged family members to marry within their own community.

Natalie's grandmother spoke Ladino.

She always cleans and sweeps out the back door, never the front.

She heard about *pan de semita* from her grandmother.

Foods are fried in olive or vegetable oil.

Her mother makes her bed quickly in the morning.

Mirrors are covered when there is a death in the family.

No music is played at the death.

Education is stressed in the family.

Natalie has charms in the shape of rams' horns.

In Puerto Rico, family and friends were called to gather with the sound of the horn.

Jewelry is removed before they say prayers at the table, and before hands are washed.

No pork is eaten on Friday or Saturday.

When a family member has died, a black curtain is hung over the door.

At a funeral, people lament by beating their breasts.

Family members put handfuls of dirt on the grave.

At a wedding, rope is put around the shoulders of the bride and groom.

Her friends always circumcise their male children during the first week.

The family says, "May the Lord keep us."

Thoughts and Feelings

Natalie married Alberto Zarza because they shared the same values about life, always looking for ways to improve, always questioning how to do things better.

When a single mother, the daughter of Natalie's friends died, leaving a child of four, Natalie adopted the child as her son, who was eight at the time of the interview.

In Spain she visited Córdoba, Seville, and Granada, and was drawn by Jewish history as she went to the synagogues.

Her life has always been influenced by Jewish people, including her Jewish babysitter. There have always been Jewish people in her life.

Her mother had Jewish friends, and Natalie worked in their store and felt comfortable eating with them.

When she heard about Jewish values and customs, she often thought about converting. She wanted to know more about the Jewish faith, because she thought she would be happier as a Jew than as a Catholic; but she was afraid to make the change for fear of reprisals from her Catholic family and community.

When she does things differently from other Catholics, she says it's because she learned those ways from her grandmother.

Her mother asks her why she doesn't take Communion, and she answers that it doesn't feel right to her.

She believes there is a strong possibility she has Jewish roots.

She feels more Jewish than Catholic.

Traveling in Spain, she felt empathy for the Jews and what happened to them.

The only synagogue in Puerto Rico is close to her mother's hometown.

She will talk to her mother, who wants to meet me. Her mother has always tended to have Jewish friends, eat Jewish food, and spend time in the Fairfax area.

Natalie will talk to her husband, and ask if he shares some of the customs discussed in the interview.

Jessie Moniz

Personal Information
FULL NAME: Jessie Moniz

AGE WHEN INTERVIEWED: 32

PLACE OF RESIDENCE: Bermuda

SURNAMES IN THE FAMILY: Moniz (father), Pereira, Simaes (mother), Tavares, Da Silva

Family History and Traditions
The family came to Massachusetts from San Miguel, the Azores (Portugal), in 1880, because of droughts.

In 1897, many members of the family moved to Bermuda, where they raised tulip bulbs.

The family has gone from Catholicism to Seventh Day Adventist belief, because of the Saturday Sabbath. Jessie thinks they were searching to form an Evangelical church.

The family has always been insular and isolationist, keeping to themselves as if in a fortress.

People in the family were encouraged to marry within their own family, such as cousins marrying cousins.

Jessie had an elderly aunt come to visit her grandmother. The aunt had an altar where she used to light two candles.

The family has always been very charitable, and charity was stressed. They belonged to the Vasco da Gama Society.

The family is very superstitious. Her grandmother said she could give people the Evil Eye.

Her maternal grandmother said, "Never tell people you are happy or that you are okay, because you could give yourself a curse if you do."

Her maternal grandmother never served pork or shellfish, because she said she didn't trust those foods.

Her father's family stressed the importance of education.

The day her father died a shelf he had made for her fell down and broke. Her aunt said that was a sign of what was to come.

She called a Portuguese genealogical society and they were very negative responding to her questions about possible Jewish roots. They said, "Why bother? It's so long ago, you couldn't prove it anyway." This discouraged her until she found an article about my research.

Members of each branch of her family (her cousins, for example) have heard that they were originally Jewish.

When Jessie's grandfather died, someone looked into his coffin and said, "He looks
like a little old Jewish man." Two cousins looked at each other and said, "What
do you mean *looks* like a Jewish man?"

Her mother's family members also say, "We used to be Jewish."

Jessie works for the *Royal Gazette* in Bermuda.

Meats were drained of blood and then were salted after being boiled by her mother.

Thoughts and Feelings

Jesse thinks the family went from the Catholic Church to the Seventh Day Adventist Church because they celebrate their Sabbath on Saturday.

Jessie thinks that her family kept to themselves to keep safe and possibly to help
them keep their culture together.

She believes she has Jewish roots and wants to know how to prove this. We talked
about words spoken in the family and the traditions that are still practiced in the
family on both sides.

Joao Calado Monteiro

Personal Information

FULL NAME: Joao Calado Monteiro
DATE OF BIRTH: September 6, 1962
AGE WHEN INTERVIEWED: 43
PLACE OF BIRTH: Lisbon, Portugal
OCCUPATION: Portuguese Guide
SURNAMES IN THE FAMILY: Pereira, Frazao

Family History and Traditions

Joao's mother married someone who was a stranger to their family's traditions.

Joao has never seen his father. He uses his mother's name.

His mother chose to work for a Jewish family because she identified with their values and the way they led their lives.

He is educated and speaks eight languages.

He was raised by an aunt and by a grandmother.

He has three aunts and four uncles.

His grandmother told him that in their family they had to bind themselves together, as if with rope, to survive and to help each other, as their family has done for centuries under despotic rule.

In December, the family eats cakes shaped like donuts, called *bolo rei*, or "the cake of kings."

Bread was always blessed in his family.

His grandmother would make a stew on Friday, to be eaten on Friday and Saturday.

The community the family lives in is very close; in fact, neighbors are often family members.

People in their town bury their dead within twenty-four hours.

They mourn for seven days.

A family member sits with the body.

Friends bring food to the grieving family.

The family uses the expression "Thank God."

The people in town eat sausages made of chicken, not pork. The sausages also include bread. They hang them over the fireplace, as they have over many generations, so the fire would singe the sausages and the Inquisitors would be fooled into thinking they were made of pork. The Inquisitors were sure that hanging sausages over the fireplace meant that the family had no Jewish roots, since they would not have had sausages in the first place.

Thoughts and Feelings

Joao studied about the Inquisition in school and was shocked to learn that the Church and the government judged people and punished them for being Jews.

He has been shocked that people don't want to talk to him about the persecution of the Jews; they say the subject is very disturbing.

He is looking further into his own family's customs and he definitely wants to know more about the history.

He uses the computer to find out about the Inquisition, because he knows that his village, in the mountains north of Lisbon, was a place where people ran to and hid.

He will talk to his mother, because there are many reasons for him to think he has Jewish roots.

Esperanza Montenegro

Personal Information

FULL NAME: Esperanza Montenegro
AGE WHEN INTERVIEWED: 41
DATE OF BIRTH: September 29, 1964
PLACE OF BIRTH: Terrabona, Nicaragua
MOTHER'S MAIDEN NAME: Carmen Rivas
GRANDMOTHER'S MAIDEN NAME: Lucmilea Flores
PATERNAL GRANDMOTHER: Julia Cardenas
HOME ADDRESS: Los Angeles, California
SURNAMES OF PARENTS' FRIENDS: Auinaga, Soca, Castilo
SURNAMES OF HER FRIENDS: Molinares, Molina, Martines
HER CHILDREN: three sons, Javier, Kevin, and Julian
HER SIBLINGS: seven sisters, two brothers

Family History and Traditions

Her parents are both from Nicaragua, where her father worked on a farm, producing beans, cows, milk, cheese, and corn. Then he bought his own farm, which has coffee beans.

Her mother baked bread and made fruit candies from cocoa, *dulces*, and prepared coconut and orange recipes.

Her mother valued education, and wanted all her daughters to go to school. The family moved from the mountains to a *pueblo* (village) so the children could be educated, unlike the mother, who couldn't read.

Esperanza prays to God first, then to Mary.

Her mother prays only to God, not to Jesus

Esperanza's grandmother has a crucifix, but her mother does not. Her mother does not like the cross, but has a bible open and displayed with flowers and candles.

Esperanza does not have a cross.

She had her sons circumcised.

Her mother had her sons circumcised.

Esperanza's ex-husband was from the city. His mother was named Flores and Peña. He does not eat pork. His parents don't eat pork, shrimp, or shellfish. Milk and meat are not on the table together, and there are separate pots for milk and meat.

Esperanza's mother also separated meat from milk, and had separate silverware for milk and meat.

At her grandmother's house, if someone used a knife for the wrong purpose, she would take the knife outside and bury it in the ground.

They trimmed fat away from meat.

They salted meat and put it in water for hours one day before cooking. This was to drain the blood.

When they slaughtered animals, they used a knife so the animals would die immediately and let the blood come out.

The family removes the sciatic vein from meat.

When a son was born, coins were given in a bag to keep for good luck.

Before Esperanza left for the U.S.A., her mother put in her hand money for her first son. Esperanza still has these coins, which came from a box in her mother's kitchen.

The family are fastidious housekeepers.

The family stayed home Friday night and Saturday, and did no cleaning, cooking, or entertaining.

They cooked on Thursday.

Grandmother said Saturday was for prayer and for God.

The people in the *pueblo* say that Esperanza's maternal grandmother was very white-skinned, with beautiful eyes. She must have come from Europe, they say. They all had respect for her because they said she was very smart.

Esperanza's mother went to the river to wash clothes on Thursday. She also changed the sheets and cooked on Thursday, reserving Friday and Saturday for God only.

The family never went to church. They prayed in the house, and only to God.

Behind the house there was a separate building, made of wood, that she would cover with leaves in October. She and her mother slept in the house in October.

Her mother and grandmother both read the Old Testament.

Her grandmother had a Torah written in Hebrew, which nobody was allowed to touch.

Her grandmother called Esperanza "Tigva," a Hebrew name.

Her grandmother talked about Moses.

Grandmother kept her head covered and stayed inside.

When someone in the family dies, the body remains in the house one day.

The body is washed by the family before burial.

The body is buried in a plain box.

When the coffin is put in the ground, the family and close friends use their hands to put dirt in the grave.

When they returned to the house, they washed their hands at the faucet outside.

All mirrors were covered during mourning.

People brought food and prayed for eight days.

The family lights a candle in a glass of water for eight days after the funeral.

During mourning, people sat on the couch without cushions.

People pray from five to seven in the afternoons during mourning.

After forty days, a stone is put on the grave.

There were no crosses on gravestones.

After one year, the last prayer of mourning is at twelve noon.

On December 31, people in the family apologize to each other.

On Friday nights, four candles are lit by women, who pray for the family.

Her grandmother and mother lit two candles on Friday nights.

Her grandmother fasted for three or four days in June.

Her grandmother and mother both cleaned all food out of their houses in April or May, every year.

Her grandmother baked very thin bread in a square shape for one week in spring, and during that time it was the only bread she ate.

In September, she cooked with honey and lit candles two at a time.

Grandmother baked bread for the priest.

Another lady in the *pueblo*, named Diega, a close friend of the grandmother, did the same.

Esperanza's friend Nieve doesn't eat pork or go to church. She has worked for Jewish people for thirty years.

The family always gave clothes and shoes to charity.

Personal hygiene was stressed.

The father put his hands on the children's heads to pray.

The father talked about being superstitious.

Grandmother had a small piece of carpet on the doorpost, which she would touch and kiss.

Although the grandmother said she was Catholic, she had pictures of the Western Wall, a silver wine cup, and a Jewish star in her room.

She never makes the sign of the cross.

Grandmother said "Oh my God" in Spanish: *"O Dios mio."*

She gave a round bread, *pan simple*, to the priest.

She would tear bread, not cut it.

The family eats eggs with onions, hard-boiled eggs inside meat, eggplant, and honey. They make sweet-and-sour meats.

The grandmother was very mysterious and wouldn't answer questions.

She was afraid to tell the truth about her traditions that were different from the traditions of the Catholic Church.

She used the word "Marrano," and said "It's Marrano," as an expression when someone did something she didn't like.

She baked egg breads.

She baked three-cornered cakes in February.

Esperanza believes in individual salvation.

The family does not have Last Rites.

Esperanza's mother was married at home. Esperanza had a civil marriage. Neither had a religious wedding in a church.

Stews are often cooked to eat on Friday or Saturday.

Esperanza's aunts have similar customs and practices.

Women braided all breads on Thursday.

Women pray with black or white covers on their shoulders.

Vegetables are dipped in salt water.

The family fries food in olive oil.

All the women make their beds right away when they get up, to keep the souls of others out.

In the past, people prayed by rocking back and forth.

Grandmother cut her husband's nails and hid the trimmings.

Esperanza believes in educating children.

Thoughts and Feelings

Esperanza says she believes her grandmother was practicing Judaism.

However, she believes her grandmother was afraid of being Jewish.

Esperanza thinks she has Jewish roots.

She will talk to her father, and to her siblings about this.

She thinks her father knows more than he's been saying.

Esperanza will discuss Jewish roots with her children

Her son Julian says he's Jewish. No one knows where this comes from, but he has a yarmulke from a friend, and he likes Jewish rules.

Tania Moreiro (Veria)

Personal Information

FULL NAME: (Persia) Tania Moreiro Veria

AGE WHEN INTERVIEWED: 46

DATE OF BIRTH: July 28, 1959

PLACE OF BIRTH: Anapolis, Goias, Brazil

MOTHER'S MOTHER: Sabino Dos Santos, Gomes da Silva

FATHER'S MOTHER: Moreira

SURNAMES OF RELATIVES: Meirreles, Batista, Ferreira, Carneiro

SURNAMES OF FRIENDS: Soares, Bastos

Family History and Traditions

Her father's family and her mother's family are both from Minas Gerais. They knew many Jews there, and their family has been there for many generations.

At age twenty-six she moved to Italy, where she married Franco Frigerio.

Her father is in Como, and her mother is in the Veneto.

Her parents are Catholic.

There are no crucifixes in the home.

They pray to God. She prays to God from her heart.

She is deeply religious, but not with the Church.

Chickens are killed and boiled so all the blood is let out.

She grew up reading both the Old and the New Testaments.

The house was swept from the outside in, and the dirt was never swept outside.

The house is cleaned on Friday.

When someone in the family dies, the body is kept at home for twenty-four hours, with the family watching.

The family mourns for seven days.

The family wears black during mourning.

Education was always stressed.

The family believes in charity, and her mother belongs to a sewing group that makes clothes for poor children.

A group called Belo Horizonte was formed in her area by people who were Jewish and who knew Jews there early.

The family uses the phrases "Oh my God" and "Please God."

She doesn't consider Jesus Christ the Messiah.

The family has never taken Last Rites.

In her family it was encouraged for cousins to marry cousins.

When there's a marriage, two cookies are baked and then joined to form one.

Thoughts and Feelings

She is anxious to learn about possible Jewish roots.

She thinks it would be a pleasure to discover Jewish roots.

She will talk to her family.

She found out that many people with Jewish roots live in her city.

She will contact the organization there to learn more and she will call with more information.

She reads about Jewish customs and life regularly.

Andre Neto

Personal Information

FULL NAME: Andre de Faria Pereira Neto
DATE OF BIRTH: December 27, 1958
PLACE OF BIRTH: Rio de Janeiro
WIFE: Egleubia Andrade de Oliveira
WIFE'S MOTHER: Naeir Melo de Souza
MOTHER'S MAIDEN NAME: Sonia Maria de Melo e Souza
GRANDMOTHER'S MAIDEN NAME: Maria da Penha Marcial de Faria
PATERNAL GRANDMOTHER: Helio Marcial de Faria Pereira
HOME ADDRESS: San Francisco, California
SURNAMES OF FRIENDS: Oliveira, Carvalho, Noguieira, Cavalcanti, Chaves, Silva

Family History and Traditions

The family was originally from Lisbon, before moving to Brazil.

Andre's wife is from Pernambuco.

He was a schoolteacher in a high school. He taught about names that represent people today who are Jewish who practice Catholicism because their families were forced to convert.

He tells students the names are ones that are close to the ground.

He taught in Rio de Janeiro. He thought that Jews in Portugal during the Inquisition who agreed to convert were sent to Africa, and those who didn't convert were killed, burned.

His wife is Egleubia Andrade de Oliveira; her mother is Naeir Melo de Souza.

His mother's father was a writer; his father's father was a judge.

Today, Andre has a Ph.D. and teaches the History of Medical Practice in the World in the most important hospital in Brazil. He is working at the University of San Francisco, translating into Portuguese the work of a renowned historian on the subject of medical practice in history. In September 2006 he will return to Brazil.

Since the 1980s, his mother has become a strict conservative Catholic, after a visit from the Pope.

His mother wanted him to be married to his first wife in the Catholic Church. Her own mother, Andre's grandmother, said that wasn't important; what was important was that he be happy in life.

His grandmother prayed to God, not to Jesus Christ.

His father doesn't believe in anything spiritual.

Andre and his son have both been circumcised, but in Brazil no one talks about this, even in the family. It is just a tradition that is followed.

Meat and milk are never served or eaten together. Andre was told they don't go together.

There are also separate pots for milk and meat, at both his mother's and his grandmother's houses. Andre's wife keeps the same tradition.

His family living in the rural areas outside of Rio de Janeiro boils meat in salt water
before cooking it.

His family always removes the sciatic vein from meat before cooking it.

His family are good housekeepers, with servants who live in separate buildings on
the colonial properties.

The cleaning was usually done on Fridays, and the beds were changed then. His
wife follows this practice.

Dirt was always put outside the back door.

Saturday was a special day when friends and family came to visit.

The Saturday lunch was always cooked on Friday, and no cooking was done on
Saturday.

When a family member dies, the body is kept either at home or in a special building
next to the cemetery, for one night, with at least one relative watching over it.

The body was washed by the family if it was at home.

The face of the deceased is turned toward the wall.

The body is buried in a wooden box.

At the cemetery, the family puts flowers on the coffin, and puts dirt into the grave.

At the funeral, relatives beat their breasts three times, saying *"mea culpa, mea culpa,
mea culpa"* (my fault, my fault, my fault), to atone for whatever they might have
done to cause the death.

When the family returns from the cemetery, they wash their hands outside, and
then they change all their clothes.

For one week after the funeral, friends and family come together to eat and to pray.

During that week, the family members do not work, and there is no music.

A memorial candle is lit for that week.

After thirty days, there is a special mass.

In mourning, the men wear black ribbons, and the women wear all black.

In December, a special bread, baked only at that time, is dipped in egg and cooked
in very hot oil, after which sugar and cinnamon are applied. This is called *rabanada*.

They always bake two breads, one for the family and one for the priest.

They cook with oil, never lard.

They eat eggs cooked with onions, figs, and meatballs.

The family believes in charity.

Andre's grandmother would have blind people come to eat at her home, and she
helped a blind organization in her city.

The family talked about magic and superstitions about keeping the devil away.

The family talked about the Evil Eye, and wore an amulet as a ring or necklace or
put one over the door to protect the family from evil.

Personal hygiene was stressed, and people took two showers a day.

Bread was always blessed and kissed, and never wasted.

When prayers were said, men would put their hands on the children's heads to bless them.

The family used expressions such as "Oh my God," "Please God," *"Gracias a Deus,"* (Thank God), and *"Se Deus oviser"* (If God wants).

Andre's wife and the other women cut excess fat from meat before cooking. Andre does this also.

His mother and grandmother each pray with a shawl.

He played *pon y saca* with dice.

The family eats vegetables dipped in salt water.

They eat chickpeas and hummus.

Andre knows about Kabbalah as the spiritual or mystical arm of Judaism.

The women in the family make the bed quickly upon arising.

Education was stressed in the family.

At a wedding, the hands of the bride and groom are tied together after rings are exchanged.

Andre is aware that widows sometimes marry their brothers-in-law.

Thoughts and Feelings

Andre feels that the expression of race is a matter of courage and bravery.

He is now sure that he has Jewish roots.

He suspected this because his name was Pereira.

He believes that his family, like so many others in Brazil and in the world, kept their Jewish traditions secretly, even though they became Catholic on the outside.

He is taken with the fact that, in spite of all his education, he had no idea why the traditions in his family persisted and were considered so important over all these years.

He has talked to his students of the three choices facing Jews during the Inquisition—to remain Jewish and die, to convert, or to leave. He tells students to think about which choice they would make, and they discuss the question.

His father doesn't believe in anything that is spiritual.

Andre knows that Jews in Portugal changed their names in order to survive.

He will share what information he has learned with his family, his wife, and his children.

His mother has stated that their name having Jewish roots is interesting.

He said he was grateful for the interview and will discuss it with others.

His friends are proud that the Dutch had an influence in the history of Brazil.

Andre brought to the interview a lot of information about what is happening for people in Brazil who are finding out about having Jewish roots.

Flavio de Oliveira

Personal Information

FULL NAME: Flavio Atunes de Oliveira
AGE WHEN INTERVIEWED: 38
BIRTH DATE: 1964
PLACE OF BIRTH: São Paulo, Brazil
MOTHER: Guilermina Ferreira de Campos
MOTHER'S MOTHER: Justina Candida de Oliveira
MOTHER'S GRANDMOTHER: Sebastina Candida Dos Santos
FATHER'S MOTHER: Maria Hose de Conceiro
FATHER'S FATHER: Joao Antunes de Oliveira
FATHER'S GREAT-GRANDMOTHER: Gliceria Neves de Moura
SURNAMES AMONG FRIENDS: De Freitas, Da Silva

Family History and Traditions

Flavio is a single father raising a sixteen-year-old daughter, whom he recently brought to the U.S. from Brazil.

Flavio's friend, whose name is Carvalho, is studying to be a rabbi in São Paulo. He brought to Flavio's attention the fact that Flavio's family doesn't eat pork, and that the name De Oliveira (of the olive tree), both indicate Jewish roots. The friend said that Flavio belongs to Judaism because he fits and feels comfortable with most of his Jewish friends. Flavio agreed with this assessment and began to look at his family's traditions. What follows here is what he discovered.

The family doesn't eat pork or shellfish, because of hygiene. Flavio's mother doesn't consider these products clean.

He looked at the names of the Jews involved in the Inquisition in Brazil and found his own name.

His family stressed the need for education, and Flavio studied medicine in Brazil. He has a master's degree in physiology and exercise.

Flavio was circumcised, by the family's choice.

Flavio was baptized because that was expected in his society.

When a family member dies in the house, the body is kept in the house and relatives take turns sitting with the body for twenty-four hours, with candles lit. Then the body is buried in a cemetery, in a plain wooden casket.

The family washes the body before it is buried.

There are emotional prayers.

Earth is thrown by the family onto the coffin.

Negative feelings are left outside the house when the family returns from the burial.

When there is a death, friends and family come to the house and bring food.

Shoes are removed and left outside.

There is no crucifix in the house.

The family does not celebrate Christmas.

Flavio's mother says the family does not believe in images.

She believes that Christ existed, but he is just a son of God in the sense that we all
    are.

She believes we should pray to God.

The family does not believe in saints.

They do not believe in Confession, and they talk directly to God.

Flavio's mother believes it's who we are inside that counts.

His parents accept who they are without labels.

His mother keeps an extremely clean house.

She believes the dead should be buried, never cremated.

Flavio's grandmother felt the same way, and was upset when his cousins were cre-
    mated.

Flavio was never taken to church.

Flavio's father said that God was present night and day, seven days a week.

Flavio's parents are very charitable.

They believe the blood in God's veins has no color. So the same is true of humans.

Flavio's mother salts meats before she cooks them, and also puts meat in vinegar.

His grandmother beats her breast when someone in the family dies.

The family eats figs and salted cod.

Flavio's mother serves hard-boiled eggs when someone dies.

At weddings, honey cakes are served, always using white sugar.

Flavio's mother asks God to protect her from the Evil Eye.

His grandmother said that no one works on Saturday.

Milk and meat are never on the table at the same time.

In Brazil, one needs a baptism certificate to attend some schools.

The family reads the Old Testament and discusses Abraham, Isaac, and Jacob.

As a trainer, he has clients, ninety percent of whom are Jewish.

His grandmother and his aunt bake flat breads.

Thoughts and Feelings

Flavio is going to tell his parents of the interview and what he has learned that in-
    dicates they have Jewish roots.

He feels comfortable around Jewish people.

He likes learning about this philosophy of Judaism.

He thinks Judaism is very positive.

He says that the Christian notion that Jews don't believe in God is all wrong. Jews
    believe more than anyone, he feels.

He feels that he comes from Jewish roots.

Phil Pasquini (Pereira)

Personal Information

FULL NAME: Philip L. Pasquini

HOME ADDRESS: Ignacio, California

SURNAMES IN MOTHER'S FAMILY: Pereira, Da Silva

OTHER SURNAMES IN HIS FAMILY: De Camora, Da (De) Freitas, Azavedo, Martin, King, Abendana, Ibn Dana, Dias de Vares.

Family History and Traditions

Phil wrote a book about his family's history, called *Indentured Immigrants*.

In 1994, Phil and his wife visited the Portuguese Jewish Synagogue when they were in Amsterdam. While he was there, he saw on the list of the building committee the name of Jacob Israel Pereyra. Since his mother's name was Pereira, he began to think he needed to find out about his roots, which might be Jewish. A woman from Tel Aviv told him Pereira was a Jewish name, confirming a long-held suspicion.

His family came from Madeira, where one had to be baptized to go to school, so that many people took Christian names when they were baptized.

The family originally came from Morocco, four to five hundred years ago, and was called Abendana and Ibn Dana.

In the eleventh century, the Pereira part of the family was in Spain, and when they were forced to leave Spain in 1492, they went to Lisbon, Portugal. In 1550, they left Portugal for Holland, but decided instead to sail to Madeira.

The family lived in the outer villages as Jews, but appeared outwardly as Christians.

They left Madeira because of poor economic and social conditions.

The family came to the island of Maui in the Sandwich Islands from Madeira in 1896. They had to work twenty-six days each month, ten hours a day, for three years to pay for their seventy-five-dollar passage to Terra Nova, the Sandwich Islands, and then to Maui, Hawaii. The working conditions were poor, with abuse by the overseers of the field hands.

PARA AS ILHAS DE SANDWICH

AVISO

O velheiro Inglés «Stirlingshire» Capitão R. Alexander annunciado a sahir Liverpool e deve chegar a este porto até o dia 20 de Novembro.

Funchal 27 Novembro de 1885

Messrs. George W. Macfarlane & Co.
Consignatorios

AN APPEAL FOR IMMIGRANTS. This advertisement encouraged the Portuguese people to come to Hawaii, also known as the Sandwich Isles, on the ship Stirlingshire.

The Pereira Family Shield

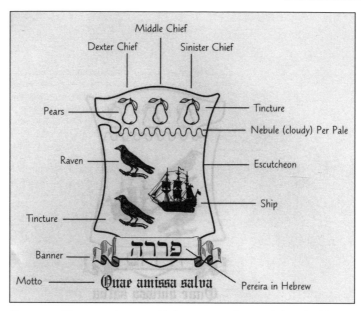

PASQUINI/PEREIRA SHIELD. *Phil Pasquini designed this shield using the family's name Pereira, with its meaning of "pears," and the ship that brought his family to Hawaii.*

The Pereira Family shield's shape is derived from a thirteenth-century Italian tournament design. Three pears are located in the tincture chief *dexter*, middle, and *sinister*, divided with a *nebule* in the *per pale*; the base is decorated with two ravens stacked one over one *dexter* and a nineteenth-century sailing ship below center *sinister* and to the right of the *nombril*—navel. A banner is located at the base of the chief and encloses the family name, Pereira, in Hebrew. The family's motto in Latin, *Quae amissa salva*, "What is lost is safe," is located below the shield.

Symbols Used and Their Significance

Pears   Three in number are symbolic of the family name.

Clouds   To symbolize the various turbulent experiences during the Diaspora and the Inquisitions.

Ravens   A Northwest Coast Indian symbol, the Transformer, able to change into anything at any time. Symbolic of the family's forced conversion and ultimate reversion to Judaism.

Ship   The ship is symbolic of the ocean voyages throughout the ages the family has undertaken to survive.

Banner   The banner is a placeholder of the family name, Pereira, in Hebrew.

Motto   Of Latin origin, *Quae amissa salva* "What was lost is safe," is symbolic of Phil's return to Judaism after the family's 500 years of posing as Christians.

PLANTATION HOUSE IN HAWAII. *A Portuguese sugar plantation manager in front of the plantation owner's house on the island of Kauai in Hawaii. Many of the Portuguese who came to Hawaii became overseers of the workers in the fields because of their ability to manage vast responsibilities and exercise unremitting care. Many of these Portuguese men had Jewish roots.*

In Hawaii, Phil's family became indentured servants. They could not vote, had to buy everything from the company stores, and labored many hours each day cutting sugar.

Phil's uncle said he wouldn't go to church, because he was a Portuguese Jew.

His mother cleaned her house on Friday to get ready for Saturday.

The family said, *"La boca serata noan entre mosca"* ("A fly does not enter a closed mouth") in the Jewish Sephardic language of Ladino.

According to Phil's grandmother, there is a curse in the Pereira family. The women (both grandmothers) were depressed for ten years. The family doesn't want to talk about the curse. Phil had visions.

They believed you have bad luck when the *fatzedas* (little people) get you.

Phil's cousin told her daughter that being a Catholic nun was not right for her, because the family are Jews, which she had known all her life from the time she was young.

Phil doesn't need Jesus Christ to pray to. He prays directly to God, with no middleman.

The family did circumcise their sons.

The family believes one shouldn't look at the *malocchi* (Evil Eye) of another person.

The family believes in fortunetelling.

In the family, hair is washed on Friday, and clean linens are put on the bed.

Cleanliness was like a ritual in his family.

The family ate pork that was pickled in vinegar. They believed eating pork showed the Church that they were true Christians, but that the vinegar would remove the bad parts of the pork and make it kosher. This was called *vinidage* (*vinho d'olilos*).

The family ate *malassadas* ("bad dough," or dough that would not rise, like matzah) at Easter.

One of the Pereiras was the Head Rabbi of Turkey and Alexandria.

Jack da Silva was a silversmith and a colleague of the City College of San Francisco.

Victor Perera, Phil's cousin, wrote about the family in a book, *The Cross and the Pear Tree*.

Phil traced his family back to the first Temple in Jerusalem through Victor's book.

His family in Madeira and in Hawaii was told to marry only within the fold. This was an old family tradition.

Phil's aunt was told not to tell anyone about the family's Jewish roots.

Denial of the roots was engrained in the family.

In the United States, some Pereiras became Perrys.

When someone in the family dies, the family throws sand on the coffin to cover it.

Charity is given when a family member dies.

The family enjoys sardines, olives, fava beans, and hard-cooked eggs.

The family ate eggplant, fried artichoke hearts, eggs with onions, radishes, Swiss chard, almond cakes, fried bread crumbs, and linguica sausage.

The family celebrated all the Christian holidays.

The celebration of Christmas is always bittersweet for Phil.

Phil believes that salvation is collective, as in Judaism, not individual, as in Christianity.

Thoughts and Feelings

Phil feels that his and his family's identity was stolen by the Inquisition and then by the experience of being indentured servants in Hawaii, which is why the family saved their money and moved to California.

He resents being told he was always a Catholic, and feels that his religion was taken away from him.

He thinks of himself as a Jewish person.

He thinks that a Jew is a person who thinks like a Jew.

He thinks that cleanliness in his family became a ritual.

Introduction to Philip L. Pasquini's book, *Indentured Immigrants*

I BEGAN THIS ADVENTURE into my mother's family's origins in July of 1994 while my wife, Elaine, and I visited the Portuguese Jewish Synagogue—the *Esnoga*—in Amsterdam. Our interest in visiting the synagogue was initially architectural and historical, but before noon that day it became a search for my hidden ancestral roots. It was in the synagogue that I discovered a plaque written in Ladino from the year 1670 listing the names of the building committee and among those listed was a Jacob Israel Pereyra. I recognized my mother's name—Pereira—immediately and in short order it was confirmed that Pereira was indeed a Jewish name. Although the spelling was different, the family shared a common ancestor.

This simple revelation coupled with my curious mind and the need to know, has now taken me around the world in search of documents, sites, and answers that have lain about for hundreds of years waiting to be discovered. It is these pieces of information that are presented here to help form a more accurate, and, hopefully, a more complete, picture of my heritage and of my many ancestors and their descendants. This story has been in the making for over twenty centuries.

A search of one's family origins is in large

THE HISTORY OF AN IMMIGRANT FAMILY. When Phil Pasquini's family came from the Spanish Madeira Islands to work in the Hawaiian Islands, they were treated as indentured immigrants, one step removed from being slaves to the sugar industry's owners.

part dependent on the keeping and preservation of records, the recollection of family stories, and a lot of hard research, coupled with a large measure of good luck. Unfortunately, records, as well as family stories, are for various reasons often not available, unreliable, or the information they contain is missing or has been subjected to much interpretation or enhancement by those charged with recording and retelling. To compound matters, my ancestors being of Jewish origin, and having been part of the first Diaspora followed by the Inquisitions in Spain and Portugal, meant that many early official records were either not kept or were destroyed. To fill in those gaps I have relied upon numerous books and historical records available today to cover early family history up to my family's arrival in Madeira in the 1500s.

The original family names of Ibn Dana, Abendana, and Pereira, whose origins are part of the Jewish tribe of Dan, is a story better told by historians and scholars of ancient Jewish history. For an in-depth look into the evolution of the Pereira family, one need only to refer to the very excellent book *The Cross and the Pear Tree* by Victor Perera. This book coincidentally was released shortly after I began my own research and has inspired me as well as having directed many of my efforts. My family, the Pereiras, can best be classified as *Conversos*, that group of Jews who were converted to Catholicism by force during the Portuguese Inquisition. Although many of the family members practiced and continue to practice as Catholics, we are first and foremost of Jewish origin. Because of this five-hundred-year-old injustice of forced conversion, I have returned to the religion of my ancestors.

A search of this sort into one's family origins and history often turns up many facts that have lain dormant for various reasons. Memories of family stories that I recollect from my youth, which then seemed like interesting historical family tidbits, have taken on new meaning as I search official historical records to help define and illuminate the ever unfolding story of the origin and direction of the Pereira da Silva family. One enters this type of research knowing that it will often take unexpected twists and lead in complicated and complex directions that in turn result in additional unexpected surprises. This entire undertaking has afforded me a renewed connection with my family's past and their lives in a new and more meaningful way. Early on I anticipated writing a complete story of the family's history going back as far as possible in time. However, not being able to discover any information concerning the family's origins in mainland Portugal, I decided to focus mainly on their later life in Madeira and continuing with their emigration in 1885 to the Sandwich Islands—Hawaii. As it turns out, all of my ancestors are derived from a single common Madeiran, Diogo Dias de Vares "The Elder" and his wife Francisca Dias.

The oral history of a family can survive only as long as the stories are retained in the memories of its members, and that is precisely what I hope this document will instill in the younger members of the family. I sincerely hope the reader will find my effort a worthy tribute.

Rafael Perez, Jr.

Personal Information

FULL NAME: Rafael Perez, Jr.

AGE WHEN INTERVIEWED: 67

DATE OF BIRTH: May 21, 1939

PLACE OF BIRTH: San Juan, Puerto Rico

SPOUSE: Maria Anita Cabral da Silva

SPOUSE'S PLACE OF BIRTH: Rio Grande do Sul, Brazil

MOTHER'S MAIDEN NAME: Juanita Velazquez Santana

PATERNAL GRANDMOTHER: Elvira Garcia

PATERNAL GRANDFATHER: Mauricio Perez

HOME ADDRESS: Lee's Summit, Missouri

MOTHER'S PARENTS: Primitiva Santana, José Velazquez

Family History and Traditions

Rafael is three generations away from living in Spain.

In 1978, he went to Brazil and married Maria.

In 1970, Maria's mother had a furniture store in Rio Grande do Sul, near the border of Uruguay and Argentina.

The boys in the family are all circumcised.

The women boil their meat in salt water to get all of the blood out, and then the meat is hung out to dry by the grandparents.

The women are fastidious about keeping their houses clean.

There is no work on Saturday.

Sunday is the first day of the week.

The family on his mother's side read the Bible every day.

They discussed the Patriarchs.

His grandfather was a barber who made coffins as a carpenter. He wrote a proverb every day on his own metal blackboard.

When a family member died, the family watched over the body and cleaned it and prepared it for burial. The body was not embalmed, and was buried the day after the death.

The family gathered around the body to mourn, before it was buried.

At the burial, each family member put a spoonful of dirt on the coffin to help bury the body.

After the funeral, men wore black ribbons in their lapels, and women wore dark clothes and no makeup.

For thirty days of mourning, there were no social functions, and men let their beards grow.

Neighbors and friends brought food.

Something black was hung on the front door.

In olden times, pebbles were put around the burial site.

There was a ceremony to put up the gravestone. Family gathered to dedicate it and to say prayers.

Women always swept from the front door to the back door and then out back.

The family kissed the crucifix as they left the house.

Charity was always stressed.

A father touches the heads of children to pray to God.

The family feared the Evil Eye, which they warded off with *Oliogrope* ("Big Eye"), the *figa*, or the hand.

The food was blessed, and the family said prayers of thanks for days and nights.

The family uses the expression "Oh my God."

They know the Old Testament and know that Mary, mother of Jesus, was Jewish.

Foods they eat include sugar cakes, fried bread crumbs, meatballs, meatloaf with egg, radishes, and onions in spicy sauce.

The family was always told they must not forget where they came from.

His father told him to look in the mirror to see a reflection of who he was in life.

Education was paramount. Although the family was poor, all four children were educated.

The two oldest children earned Ph.D.s. Rafael's uncle is an engineer, and his father is a professor and a lawyer.

Rafael believes in individual salvation.

He believes Christ was circumcised.

He confesses to God, not to a priest, and believes that God listens to all.

His wife braids challah.

The family ate a stew of meat (beef), potatoes, and vegetables Friday to Saturday.

He played *pon y saca*.

The family dips vegetables in salt water.

The grandmother made three-cornered pastries.

The family beat their breasts (*mea culpa*) when they atone.

People in Brazil gathered on Saturday to socialize.

The family remove their jewelry to wash their hands before eating.

Thoughts and Feelings

Rafael has never wanted to work with someone who wasn't Jewish.

He appreciates the Jewish way of living and feels he understands it.

When invited to a Passover Seder, he feels completely comfortable.

He has been told that he should be a Jew.

He says Jews are God's chosen people. He thinks they work hard and have survived because of all they've gone through. He says Jews are the best at anything they do, be they bankers, taxi drivers, or whatever.

He believes his grandfather was right to rebel against the Catholic priests and dispute them in the town square. That grandfather was so angry he became a Protestant.

Rafael believes he has Jewish roots.

He feels Jewish.

Isabel Raygoza

Personal Information

FULL NAME: Isabel Cristina Raygoza

AGE WHEN INTERVIEWED: 20

DATE OF BIRTH: October 15, 1985

PLACE OF BIRTH: Zacatecas, Mexico

MOTHER'S MAIDEN NAME: Galvez

GRANDMOTHER'S MAIDEN NAME: Romero

PATERNAL GRANDMOTHER: Martinez

HOME ADDRESS: Kamuela, Hawaii

SURNAMES OF FRIENDS: Ortega, Motta, Palos, Phavez

Family History and Traditions

The family came to Mexico while the French were there.

In her village in Zacatecas, there are 300 people, all related to each other.

Isabel's family prays to God.

There are no crucifixes in her house or on it.

All the boys in the family are circumcised.

There are separate pots for cooking milk and meat.

Meat and milk are not served on the table at the same time.

The meat is always boiled in salt water before it is cooked, especially the pork, and is then hung.

The family keeps a very clean house.

Isabel's mother reads the Old Testament and tells stories of Moses, Jacob, Isaiah, Abraham, and David's Psalms.

When someone dies, the body stays in the house for twenty-four hours. The family stays with the body, and they wash it.

Then they carry the body to the cemetery.

All the mourners put dirt on the grave.

People wear black to the burial.

The family mourns for a week.

When Isabel's grandfather died, friends and neighbors came to pray with her grandmother.

Isabel's mother fasts when she wants to wish for something good.

The family blesses their bread.

They put rocks and pebbles on graves.

The family belongs to a benevolent society.

They stress personal hygiene.

They believe that there are curses.

Isabel's mother says that the Jews have been treated badly.

The mother talks about Israel.

Isabel's grandmother prays with a shawl.

The women trim excess fat off all meat.

They eat eggs with onions.

Isabel's grandmother believes in Last Rites, but her mother does not.

The family kills their animals humanely, so they will not suffer.

The family played a game with a top called *pirinola*, or "put in and take out."

They don't eat shellfish.

Education was always stressed.

Some expressions used in the family are "Oh my God, "Ay ay ay," "May the Lord keep us," and "God is King."

At weddings, the groom is lifted up by the men.

Thoughts and Feelings

Isabel will definitely talk to the family about the questions raised in this interview.

She's glad we did the interview.

She now thinks her roots might be Jewish.

Gifelle (Gizelly) Ribeiro (Hibeiro)

Personal Information
FULL NAME: Gifelle Ribeiro

AGE WHEN INTERVIEWED: 50

MOTHER'S NAME: Vieria, from Oliveira

PLACE OF BIRTH: São Paulo, Brazil

OCCUPATION: lawyer and teacher of English

SURNAMES OF FRIENDS: Perreira, Pinhero, Gomes

Family History and Traditions
Gifelle's father's family is Portuguese.

Her mother's family (Jacoma) is Italian, from Livorno.

She thinks her family dealt in coral and exported it as merchants and traders.

Her family has been in Brazil for many generations.

She knows about Kabbalah and has a copy in English from her friend, Mark.

Her family has always stressed education.

She lives outside of São Paulo, where her children are safe.

Her friends have been interested in Judaism, and she knows that their names are often associated with Judaism.

Thoughts and Feelings
From the time she was a small child, she has been fascinated with Judaism.

She feels an affinity with Jews and she feels Jewish, although she has nothing to prove it.

She wants to read the Kabbalah in Portuguese.

Esperanza Salas Sandoval

Personal Information
FULL NAME: Esperanza Salas Sandoval
AGE WHEN INTERVIEWED: 78
BIRTH DATE: January 17, 1927
HOME ADDRESS: Aguascalientes, Mexico
MOTHER'S MAIDEN NAME: Manuela Ibarra
FATHER'S MOTHER'S NAME: Marceleena Franco, from France
NAMES OF FRIENDS: Carmen Dias, José Pena
SISTERS' NAMES: Consuela Villapanda, Alicia Regalato

Family History and Traditions
Esperanza's grandmother and grandfather were from Zacatecas.

Pan dulce was served in the home.

The family never mixes milk and meat. Her mother told her that mixing them would be bad for you.

The woman drain the blood out of the meat before it is cooked.

The sciatic vein is removed from meat.

Esperanza prays to both God and Jesus Christ.

The family is fastidious about cleaning. The people are poor, but very clean.

Her paternal grandmother told her stories from the Bible, and said the world would be saved for all.

When someone in the family dies, the body is kept at the house for twenty-four hours, with the family watching over the body. They don't leave the body while the soul is still there.

The family puts coins wrapped in a red cloth in the coffin.

At the burial, family members each put a handful of dirt on the casket, as a sign of respect.

After the funeral, the family wash their hands at the cemetery, before going home.

During mourning, a black ribbon is put on the door.

The family mourns for seven days, with friends and neighbors bringing food.

During mourning, there is no radio or television.

During mourning, the family wears black.

Her father's mother covered the mirrors in rooms.

A candle is lit for seven days.

When Esperanza was pregnant, her father-in-law brought her a red ribbon to protect her.

On her father's side, there were fast days.

The family eats *banuelos* (donuts fried in oil) on days in December, both in Los Angeles and in Mexico.

They eat *semita*, a flat bread, in April.

The family believes that the Evil Eye is given by people who are envious.

They make the bed immediately in the morning, to keep bad spirits away.

In Mexico, her *padre* tells her that Jesus Christ was King of the Jews.

The women always trim the excess fat off their meat.

Relatives always took a pinch of bread to give to their priest.

She remembers hearing people called Marranos, in a nasty way.

Her cousins make meatloaf with a hard-boiled egg.

She believes salvation will be for everyone.

There is a charity box in the home, which is passed from person to person, and then from house to house.

The family is encouraged to marry people with the same values, to keep the traditions together.

Esperanza heard that if you moved from place to place, you were a *Judio*.

When the family killed chickens, they cut the throat and then ripped off the head.

After dinner, the family often plays a game called *pirinola*, which is like the Portuguese *pon y saca*, with a top, which they know to be a dreidel.

They make a beef stew with garbanzo beans.

Their friends sway back and forth to pray.

Education is stressed in the family.

October is considered a festive month of abundance.

The family removes their rings before washing their hands at meals.

Esperanza remembers seeing her neighbor kissing the doorpost of her house when she was a child.

Thoughts and Feelings

Esperanza definitely feels a Jewish tradition or connection.

She feels she has Judaism in her background.

Her great-grandmother, Patricia, who arranged this interview, knew of the possibility of Jewish roots from hearing of Jewish traditions.

The family would like to come to a Passover Seder.

Jaime Saucedo

Personal Information

FULL NAME: Jaime Saucedo

AGE WHEN INTERVIEWED: 48

MOTHER'S MAIDEN NAME: Pedraza

FATHER'S MOTHER: Martinez

PLACE OF BIRTH: Colima, Mexico

SURNAMES IN FATHER'S FAMILY: Navarro, Flores

Family History and Traditions

The family prays to Jesus and to God.

Jaime's parents raised tomatoes on a farm as laborers.

When a family member died, they buried the body after it was kept at home for one day, wrapped up on a table and watched over by the family.

The family mourns for nine days.

A memorial candle is lit during the nine-day mourning.

Men wear black armbands or a ribbon that is cut. The immediate family— siblings, children, parents, husband, and wife—all wear ribbons and some black to show mourning.

When someone dies the mirrors are all covered.

At the funeral, each person puts a handful of dirt on the casket.

When the family returns from the cemetery, each person must bathe or shower.

Women put meat in water with salt to get the blood out of it.

They cut fat away from the meat before cooking it.

There are different pots for milk and meat, and the two are never mixed.

In December, the family eats a special sweet bread that looks like a donut.

Honey cakes are served at holidays and weddings.

A piece of bread is given to the priest when the family goes to church on Sunday.

Sheets are changed on Friday or Saturday.

They read the Old Testament and talked of Abraham, Moses, and Jacob.

The family puts a red ribbon on a baby's basket or crib to keep out evil.

The family believes in the Evil Eye.

They put an unopened egg in a glass of water for a baby, then they open it. They pass the glass by the baby for good luck.

The family uses the expressions "Please God" and "Oh my God."

The family talks about the stars and the moon.

Adults put their hands on the heads of the children to pray before meals.

Education is considered very important.

Thoughts and Feelings
His roots in Mexico go back many generations
He thinks he might have Jewish roots.
He will discuss the subject with his children.
He needs to dig deeper into his family history.

Maria Angela Nunes Candido da Silva

Personal Information

MAIDEN NAME: Maria Angela Nunes Candido da Silva

MARRIED NAME: Angela da Silva Gruber Pereira

MOTHER'S NAME: Albertina Mauricio Nunes

PATERNAL GRANDMOTHER'S MAIDEN NAME: Marianna Augusta Medeiros

PLACE OF BIRTH: Lisbon, Portugal

EX-HUSBAND: Joao Manuel Gruber Pereira

EX-HUSBAND'S PLACE OF BIRTH: Lisbon, Portugal

OCCUPATION: secretary

EMPLOYER: Portuguese Tourism Trade Commission

HOME ADDRESS: Fremont, California

SURNAMES OF FRIENDS: Oliveira, Pizarro, Monteiro, Aranes, Bettencourt

SURNAMES OF PARENTS' FRIENDS: Eladid Dos Santos, Sampao, Benavides, Oliveira, Marques

OFFSPRING: Sebastian, a son, and Pinheiro de Almeida, who lives in Evora, where his mother lives

Family History and Traditions

Maria's family is from the north of Portugal, near the Douro River.

Her father is a professor of engineering.

She belongs to a benevolent society, a charity called The Holy Ghost.

The family prays to God, the saints, and the Holy Ghost.

Her mother-in-law wanted the grandson to be circumcised, but Maria decided not to do it.

Her mother has separate pots for milk and meat.

Milk and meat are never put together, because she says they would not go together.

Her family are Roman Catholic.

Her mother trims the excess fat off the meat.

On Saturday the family relaxes or does small projects.

They read the New Testament and talk about the rules of God's Commandments. They also discuss Moses.

When a family member dies, the body is kept at home at first, usually for one day.

Someone keeps the body company. This happened with her grandfather's body.

The family washes the deceased's body.

She has seen people put dirt on the graves.

She has seen mirrors covered during mourning.

During mourning, men wear a black ribbon called a *fumo*, and women wear black.

Flowers are brought to the family to show respect.

The family mourns for one week, with no work, and depending on the relationship, the widow or widower wears black for six months, then black and white for another six months.

The clothing of the deceased is given to family or to a charity.

Education was stressed in her family.

During December, dough is fried and it expands with air inside. On Christmas Eve, *malassadas*, or donuts, are eaten.

On the farm where her family bought bread and milk, the bread was blessed and a small amount was given to the local priest.

When praying, her father would put his hands on the heads of the children to bless them.

Her family is very charitable.

Her father says that numbers, and the sequences of numbers, are important in life.

The family considers the movement of the stars important.

The family discussed the turmoil surrounding Christ and why he was put to death, to die for all men's sins.

Her family discussed Jonah and the whale.

The family eats almond cookies and honey.

Her family ate chickpeas with onions and parsley, fried in olive oil.

She has put a hard-boiled egg inside a meatloaf, just because she felt like it.

Her mother puts an egg in veal.

A stew is often cooked on Friday, so her mother doesn't have to cook on Saturday and can relax.

The family uses the word *Judio* when talking about Jewish subjects.

Her mother and father are distant cousins.

Her aunt also married a cousin.

Her family played the game *pon y saca* with both a top and dice.

Dirt was sometimes swept under the carpet, but never outside.

Her family removes jewelry before washing their hands before dinner, but she thinks it is a physical thing.

They use the expression "Please God."

At a wedding, the bride's and groom's hands are tied by a priest.

Thoughts and Feelings

Maria spoke with her mother, who said no one ever brought out the subject of the family possibly being Jewish.

She thinks that the roots could be there, because of all the things that the family does that resemble Jewish rituals and traditions.

She is definitely going to talk to her mother and ask her the questions that she, herself, could not answer during this interview. She is also going to talk to her son.

Doris da Silva Naumu

Personal Information
FULL NAME: Doris da Silva Naki Naumu
AGE WHEN INTERVIEWED: 73
BIRTH DATE: March 2, 1931
BIRTH PLACE: Lahaina, Maui, Hawaii
MOTHER'S MAIDEN NAME: Da Silva
GRANDMOTHER'S MAIDEN NAME: Charlotte (Carlotta) Texeira
MATERNAL GRANDFATHER: Antone da Silva
PATERNAL GRANDFATHER: Dalhousie
GREAT GRANDFATHER: José Correia-Picanco
GREAT GRANDMOTHER: Maxima Julia Texeira
SURNAMES IN THE FAMILY: Porreia, Picao

Family History and Traditions
Doris's paternal grandfather came from the Azores in 1882.

When someone dies, a pair of scissors is hung from the front of the entryway of the house to show that something has been cut away.

All the sons in the family have been circumcised.

When the house is cleaned on Friday, the dust is not thrown out, but collected and put in a pile to be thrown out at another time.

The family eats almond cookies, eggs with onions, radishes, olives, figs, and dates.

Doris's grandmother has a special shelf for fruit, where she also kept candles to light at certain times, especially during the holiday season.

Her grandmother had statues of the Virgin Mary and the Baby Jesus.

Her family disowned one of the grandmothers because she was not going to marry another person of Portuguese descent. She was told she must marry someone who was like the family.

When someone in the family dies, salt is put on the body for preservation in the casket.

The family sits by the body all night.

Dirt is thrown on the casket.

Food is brought by family and friends.

For three days after the funeral, no one works, and black clothing is worn for a few days.

At the beginning of the new year or at the end of the old year, family members went to one another to ask for forgiveness.

In the summer in the Azores, many Portuguese families, including Doris's, would take their dishes to wash them in the sea.

They thanked God for bread.

Meat, especially pork, was often soaked in vinegar before it was cooked.

A favorite saying in the family was "Oh my God."

Charity was very important to the family. Her relatives helped with the beneficent society, developed early in Hawaii by Portuguese from the Azores.

Doris is president of the Portuguese Genealogical Society in Hawaii, based in Honolulu for twenty-five years.

Today Doris belongs to the Mormon Church, although she was born a Catholic. She felt the Catholic religion was too strict, and she didn't identify with its precepts.

There was much superstition in her family, who were fascinated by the new moon and the movement of the planets.

The family fasted to let revelations in.

Before bed, the family prayed to God.

Thoughts and Feelings

Doris says she feels a connection to Jewish roots.

She had me speak to the members of the Genealogical Society to help those who have Jewish traditions and customs see how those traditions and customs lead back to their roots.

The Portuguese community is now beginning to accept that they do have Jewish roots and now are not as vocal about not being Jewish, because some are starting to read and ask questions about the Jewish heritage.

Antonio Julio Pereira Lourenco Simoes

Personal Information

FULL NAME: Antonio Julio Pereira Lourenco Simoes

AGE WHEN INTERVIEWED: 76

DATE OF BIRTH: January 1, 1926

PLACE OF BIRTH: Roriz, Domino Province, Barcelos, Portugal

ADDRESS: Chino, California

PROFESSION: physician. He is a cardio-thoracic surgeon.

MOTHER'S MAIDEN NAME: Pereira.

GRANDFATHER'S NAME: Lourenco

GRANDMOTHER'S NAME: Pereira

SURNAMES IN THE FAMILY: Silva, Castro, Melo, Rocha, Marques

Family History and Traditions

Antonio is married to Mary, whose family came from the Azores, although she was born in Corona, California. She was a dairy farmer, as her family had been in the Azores. The family now are in Chino, with 4,000 head of dairy cattle.

His father was born in Portugal in 1897. He was educated in Portugal, then came to America through Spain and Cuba. He never went back to Portugal to live.

His father went back only once, when Antonio's parents were married in Portugal. Antonio was their only son.

Antonio was raised by his maternal grandparents.

He still has family lands, left by his grandfather and grandmother.

He was educated in a private boarding school in Oporto, Portugal, and at lycee at the age of sixteen.

He graduated from medical school at the University of Coimbra at the age of twenty-five, having completed seven years of school in three years.

He came to America to meet his father and studied medicine at New York Hospital.

His grandfather served fish, and a fish is a symbol of a Jew who has become a Catholic.

Antonio met Jerry and Debbie Hamburg in Philadelphia when he was practicing medicine.

He felt totally comfortable being in their Jewish home.

He began to read about the Jewish holidays and religion and felt a social and intellectual affinity.

He started to celebrate Jewish holidays after his wife died, fifty years ago.

He began to pray to God.

His grandmother kept a very clean house on Sundays. She and his aunt cleaned, but never on Saturdays.

When someone in the family died, the body was kept at home for twenty-four hours and then taken to the cemetery.

A priest administered Last Rites.

The family puts dirt on the coffin at the burial.

Mourning lasted seven days.

Friends brought food, since the immediate family couldn't cook.

All washed their hands before coming into the house of mourning.

Pork was not eaten at his grandmother's house, because she said it wasn't healthy.

The family ate sardines.

They did not go to Confession.

They felt it was their responsibility to give to charity. They were very charitable. Antonio's mother is also very charitable.

The family discussed Moses (called Moise in Portuguese), and the Ten Commandments were emphasized in the grandparents' home.

Antonio was not circumcised.

His mother believed in and talked about the Evil Eye.

There was no crucifix in the house.

His grandfather put his hands on a child's head to bless the child.

His grandmother cooked all day on Friday, but not on Saturday.

Antonio's wife, Mary, also cleans the house thoroughly on Fridays.

When his mother died, she was kept at home, washed, put in a shroud after twenty-four hours, and then buried in a wooden box.

Thoughts and Feelings

Antonio feels Jewish, intellectually and socially.

He admires Jewish culture and religion.

He feels Sephardic.

He speaks to the Rotary Club about Portuguese Conversos.

His favorite books are *Judeus em Portugal*, by Atunes, and *Hebrews of the Portuguese Nation*, by Miriam Bodian.

His most admired Portuguese person is Aristides de Souza Mendes, Consul General in Bordeaux, France, who saved 30,000 Jews from the Holocaust.

Harvey Teves

Personal Information

FULL NAME: Harvey Alfred Teves

WIFE'S NAME: Julie

PLACE OF BIRTH: Honolulu, Hawaii

MOTHER'S MAIDEN NAME: Adeline Sousa

MOTHER'S GRANDMOTHER: Maria Martins

FATHER'S MOTHER'S MAIDEN NAME: Maria Gloria Repoza

FATHER'S GRANDMOTHER: Maria Isabel Rodrigues

HOME ADDRESS: Kailua, Hawaii

SURNAMES IN THE FAMILY: Tavares, Machado, Mendes, Costa, Baptiste

SURNAMES OF FRIENDS: Ventura, Mederios, Nunes, Sousa

Family History and Traditions

Harvey's father's family (Rodrigues) is from Madeira.

His mother's father is from San Miguel, Azores.

Other family members on his mother's side are from the Azores. Her father was Cartano Repoza Teves from Lagoa, the Azores. Her mother was from the Azores and the name was Martins.

With the help of a hired genealogist, the family had a reunion of two hundred people.

Teves is a Flemish name. In San Miguel, Azores, many Portuguese Jews also had Flemish names, because Flemish people came there as well.

Whole Portuguese families came to Hawaii, giving up their language and their culture, thereby losing their identity.

Harvey's father worked on a plantation in Kauai raising sugar cane.

His grandfather, Joseph, worked with a debt to the Kea Lia company store. He helped to order brides for his fellow workers.

His mother's father worked as a mechanic on a sugar plantation.

Harvey is a retired building contractor in Hawaii, having previously worked for the National Security Agency in Washington, D.C.

He has a bachelor's degree from Chaminade University, Honolulu, and a master's degree from the University of Hawaii.

His sons have been circumcised.

The women in his family are very clean.

There were no cremations prior to Harvey's generation.

Before his generation, when someone in the family died, the body was at home for two days.

The family watched the body.

A candle was lit for the deceased.

The family put handfuls of dirt on the grave.

His great-grandmother fasted and beat her chest in mourning.

Harvey believes in charity. He belongs to a beneficent society called San Antonio.

The family believes the Evil Eye is to be reckoned with.

Women in his grandparents' generation did not sweep dirt out of the house. It had to be taken out the back door.

Harvey ate bread with hard-boiled eggs (*pan deuce*).

The family's bread was always blessed.

They did not read the Bible.

Some foods they ate were figs, olives, chickpeas, and braided breads.

Family members were encouraged to marry within their own community

Up to his parents' generation, cousins married cousins in Harvey's family.

Widows in his grandparents' generation were encouraged to marry their single brothers-in-law.

Education was stressed in the family.

The family is made up of high achievers, including doctors, and they are proud of their accomplishments.

They used the expressions "Please God" and "Oh my God."

The older generation of the family gathers on Saturday.

The family gave bread to the priest on a regular basis.

There are relatives in São Paulo with the names Sousa and Martins.

Harvey knows that his great-great-grandfather from Oakland, California, was related to John Philip Sousa.

He says that his family in San Miguel are Portuguese Jews.

Some relatives now live in New Bedford, Massachusetts; others live in Brazil.

Harvey believes in a common salvation.

Thoughts and Feelings

Harvey will talk to his cousins, aunts, and uncles about this interview to get their information.

He has been reading about the Spanish Inquisition.

He thinks there is something to all the feelings and traditions that could indicate that the family has Jewish roots.

A Letter from Harvey Teves

Sandra,

As a result of meeting you and resulting from your presentation, I began inquiring and Internet-researched enough information about the Spanish Inquisition and the plight of the Sephardic Jewish people. I visited the Bibliotecha in Ponta Delgada, São Miguel, and while there learned that: 1) perhaps 25%–30% or so of the population that originally migrated there in the 16th century were Sephardic Jews or "Novo Cristos" from Portugal. 2) Many of the surnames you sent me that are of Sephardic origin are the names of relatives and friends of our Portuguese community that migrated to Hawaii, New Bedford, Mass, Brazil, and New York, especially during the 1850s through the end of the century.

It is quite interesting to learn that "Ponta Delgada," the Capital of São Miguel, Azores, was called "Jew-town" prior to being called "Ponta Delgada."

In all my years and my entire education I had never heard that the Portuguese in Hawaii were or may be of Sephardic Jewish origin. I learned that from you. Since meeting you my interest was awakened and the tools of the Information Age have enlightened and enhanced my learning about the Spanish Inquisition and the very likelihood of myself and many members of the Portuguese community in Hawaii being of Sephardic Jewish lineage. My appetite to learn more about this aspect of my heritage is very strong.

Thank you.

(signed) Harvey Teves

Erma Souza (Trowe)

Personal Information

FULL NAME: Erma Trowe

AGE WHEN INTERVIEWED: 89

FATHER'S NAME: Antonio Bernardo Jeremias (Souza in the Azores)

PLACE OF BIRTH: Southwest of Fresno, in Lenore Summit Lake, Tulare Lake area

MAIDEN NAME: Simas

MARRIED NAME: Craveiro (husband is deceased)

SURNAMES OF CHILDHOOD FRIENDS: Costa, Coelho, Correia, Freitas

SURNAMES IN MOTHER'S FAMILY: Bettancourt, Ferreira, Pereira-Simas

SURNAMES IN FATHER'S FAMILY: Jeremias, Sousa, Vielo

SURNAMES IN HUSBAND'S FAMILY: Machado, Silveiro

Family History and Traditions

Erma's father's cousin was Jacob Pereira from the island of Flores, in the Azores. She visited relatives in the Azores whose names were Signora and Signor Sousa.

Erma's three sons were all circumcised.

Her father's family was very interested in culture.

Her mother's family was spiritual.

Her father was born on the island of Flores, in the Azores, where Erma knows people with Jewish roots lived.

Her father was born when his mother was fifteen. At seventeen he left the Azores to work in Idaho as a shepherd.

In 1915 he came to Fresno.

Erma's mother came from the Pico Island in the Azores, where Dutch people lived, where cheese is made, and where there are windmills.

The family brought a crucifix from the Azores.

Erma remembers that her family's neighbors made their sausage out of chicken, not pork. Her own family did not use chicken for the sausages, but she was told that the family in Flores Island did use chicken for sausage.

Her family in America made sausage out of pork.

Family cleanliness was important, but living on a dairy ranch with many children often made changing linens very difficult.

When a family member died in the Azores, the family kept the body home for one day and then buried it in a wooden box.

When her father's mother died, he wore a black armband for thirty days. His armband was brought from the Azores, following the family's tradition.

Mourning was a deeply sad time in his life, with no music or gaiety.

Her father was very intelligent, with a well-developed mind. He looked at everything in depth.

CRAVEIRO FAMILY PORTRAIT. *Erma Craveiro Trowe's family came from the Azores island of Flores. Today, Erma still lives in Fresno, California, where her family farmed after arriving in America.*

The family's bread at Easter time was baked with a hard-boiled egg inside.

The family fasted at Easter. Erma was told this was good for the body and for the mind.

The women in the family salted their meat before it was cooked.

Education was given high priority in her family. All of the children were given a chance to go to college in America.

Her father stressed a love of music in the family. Although poor during the Depression, he managed to buy a piano for seventy-five dollars and gave his children lessons. Erma's brother also received a cornet, and her sister received a violin, which they learned to play.

Before she could read, Erma's father began telling her the story of Moses.

The family did not own a bible.

The family was very charitable, giving contributions through their church to its beneficent society.

At the funeral of a lodge brother, a group of men would come to stand at the service to pray for the deceased. This ensured a good number of people would be present.

Her family has always stressed the fact, when they heard disparaging remarks about Jewish people, that Jesus Christ was also Jewish.

In order to increase milk production, Erma's oldest son, Jerry, helped to develop the scientific feeding of Holstein cows by looking at, and adopting, the practice in Israel of milking three times each day, instead of the customary twice a day in the U.S. He also developed registered stock with good genes that produced more healthy cows.

Even as a young child Jerry was intellectual and a leader.

The family serves sugar cookies, eggplant with onions, Swiss chard, and lamb at Easter.

Her father's cousin, Sousa, was told by his mother to get educated, to go to San Miguel (the Jewish island), and to become a priest. He left but then returned home, having decided not to pursue this plan. His mother told him she would commit suicide if he did not become a priest. He agreed only if he could also study medicine and become a doctor, because the island of Flores needed a doctor.

Thoughts and Feelings

Erma exchanged thoughts with her father, who had educated himself about always doing the right thing.

She learned that she must have a developed mind.

She always gravitated toward learning about Jewish culture.

At times she sees Jewish doctors because she feels comfortable with them.

She has always liked having Jewish people around, as she is drawn to them and admires them.

She thinks Judaism is passed down in her DNA and in her soul, and so she has investigated this to get her answers.

Erma is convinced that she has Jewish roots.

She thinks her boys had a different perspective on life because the family has Jewish roots. They were always curious to get to the bottom of the issue to find answers. Her boys are all intellectual.

All the learning for the Portuguese community took place in her parents' home, with Father Doud coming from seventeen miles away to teach the Catechism, the rules and prayers of the Church.

She thinks like a Jew and she feels like a Jew, and all of her children know how she feels.

She believes that the Messiah will return for all people, not for individuals.

Her family is very close, and Erma created a book of photographs and stories of the family to give each child.

Her search for Jewish roots has been happy because she has always known that she was on the right track.

Elisabete Viera

Personal Information
FULL NAME: Elisabete Viera

BIRTHDATE: 1977

PLACE OF BIRTH: Recife, Pernambuco, Brazil

OCCUPATION: She is a professional guide. She speaks five languages.

Family History and Traditions
Her family has always found friends who are Jewish.

She has learned to cook Jewish recipes, like potato pancakes.

They eat matzah for Passover.

The family is very charitable.

She does not eat pork.

They make sausages out of chicken.

The family played with a top that spun, and people would put in and take out, depending on which side the top landed.

The family is still considered to be Catholic, even though they don't believe in saints and never go to church.

The family prays only to God.

Thoughts and Feelings
She believes she is Jewish because of her roots.

She says people who were forced to be Christian were robbed of their Judaism.

She sends her daughter to a Jewish day school.

She has always felt comfortable with people who are Jewish, not with Catholic people.

She buys books and reads as much as she can about what it is to be a Jew.

She has taken classes about the Jewish faith.

She told me about the driver of our van, who also had Jewish roots. He did not speak English.

She knows what a mikveh is used for.

She feels more natural and happy knowing her roots are Jewish.

CHAPTER SIX

The Remarkable Findings

A FTER INTERVIEWING NINETY-PLUS individuals or families, some interesting facts came together.

In death rites, most interviewed told of a body being washed, put into a white shroud or garment, laid out in the front or formal room, prayed and watched over by relatives for approximately twenty-four hours, and then buried in a plain box in the ground. Often, the people who told me of this tradition assumed that all Catholic people must also do this, until I reminded them of popes, who sometimes weren't buried for more than a week.

Many people told me that their families didn't mix milk and meat products on the same table or in the same pot at the same time because Grandma told them it was bad for their physical health, and they were likely to become ill.

I told them that the real reason included the thought that one would never want to cook a calf in its mother's milk because that would be disrespectful. That was really just a signpost to alert one to be respectful to oneself and to one's family, friends, and the community; if people all did this, it would be a better world.

More than half of the people I talked to told me that their families' houses, and theirs, were always cleaned on Friday to prepare for the most important day of the week, Saturday, when the Old Testament was read and friends and family came to visit. Along with a clean house came changing the bed, and wearing clean (often white) clothes. I told them this was done to honor the Sabbath Queen—a special day of rest from the chores usually done during the rest of the week.

Some families told me that the Saturday meals were cooked on Friday so that no cooking needed to be done on Saturday. It was so interesting to me that the Jewish Sabbath was celebrated and was considered the most important day, rather than Sunday, even though many still went to church on Sunday.

Many families told of circumcising the sons of the family, even it if was done in secret. I told them that circumcision was the first covenant for Jewish men with God. Often families encouraged sons and daughters to marry only within their own family (cousins) and their own circle to keep their traditions alive.

Almost all of the people I interviewed said they should keep the family close, because in numbers there is strength to keep traditions and to survive. That's what one generation had told to the next one, over the years and often right up to the present.

Although a few people expressed concern that they were, perhaps, looking for the wrong conclusions at the beginning of the interview, and that they probably weren't really Jewish, by the end of the interview the doubts were turned to more questions about more places to find their genealogy. Because I am not a genealogist, I offered information about places I knew that might be able to help them. Most of the people had no idea of the history of the development of the Inquisition, so part of my introduction to the interview included the facts that led to their families' becoming Catholic centuries ago. I talked of the participation of the rulers in the Spanish states and that of the Catholic Church and the laws (bulls) that came from the popes themselves—and of course, of the horrors and fears that arose for individual families and whole communities of Spain, Portugal and their colonies.

I explained the reasons for the traditions practiced by each family, as they were cited. The listeners often took notes as I spoke, and there were often pauses while the interviewees pondered my questions. In many instances, people made phone calls to family and friends, even as far away as Brazil and Portugal. The nicest occurrences happened when those interviewed became my personal friends.

It was often hard for me to keep my own emotions out of the questions and answers I gave, but sometimes because I felt so badly about the victims of the Inquisition, my own feelings were told. After all, it's because of my feelings that arose from my research on the Inquisition that this project was conceived, came into being, and formed the most important part of this book—the interviews of the descendants of those whose lives were brutally changed, sometimes forever.

As I asked the questions of the interviewees, the responses I received about the traditions in their homes were as varied as the people themselves. I was asking them to think not only about their own lives, but about the customs of their parents, grandparents, and other family members as well. The interesting part of these interviews was the unfolding of memories and stories that I was told, sometimes even before all of my questions were asked. People would say, "Is this tradition something Jewish?"

The categories I concentrated on included religious rites, death and marriage rites, food preparation, social responsibility, charity, education, mysticism, amulets, moral teaching, and personal beliefs.

Some had more to say than others, but all had something to say about their belief in the Jewish connection in their history and in their lives. Often, a person could only express that a feeling existed of not being comfortable in the religion they were raised in—but saw that they felt at home in the religion of a friend who was a practicing Jew. Sometimes a person would notice that his or her belief or tradition was just like the belief or tradition of a Jewish friend, neighbor, or work colleague, and then the person would begin to have stirring feelings that led him or her to wonder "Am I also Jewish?" Many times I was told that some research had been done to verify feelings of Jewish lineage, but because most often individuals didn't know how to ascertain that information, they were still searching for a better understanding. That's why the interview process was so welcome: questions I asked and the answers they gave filled in the gaps.

Almost all of them were going to explore further, and almost all of the people interviewed were going to discuss the information learned from the interviews with their children, parents, or extended families.

As I explained the reasons, which were most often lost, for the family traditions that were Jewish, the interviewees were like sponges, soaking up every word I said. They were eager to ask and learn more and excited about knowing why they did what they did. In a sense they were returning to their Jewish roots—even if it was only by hearing the explanations I gave them.

The seed that was planted was sprouting, and some of the people were planning to add Jewish holidays to their year. Others were planning to make Judaism their own religion in practice and come back to their original roots.

Some showed tears and even anger at having been deprived of their rightful ownership of Judaism; and always with or without that anger, joy was exhibited at being a part of an old, and although often persecuted, important religion in the world. And the thank-you's I received were sincerely grateful.

I hope others of Latin heritage who read these interviews will look into their own pasts to see if they too have traditions that are wanting to be explored and put into context, for they too have a right to know their roots.

True and certain it is that there is one God,
And there is none like unto Him.
It is He who redeemeth us from the might of tyrants,
And preserveth us from the hand of all oppressors.
Great are the things that God hath done;
His wonders are without number.
He brought forth the children of Israel from Egypt,
And delivered them from slavery unto freedom.
In all ages the Lord hath been our hope;
He hath rescued us from enemies who sought to destroy us.

—Responsive Reading, adapted from the Hebrew
from Evening Service, Yom Kippur

Sephardic Judaism in the World

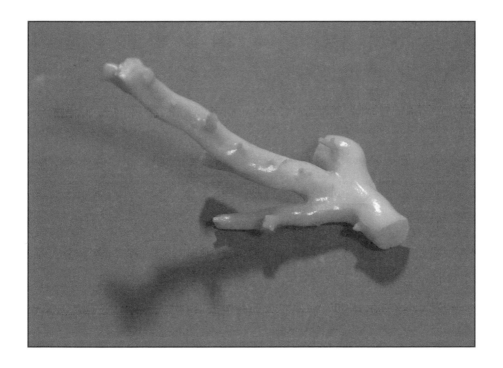

Those Sephardic Jews who survived, whether they remained Jewish on the outside or converted to Christianity to the outside world, made many contributions. In spite of all the threats by the Spanish and Portuguese courts, the harassment by the Catholic Church, and the fears of the autos da fé, the people represented here are just some of the successes the Sephardic people accomplished worldwide. Some of these Jews were merchants, scientists, doctors, translators, advocates, authors, artists, and astronomers. Some even accompanied explorers like Columbus on their voyages to the New World.

Those Jews acting as New Christians, or Marranos, were creative, industrious, and ready for a challenge, even with the threat of Inquisitional Boards hovering around and looking for any reason to bring them to defend themselves because they were acting improperly by Christian law—practicing Jewish traditions. If caught, the punishment was often death, and a person's whole family might also be dealt with in the same way.

Even in America there was a period of time when the Spanish were a threat to the Jews. The colony of Georgia was created out of the wealthy colony of South Carolina, when the Spanish were threatening to come up there from their lands in Florida. Even after the creation of Georgia in the eighteenth century, the Sephardic Jews in Savannah left because of possible Spanish encroachment which might also bring the Inquisition with it. Those Jews went to either South Carolina or Virginia, and some even traveled as far north as Philadelphia. Only after the Spanish stopped trying to come north to Georgia did the Sephardic families return to Savannah. Still, the Sephardic Jews in America continued to create a role that only added to the growth of America.

There were also Nuevos Cristos with Jewish traditions in many other parts of the world. For example, Jews settled in Cairo, Egypt; Jerusalem and Safed, Israel; Damascus, Syria; and Salonika, Turkey. Marranos also settled in Pisa, Florence, Sicily, Sardinia, and Naples, in what was to become unified Italy. Marranos were in Bordeaux, Bayonne, Toulouse, Lyons, Montpellier, La Rochelle, Nantes, Rouen, Biarritz, Bidache, Peyrehorade, and Saint-Jean-de-Luz in what was to become unified France. At one time in the sixteenth century Marranos lived in Antwerp, with Judaism being practiced but only in a restricted fashion.

Nuevos Cristos were on all of the inhabited continents in various cities and ports. How well they lived depended on the cities and countries in which they dwelt and the times in which they resided there, as they took with them, wherever they went, their Jewish ancestral traditions, even if they had to keep and observe those traditions secretly.

CHAPTER SEVEN

Sephardic Society Throughout the World

D ESCENDANTS OF THE JEWISH POPULATION who were forced to leave Spain and Portugal because of the Inquisition and the punishments associated with it consider their ancestors' history to be a tragic and forced Holocaust and Diaspora—as important and crucial to the Jewish people involved as both the Babylonian and the Roman dispersions of Jews from Palestine, approximately 3,000 and 2,000 years ago. Like then, the Jewish immigrants' lives were disrupted in every way. Many of the families and individuals involved have, over the last five centuries, to this day continued to mourn the loss of their roots in the Iberian Peninsula.

This fact is even more evident for the individuals and families who, although Catholic or practicing other religions today, have begun to recognize that many of the traditions they have reveal that they have Jewish roots. Their identity as Jews was taken away from them by the fear and rule of the Inquisition when they became Nuevos Cristos or Marranos in Spain, Portugal, and their colonies.

For these descendants of Nuevos Cristos, New Christians, or Marranos, there is much to be learned, not only about their own particular family roots, but also about the religion that was left behind when their families were persecuted. These descendants also have much to learn about the countries they live in today, and about what is being done to encourage this kind of investigation. Looking at countries, starting with Spain and Portugal and their respective colonies where the Inquisition began, it is easy to reference the Jewish presence, whatever it might be, that would possibly make it inviting for the descendants of Marranos to identify with Judaism.

It is also important however, to see what exists for Jews today in England, Holland, France, Turkey, Greece, Italy, Gibraltar, India, Morocco (North Africa), Safed, Israel, India, the Philippines, China, Germany, Sweden, and the United States, because these countries also played a role during the Inquisition's long reign of terror. For information about Sephardic communities and synagogues throughout the world today, see the list that apears at the end of this chapter. The lists may be incomplete, as communities change through time, but they do illustrate an overview of how widespread the Sephardic Diaspora is. What follows here is a descriptive summary of the state of Sephardic populations in those countries, country by country.

Spain

Because of the Inquisition and its punishments, forced conversions, and expulsions, the Jewish population in the Iberian Peninsula today is quite small.

The Jewish population, acting as Christians or Marranos in Spain, played an important role in the organization of the first voyage of Christopher Columbus. Abraham Zacuto, who fled from Spain to Portugal in 1492, and José Vizinho helped to develop the astronomical instruments that were used by Columbus in calculating his route to the New World.

When Columbus wanted to convince Queen Isabella of Spain to allow his voyage, he turned to another Marrano—Luis de Santangel, whose grandfather had been an openly practicing Jew. Santangel was comptroller for Isabella's household and he not only framed the voyage in a positive light, he also personally helped to finance the trip.

When Columbus finally sailed on the three ships, there were Marranos present, including Rodrigo Sanchez de Segovia, Luis de Torres, and Luis Bernal. Rodrigo Sanchez de Segovia was chosen personally by Queen Isabella to serve as a comptroller for the expedition, while Luis de Torres was to be the interpreter.

TOLEDO SYNAGOGUE INTERIOR. *Originally a Jewish synagogue designed in the Mudejar style, its beauty can still be seen in its architectural features, but with a cross at one end of the building now!*

In Spain, which today has a general population of approximately forty-three million, only about 40,000–50,000 of this population are Jews. The synagogues that once abounded in many cities are now just buildings that are void of what made them Jewish edifices in the first place, including the arks, which would have held the Torahs, and the *bimahs* from which the Torahs would have been read to the congregations of Jews who believed in the Five Books of Moses, the laws governing Judaism, contained in those Torahs.

For example, the Samuel Ha-Levi synagogue in Toledo was turned into a church with a tomb, which would never have existed in a Jewish house of prayer. Today it still exists as more of a church than a synagogue.

There is a small museum attached to it with some remnants of cemetery stones and artifacts that were part of the Jewish world before the expulsion—and a sign with words that relate the fact that Spain had no tolerance for Jews and usury and that was why they needed to be eliminated from Spanish society.

In Córdoba, the home of Moses Maimonides, the little synagogue is on "Jew's Street," called Judias at the western part of the old Jewish quarter near the Jew's Gate.

CÓRDOBA SYNAGOGUE INTERIOR. *The synagogue in Córdoba, Spain, in the Mudejar style, was used by Jewish residents until the expulsion in 1492. There are still Hebrew inscriptions on the interior, although the Spanish government has not restored the building to show what it looked like when it was a functioning religious building. There is not even a picture to show visitors what it would have looked like.*

CÓRDOBA JEWISH QUARTER. This street in Córdoba, Spain, leads into the old Jewish quarter by the synagogue building, and the statue of Moses ben Maimonides.

In 1965, a bronze statue of Maimonides was put in the plaza opposite the synagogue and a mezuzah was put there in 1985 to commemorate the birth of Maimonides on his eight hundred and fiftieth anniversary. There is no ark or *bimah* put back in the synagogue, but the walls on the upper level are still lined with Hebrew words. At one time the small synagogue was used as a hospital, and then in 1588 it served as a shoemaker's church used for a Mass once a year to celebrate the feast day of their patron saints, Crispin and Crispinian, whom Shakespeare referred to in his play *Henry V* as Crispin and Crispian.

Although the Inquisition in Spain ended in 1834, it wasn't until 1869 that non-Catholics were given the rights of both residence and freedom to practice their religion. After 1869, some Jewish people came back to Spain because the law to disallow the building of new synagogues was abolished.

The old synagogues have not been restored, and in some cities, like Girona, the Catholic cathedral that was built on top of the site of the old Jewish quarter is still there. But the Call (center of the Jewish community) in which Jews resided in the fourteenth century has been excavated and the mikveh (ritual bath) was found there as well. Here also was a hospice for the poor, the bakery, the butchery to kosher the meat, as well other community services, all of them being restored with private funds. Here also are the remnants of Jews who had been either expelled or converted, as New Christians, who continued to form the mystical interpretation of God that is called Kabbalah. Girona was a center of Jewish learning in the thirteenth century. It was in Girona that the Kabbalah first appeared in Spain, and contributed to the basis for Jewish mysticism. Even after the Call was sold in 1492 after the expulsion, Girona was still considered the first center of Kabbalistic studies. Today there is the Nahmanides Institute for Jewish Studies.

The city of Girona, which is walled, is where Jews resided for 600 years, starting in the ninth century, before the Inquisition. By paying taxes to the local monarchy, Jews were able to have royal protection at times.

While living in the Iberian Peninsula, Jewish people often adopted the beautiful architecture that came from the Moslem (Arabic) community. Known as Mudejar, this architecture derives its name from the pre-Islamic Moorish people who were called "Mudajjan," which means "permitted to remain." Today the term Mudejar is used to describe a building made in the Arabic style but for usage that is not Arabic. Hence the synagogues and houses and community buildings in the Arabic style used by Jewish people are called Mudejar. Such buildings are known for their impressive arches and columns, their tile roofs, and a number of elegant ornamental elements on the interior walls, such as ceramic tile, intricate geometric patterns, and stylized calligraphy.

Today about 5,000 Jews live in Barcelona; 3,500 in Madrid; 1,500 in Malaga, Valencia, Palma, and Alicante; and the rest are scattered throughout Spain. There are new synagogues in Madrid and Barcelona, and there is much security guarding them. There are also Jewish day schools established for the handful of Jewish students. In 1996 in Barcelona, the two-room Sinagoga Mayor, thought to be one of the oldest in Europe, was excavated. A Jewish cemetery with 500 gravestones that has existed for more than 1,000 years is in Montjuic with dates that go back to 1034 C.E.

To the average Spanish person on the street, the Inquisition and persecution of the Jews never happened. To them no Jews were burned alive and no confessions were extracted. It is all a myth in their minds, because this history is not taught in schools. There has been in Spain no attention paid to educating its citizens about the horrors done to the people of the Jewish religion during the Inquisition, just because they were Jewish.

In 1995 I wrote to the King of Spain regarding this lack of information and education about the persecution of Jews during the Inquisition. I received a brief and dismissive response from a government official.

Jews today keep a low profile in Spain, although King Juan Carlos in 1992 made an attempt at an apology to the Jewish communities in Israel and the United States. But to the hundreds of thousands of descendants of expelled Jews and converted Jews of Spain, the stigma of that horror still exists today.

Sandra Cumings Malamed
POST OAK LECTURES
345 N. Maple Drive, Suite 320
Beverly Hills, CA 90210
310.278.5888 Phone
310.278.5316 Facsimile

September 6, 1995

King Juan Carlos de Bourbon
Palacio De La Zarcula
Madrid, Spain

Your Highness:

This summer my family and I decided to come to Spain. I felt comfortable in this decision because of your apology to the Jewish people for the atrocities perpetrated against them during the Inquisition period of Spanish history, and because you officially reversed the Inquisition laws and opened the records for all historians, such as myself, to study.

I am an American, Sandra Cumings Malamed, and I am curator of American History, specializing in the American Jewish Colonial Experience, 1654 to 1840. I curate for the American Jewish Historic Society on the campus of Brandeis University in Waltham, Massachusetts and for the Skirball Museum, an arm of the Hebrew Union College in Los Angeles, California. I also lecture on this subject, fourteen different presentations with slides, to illustrate the many contributions of the Jews who lived in America during the early period. More that half of the people about whom I speak come from families who were called "marranos" in Spain and "conversos" in Portugal. Their dedication to America showed in their outstanding participation in the mercantile trade, medicine, industry, science, the arts, political reformation and social reform. Their deeds were vast and far reaching into today's present society. Often these people had to regain their Jewish roots, including the rite of circumcision for the male line. As new Americans, these Jews never forgot their Spanish home that they had lived in and flourished in for many centuries. Their synagogues (sinagogas) reflect the beauty of the culture they were forced to leave behind.

My family and I are now home and reflecting back on our summer trip to your country, we found Spain today, to be quite extraordinarily beautiful and the people warm and friendly. We realized the pride that is felt by them for their history and for the culture is deep and it is real.

However, we were also dismayed by the lack of knowledge of many of the citizens of Spain as to the plights of the Jewish community in Spain from 1391 onward.

People, guides, actually told us that for the Jews being a Catholic was a good change and that Jews had not suffered any persecution, torture or death by the Inquisition - that was just a rumor. We were shocked at the lack of education on the subject for some of the Spanish licensed guides we met.

If that was not enough, we visited Seville where there was a large and active community and synagogue in 1492 - only to find that now there is a cross on the cemetery property and no mention of the Jewish people who once called it their home.

September 6, 1995

When we reached the old synagogues in Cordoba and Toledo, we could not believe the lack of attention to restoring those edifies to their original interiors with a proper Aron Dodosh (Holy Ark) and the Tebah from which the Torahs were read to the congregation.

Even though you call it a "sinagoga", only the remnants of the church are still in place, very confusing for anyone to visit, or understand what should be in place and how as a Jewish people, there was worship there.

The most disturbing of all was the Sephardic Museum in Toledo. The English words that were written there are insensitive and, you may not realize, offensive, both the Jewish history in general as well as to the specific Jewish Spanish experience. The lack of understanding of what Judaism stood for then and what is has represented for thousands of years was not obvious in the representation of Toledo.

I know that you must not be aware of these problems (insults) because I know if you were you would not let them be as they are, they are wrong and misleading. It is my hope that you can initiate the process to help improve these conditions with more education for the Spanish people, including the guides who present the Spanish history to families such as mine this summer. The Inquisition period was a tragedy and the story should be told that way. I will be writing a new lecture on Spain in 1492 and Spain now. I would appreciate hearing of any changes that will occur so that I can present them as well to my many classes and audiences. I believe attention to these types of issues will lead to an expanded tourism from world wide Jews to Spain.

I would be more than happy to assist you in attending to these goals. My family and I are looking forward to a return trip.

Very sincerely,

Sandra Cumings Malamed
Curator and Historian

A LETTER TO THE KING OF SPAIN. The author (with the help of Rebecca, Laird, and Elizabeth Malamed) wrote this letter to King Juan Carlos of Spain, expressing anger and disappointment at the obvious lack of education and understanding by the people of Spain on the subject of the Jewish Inquisition.

CASA DE S. M. EL REY
SECRETARIA GENERAL
SECRETARIA DE DESPACHO

Palacio de la Zarzuela
MADRID, 16 de Octubre de 1995

Cumpliendo las órdenes recibidas de SU MAJESTAD EL REY con esta fecha y número 15.719 se ha dado traslado de su escrito al MINISTERIO DE CULTURA para que por el Departamento u Organismo correspondiente se estudie su petición.

Atentamente le saluda,

nv.

SR. SANDRA CUMINGS MALAMED

BEVERLY HILLS, CA 90210

THE SPANISH GOVERNMENT RESPONDS. The author's letter to King Juan Carlos was answered by the Spanish Minister of Education and Culture stating that the petition was going to be studied.

RUA DA JUDIARIA, EVORA. The sign in Evora, Portugal, indicating the street (Rua) where the Jewish community originally lived. Judieria is the word in Portuguese for Jewish. As with many proper names in Portuguese, there are a number of alternate spellings.

Portugal

As in Spain, the population of Jews in Portugal is tiny compared to the general population; there are only about a thousand practicing Jews among approximately ten million people in Portugal today. Six hundred are in Lisbon, 180 in Belmonte, 120 are in the area of Porto, and several others are scattered in smaller cities.

The Jewish community is mostly upper-middle-class, with businessmen, engineers, doctors, economists, and professors. Most of the Jews in Portugal live in Lisbon, its capital, and a small number in Oporto, Tomar, Algarve, Guarda, and Belmonte.

Lisbon has two synagogues, one that is Sephardi, Shaare Tikva, and one that is Ashkenazi, Ohel Jacob—and one rabbi. There is also a kosher kitchen, a Jewish community center, a youth organization, and a Jewish home for the aged.

The main section of traffic in Lisbon surrounds an area called the Rossio, or central square. There is theater built in the nineteenth century on the site of the Ministry of Justice, where in 1497 the forced baptisms of Jews took place and where the autos da fé of the Inquisition were carried out. All that remains today of the Jewish synagogue in the Jewish neighborhood called the Alfama is a pair of arched windows near the top of a high wall. It is reached through the Arco de Rosario. It was here that many of the Jews fleeing Spain in 1492 settled.

In the Tras-os-Montes region of northern Portugal less than thirty miles from Spain, descendants of original Nuevo Cristos or Marranos still live in and around

PLAQUE REMEMBERING THE JEWS
EXPELLED FROM PORTUGAL. *This
plaque in Lisbon is in memory of all
the Jewish victims of the Portuguese
Inquisition and autos da fé, and is a
form of apology for the expulsion
of the Jews from that land.*

the town of Belmonte, where there is a foundation of a stone synagogue that dates to 1297 C.E., long before the Spanish expulsion. Many Jews from the Spanish Inquisition fled to towns like Belmonte, and many Jews from the large towns in Portugal itself ran to the mountain towns to escape the Inquisition. For the most part, the older generation is still uncircumcised, baptized, but many still practice some form of Judaism in secret, with shades pulled down in their houses when they light their Sabbath lamps in the cellar or bake their unleavened breads. Over the generations since they settled here, the Jews have arranged marriages for their children to keep Judaism alive, says Elias Nunes, past President of the Belmonte community. The Jews of Belmonte and Covilha did not eat pork and never ate scale-less fish, rabbit, or any animal with blood still intact. They purposely celebrated Jewish holidays on the wrong dates so as not to be detected as Jews. Men and women prayed separately or the prayers were led by women only, not in the city, but out-of-doors and away. They used the new moon to calculate their calendar and the many fast days they celebrated. The only Hebrew word they remembered and used was *Adonai*, which means "God."

They continued to go to the church, although they quietly disavowed the Host (bread), given by the priests at the Mass, and the images of Christ, the Madonna, and other religious portraits in both paintings and stone. They continued to put crucifixes on their cemetery stones and on the walls of their houses. They only married within their own communities, and their neighbors call them the *Judeos,* which is Portuguese for "Jews."

Although discovered in 1917 by Samuel Schwartz, a Polish mining engineer, the Jews of Belmonte were still not paid attention to until 1982, when the neighboring town of Guarda was paired with the sister city of Safed in Israel.

The older Jews of Belmonte still celebrate a form of Passover that is not complete in its form, since there were no teachers or books to instruct them; only orally has the tradition for them been carried on. They have gone down to the river for 500 years and still carry their dishes on the days of atonement to wash them in the ritual style of cleansing, and they also wear white garments at those times.

The women said special prayers and then taught them to their daughters and referred to the prayers as *oracoes.* The prayers were separate from the rituals that were organized by the men. The new younger generation has learned the complete ways of celebrating Judaism and in a storefront has put together a synagogue to attend. Those members of the older generation who are still living, however, prefer their old ways.

Nowhere else is a return of a whole community evident, as is found in Belmonte. Elias Nunes says that they survived with vestiges of Judaism not only because they married only within their own community, but also because the Inquisition never had a presence in Belmonte. Today everyone comes out to celebrate Shabbat. In 1989, thirty-two men from Belmonte were circumcised by a *mohel* from Lisbon, as reported by Shlomo Pereira, a professor of economics in California and the community's representative.

There is today, on the banks on the Nabao River, the city of Tomar with its original Rua da Judiaria 73 (Jew Street 73) and its fifteenth-century Sephardic synagogue still in existence. Although at one time it was used as a prison, the building was purchased by Samuel Schwartz in 1923, after it had been declared a national monument in 1921. The original mikveh has been excavated in Tomar and there is a small museum.

In 1993, five centuries after its forced closure, on Yom Kippur (Day of Atonement) a service was held in the historic and restored synagogue. There were prayers of reconsecration, and a Torah, brought from London, England, was put into its ark (its *halel,* or designated sacred place for the Torah). Many people from Portugal, Britain, and America, as well as from other parts of the world came to see this memorial to the Sephardic Jews who were so important to the economy, science, exploration, and medicine of fifteenth-century Portugal.

It is doubtful that a permanent Jewish community will ever live there, but Tomar represents the beauty of a Jewish community that once existed there before the Portuguese Inquisition forced Jews to convert to the Christian faith.

The city of Evora is one of the most important parts of Portugal in terms of Inquisition history. Here is the Court of the Inquisition where the Jewish trials took

THE INQUISITION BUILDING IN EVORA. There are no signs on this building in Evora, Portugal to indicate the Inquisition trials that took place there. Unless someone were to tell a visitor or tourist of its raison d'être, *the building's original use would never be known.*

place before the Jews were taken to Lisbon for the imprisonments or punishments. Beautifully tiled and yet somber today, the courtroom of the Inquisition sits in a large building that also houses the tiled Inquisitors' office. Many of the designs of these blue and white tiles comes from the time of King Manuel I, who first forced Jews to become New Christians. Perpendicular to that building is the Inquisitor's house and the Inquisition administration office. On both of these buildings there is the sign of the Inquisition, the Holy Office, which includes a cross, a sword, and the olive branch.

The city of Evora also has remnants of the old Jewish quarter in the narrow streets and alleyways, a presence from before the Inquisition was there. There were two synagogues, mikvehs, and a hospital. There still exist today the pillars of one of the synagogues, the doorway of another, and indentations in the doorposts of some of the houses where the mezuzahs were once placed. At the Evora museum is a stone with Hebrew words that is dated 1378 C.E. In the Evora public library is a copy of the first edition of the *Almanach Perpetuum* by the Nuevo Cristo Jewish scholar and scientist Abraham Zacuto.

At the Evora tourist bureau, Rose Cato said these words: "We have all here mostly Jewish roots, for those families who have lived here for hundreds of years, although we don't talk about it because the Catholic Church is still very much strong here in

Evora." She also said that "Even though people don't speak about being Jewish, we all know who is because of their names, that represent nature, and because of the families who stick closely together and marry within their close community. Many have Jewish roots and are named from the Bible, like Jacob and Merriam. The Jewish streets are called Rua Judiaria." She says she knows that her roots are Jewish and she is glad that what she says is going into a book to tell the story.

There are many other cities as well where there are signs of a Jewish presence before the Inquisition in Portugal, such as Castelo de Vide, Monsaraz, Marvão, Sintra, Coimbra, and Porto.

In addition to the two Jewish cemeteries in Lisbon, there is one in Faro. In 1991, in the Algarve, Mr. Cabrito Neto received permission from the British Library to reprint the Gacon Five Books of Moses (the Pentateuch). It was originally published in 1487 by Samuel Porteiria Gacon there. That was also the first time that the Five Books of Moses were printed anywhere in Portugal. One thousand copies were printed, and the publication was presented in Faro on May 21, 1993, at the same time the cemetery of Faro was rededicated to the State President of Portugal, Dr. Mario Soares, and Portuguese representatives from many communities throughout the world. Dr. Soares stated then that "different people can live in peace and harmony despite the terrible mistakes of the past."

Jews began to return to Portugal just before 1810, settling in Lisbon, in the Azores (Portuguese islands about 1,000 miles from mainland Portugal), and in 1830 in the Algarve, with the effects of the Inquisition still in existence in all three areas, according to Jeroniso Martins, a well-known Jewish Lisbon grocer.

The first Jews who returned to Portugal came from Gibraltar, which was first a Spanish territory that became British, and from Morocco, which is in North Africa. All were Sephardim whose ancestors had been expelled from Spain or Portugal or both.

Jewish communities were organized in Lisbon, Faro, the island of Madeira, and in the islands of the Azores, each with a synagogue and a cemetery.

Today, the constitution of Portugal prohibits any form of discrimination based on race, religion, or political views and guarantees the inviolability of conscience, religion, and culture.

A recent Portuguese tourist board publication, "The Jews of Portugal," lists Garcia d'Horta, a sixteenth-century botanist, and Pedro Nunes, a mathematician, as New Christians (Nuevo Cristos), both of whom were originally Jewish in their heritage, as a way of honoring the many pre-Inquisition-era scientists, mathematicians, and scholars who contributed so much intellectual material to Portugal's esteem.

Today, many Portuguese people still retain surnames with meanings of animals, plants, and trees and other things in nature that they took when they were forced by King Manuel to take new surnames and to convert to Christianity. Examples of such names are Pinto (horse), Coelho (rabbit), Pinheiro (pine tree), and Pereira

Some Portuguese Marranos Who
Held Important Posts in the World

1664	Isaac Nunes Belmonte in 1664 was Agent General for the King of Spain in the Netherlands.
1690–1700	Daniel and Jacob Abensur were representatives of the King of Poland.
1650	Gabriel Gomez was an agent of the King of Denmark.
1746	Joseph d'Oliviera represented the King of Portugal in Tuscany, Italy.
1690	Joseph Tesuran Lobo was the Spanish Consul to New Zealand.
1740	Joseph Manuel de Acosta was the Spanish Consul to New Zealand.
1658	Jacob Cohen was an agent at Amsterdam for Prince Maurice of Nassau.
1670	David Bueno de Mesquita acted as President for the Margrave of Brandenburg and conducted missions for the Sultan of Morocco.
1684	Miguel Osorio was the representative in Holland for the Queen of Sweden.
1684	David Salom d'Azevedo represented the Court of Algiers.
1680	Agostino Coronel (Chacon), one of the founders of the Anglo-Jewish community, was the Portuguese Agent in London. He helped to gain a footing in India for the British.

(pear tree). Most importantly, from the fifth grade on, Inquisition history is taught in Portuguese schools.

In the northern areas, some priests still espouse anti-Semitism, while the Jews in Lisbon can openly practice without fear of reprisals and accusations. They do no work on the Sabbath, and they fast on Yom Kippur, the Fast of Esther, and Passover. Antonio Pereira's family lives near Belmonte, and he returned to Judaism while studying in the United States.

Another president of Portugal, Jorge Sampaio, has said that "while history cannot be rewritten, it should be appraised as the basis on which to build a future, taking away if possible the national calamity caused by the Edict of Expulsion and the Inquisition that followed it."

Israel has an embassy in Lisbon, and many Portuguese Jews have emigrated to Israel, although Portugal does not have an embassy there.

West Africa

There is one area in the Portuguese-colonized world that represents an immigration of Marranos or Nuevo Cristos that was different for these hidden Jews. Unlike the other parts of the world, where Jewish Marranos ran or escaped to out of fear of reprisal from the Inquisition, the west coast of Africa was a place the Portuguese government encouraged or even enticed Marranos to populate. These western African areas included Portuguese Guinea, Angola, Cape Verde, São Tomé, and Príncipe Island. The Portuguese had been in these areas since the middle of the fifteenth century; for example, there were Portuguese trading posts as early as 1446 in Guinea where slaves were sold. Portugal ruled in Guinea, often fighting off both the French and the English in order to keep her power and control over Portuguese Guinea.

Portugal was the first nation to have a maritime empire out of Europe, and Africa was a large part of it. The Portuguese had come to Africa in search of gold and slaves.

As in Guinea, Portugal looked for slaves and gold in Cape Verde, São Tomé, and

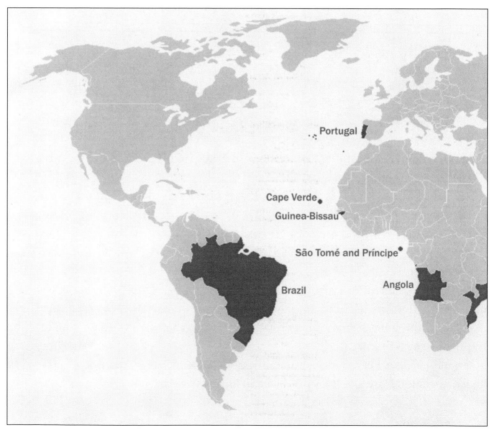

AFRICA AND SOUTH AMERICA. *This map shows the cities colonized by the Portuguese from which slaves were taken to Salvador, Brazil, to be dispersed and sold.*

Príncipe. The Marranos became important in these areas because they were known to be proficient merchants, and so they were brought to Africa to do the Portuguese King's work. The Crown needed money to colonize and explore the world, and Africa was a place to raise these funds. Although the Jews were promised, at first, "religious freedom," they were charged many *cruzados* to go to Africa, and eventually the Inquisitors were there to haunt them as they had in mainland Portugal.

The King had said the Marranos could be merchants searching for riches, but mainly, they were to trade and sell slaves.

By the sixteenth century, the Portuguese, along with the French, the British, and the Swedish, had set up a slave trade up and down Africa's west coast. Approximately ten million slaves left from there, mostly to go to Salvador, Bahia, the port of entry for slaves into Brazil.

Often the Portuguese men married native Africans. Children who came from these unions were not considered to be slaves to be traded. Often the descendants of these marriages had Portuguese names like Pereira, Pinto, Da Silva, Carvalho, and Fonseca.

The Portuguese language in Africa became a Creole language, slightly different from Portuguese spoken in the mother country. The Portuguese in Africa were called Creoles.

Today, the official language in Angola, Guinea-Bissau, Cape Verde, São Tomé, and Príncipe is still Portuguese. Most of the people are Christian, but some are Jews whose ancestors escaped the wrath of the Inquisition.

At one time in the Portuguese control over Cape Verde, Africa, Jewish Marrano merchants were forbidden to develop their own industries for fear by the Portuguese that those jobs could require slaves and that would take money away from the Portuguese Crown. It was in Cape Verde that Marranos traded slaves, but they did it mostly for the benefit of the Portuguese kings, who encouraged and benefited the most from the trade.

As successful as the Marranos were for Portugal, still they had to deal with the Inquisition's investigations and punishments; and it wasn't until the nineteenth century that the official oppression in Africa ceased.

On September 10, 1974, Guinea gained independence from Portugal; and the same was true for the Angolans, who in 1974 also became free of Portuguese rule.

Gibraltar

Originally the Moors of North Africa in 711 C.E. had used Gibraltar, at the southern tip of the Iberian Peninsula, as a stepping stone to conquer Spain. For 600 years they controlled Gibraltar, until 1309, when the Spanish states took over. In 1333 Spain lost control to the Moslems, but by 1462, the Spanish again took over Gibraltar and forced the Moslem community to leave.

The first Jews in Gibraltar were Sephardim who came across the border from Spain in the fifteenth century, starting in 1474, running from persecution that they experienced in the cities of Córdoba and Seville. There were 4,350 Conversos who arrived in Gibraltar because of the favors of the Duke of Medina Sidonia. By 1476, all of the Conversos were expelled, after having had to build their own houses and import food and objects by ships over perilous seas in the two years they were Gibraltareans.

After the Jewish expulsion of 1492 from Spain and Gibraltar, the history of Jews in Gibraltar ceases to exist for more than 200 years. Many of the Jews who left Gibraltar after the expulsion went to live in Morocco, North Africa, and other welcoming communities, including Turkey and Greece. The British captured Gibraltar in 1704. Then, in 1713 England signed the Treaty of Utrecht, which made Gibraltar a British dependency. Although Spain's part of the Treaty of Utrecht called for no Jews or Moslems in Gibraltar, the English authorities signed an agreement in 1729 with the Sultan of Morocco, permitting the Jewish or Nuevos Cristos subjects to return to Gibraltar to trade and eventually organize a community, which is still there today. Most of the Conversos who came to live there then, like their predecessors, had to bring their own supplies by ship and build their own houses.

In 1749 Jews numbered 600, about one-third of all Gibraltar's citizens. By the nineteenth century, there were 2,000 Jews there, and they mostly worked in the retail trade.

The Jews were evacuated to Britain during World War II. Some never returned.

Many of the Jews who returned have served as cabinet government ministers and Sir Joshua Hassan was first mayor and then Chief Minister for thirty years. Several Jews were even made diplomatic representatives to foreign governments. Most of the Jews of Gibraltar today are observant of the Jewish rituals, laws, and holidays.

The Jewish stores along the main street are closed for the Sabbath. There are four synagogues where the Jewish residents take Sabbath meals and then stroll the narrow streets, visiting each other's homes according to Manfred R. Lenman. He witnessed the Levy family singing the traditional Sephardic song called "Bendiganos."

Today the Jewish Gibraltar community has two Jewish day schools and six Hebrew schools. Gibraltar's Jewish heritage is being documented by the Survey of the Jewish Built Heritage.

The Jews of Gibraltar live in great harmony with people of other denominations who live there. Religious differences are respected in Gibraltar. Often Jewish children attend Catholic schools and there is great attention paid to nurturing feelings and stamping out prejudice among the students, an idea that permeates throughout Gibraltarean society today. The synagogue Shahar Hashamayim, that was started first in 1797, is decorated in the Mudejar style and, although rebuilt after a fire of 1911, still retains the women's gallery upstairs, which is supported by six columns of Carrara marble. These columns were salvaged from a ship that went aground at Punta Carnero.

JEWISH WOMAN OF GIBRALTAR. *A Sephardic Gibraltarean Jewish woman in a* fiesta *dress. The Jews of Gibraltar at times were forced to move to Morocco, or to England, before their community came back to stay and thrive as they do today.*

The *tevah* (reading desk) is made of wood and placed in the center of the synagogue, much like the old Sephardi synagogues in Amsterdam and London. When first inaugurated in 1800, the synagogue was known as Esnoga Flamenca or Flemish Synagogue. The most well-known Jewish families of Gibraltar are the Benoliels, Elmalehs, and the Abudarhams. There were also the families of Abraham Benatar, Emanual del Mar, Don Aaron Cardoz, Attias, Sertaty, Cazes, Gabay, Benabu, Conquy, Massias, Bensusan, Benzaquen, Benselum, Benaim, Aboab, Marrache, Balensi, Benabu, Benain, Sequerra, Migueres, Sananes, Edery, Schocron, Cohen, Beniso, Hassan, and Abecasis.

Rhodes Synagogue. The Jews and Marranos who ran from the Inquisition were welcomed into Greece. Some settled there on the island of Rhodes, where they had a very active community until the Nazis took control.

Greece

Jews were in Greece after 323 B.C.E., when Alexander the Great died. By 100 C.E. there were synagogues in many cities in Greece. Under the Byzantine emperors, there was much persecution, even though parts of the Jewish scriptures were translated into Greek as, in 285–247 B.C.E., when Ptolemy II, the Macedonian King of Egypt, according to legend, hired seventy Jewish scholars to translate the Torah (the Five Books of Moses) into Greek. Eventually all of the Old Testament was also translated into Greek, and was called the Septuagint.

The communities in Greece where the Jews lived included Sparta, Delos, Sicyon, Samos, Rhodes, Kos, Gortynia, Crete, Cnidus, Aegina, Thessaly, Boeotia, Macedonia, Aetolia, Attica, Argos, Corinth, and Cyprus. The Jewish communities for the most part were very successful.

The Jewish philosopher Philo (ca. 30 B.C.E.–45 C.E.) was part of the elite of Alexandria, and wrote his works in Greek.

In 331–1453 C.E. the Christian Roman rulers in Greece restricted the rights of Jews. In 1453 C.E. when the Ottoman Empire began to rule over Greece they brought a more tolerant religious system for the Jewish population.

In 1492, after the expulsion from Spain, the Judeo-Spanish language called Ladino was brought into Greece. Most of the Spanish refugees settled in Salonika, an important area for Jewish culture. In the Greek war with the Ottoman Empire for

Greek sovereignty, from 1821–1829, many Jews lost their lives when they fought on the side of the Turks.

At the beginning of World War II there were 77,000 Jews living in Greece. Under German occupation, 43,800 Jews from Salonika were deported and killed at Auschwitz and Birkenau. By the end of World War II, there were only 11,000 Jews left in Greece.

Today there are only about 5,000 Jews in Greece, mostly of Sephardic origin. Athens has 2,800, while Salonika has only 1,100, Larisa has 400 and there are small pockets of Jewish people in Chalcis, Corfu, Ioannina, Trikkala, Florina, Veroia, Kavalla, Rhodes, Karditsa, and Patras. The beautiful Sephardic synagogue in Rhodes is still used and open to the public.

On January 27, 2004, the Greek government created a national day of remembrance for the Jewish-Greek victims of the Holocaust.

Morocco

Morocco, located in North Africa, was populated by Sephardic people after both the expulsion by Spain in 1492 and the passage of strict laws in Portugal after 1497. It was here that the seeds of Kabbalah (mystical devotionals) like in Spain were planted at the end of the fifteenth and beginning of the sixteenth centuries.

Moroccan Jews worshiped the graves of the *tzaddikim* (learned men) of Judaism and often prayed to them for everything from their own personal health to a peaceful running society in the *mellah* (the Jewish quarter).

Moroccan Jews took part every spring in a Mimouna, a springtime celebration involving walking through gardens, enjoying picnics, and visiting each other's homes. They shared faith that someday, when the end of the Inquisition came, they would be redeemed from their exile in Morocco, and be able to return to their be-

THE TOMBSTONE OF MAIMONIDES. *This stone marks the grave of Moses ben Maimonides, who fled Córdoba, Spain during the Inquisition, lived in many other countries, and died in Morocco.*

loved homeland in Spain. The Zohar, the collection of mystical writings from the Kabbalah, was revered more than the Torah in Morocco, as it contained practical ways to reach peace within oneself. This was important as the Jewish community was surrounded by the Moslem community, and although the Jews always tried to include Moslems in their festivals, as they did in the Mimouna, still there was always the fear of being attacked by them. The Zohar gave the Moroccan Jews the ability to be close, personally to their one God. This was especially important in the house to protect where a newborn lived, or to give benefit to an ill person. Zohar books were borrowed from the synagogues and returned with formal processions and hymns because of their importance. The Torah scrolls on the other hand, once brought into a synagogue, are never taken out.

Sephardim in Morocco adopted the wearing of Moroccan dress and lived in homes that included Moroccan design and decorative arts, from furniture to paintings. The artist Delacroix often included Jewish women in his paintings. He emphasized not only the ways in which Jewish life was constrained, but also unity of the community and its intense family ties. He depicted this as he painted daily life in Morocco with its rich colors, flowing fabrics, and the elegant interior rooms of Jewish homes, including carpets, tiles, and pottery.

During Passover, as well as during the Mimouna, Jews opened their homes to not only themselves, but to their Moslem neighbors. Their tables would have flowers, stalks of green barley, and orange blossoms. Neither coffee nor meat was served. Only fish was eaten. People greeted each other saying a blessing, "May you profit and be happy."

Rabbi Hayyim Pinto, of Portuguese descent, moved to Essaouira in Morocco and died there in 1845. He had a synagogue on the second floor of his home. Today, the home and synagogue have been preserved, as has his tomb. Moroccan Jews today make pilgrimages to both sites.

There are approximately 7,500 Jews in Morocco now. Their challenge is to preserve their synagogues, like the one in Fez, called Sa'adon synagogue. Working with the World Jewish Congress, they are preserving an essential part of their history.

France

After their expulsion from Spain in 1492, many Jews went to live in Bayonne, in the southwestern part of France. Some of the names of Sephardic families who lived there included Soarez, Silveyra, Pereyra, and De Silva.

In 1536, after the Portuguese Inquisition was instituted, Portuguese Sephardim also came to live in Bayonne. The names of families there included Wañes, Castello-Mendes, Curiel, Da Costa, Cardoso, De Avila, Vaez, Villaréal, De Paz, Lindo, Lopes, Sasportas, Ravelo, Meldola, Tavarez, Fonseca, Gradis, Azevedo, Furtado, Abarbanel, Colaso, D'Oliveira, Peixotto, Alvares, Rodrigues, Suares, Brandon, Azoulay, Medina, De Crasto, Salzedo, Nunés, Pereira, Carvaillo-Navio, Florés, Peyrehorade, Gardoze, Gomes, Brito, Ferreira, Henriqúez, Cuidad, Fonseque, Pinéde, and Meldola.

Sanhedrin Welcomed by Napoleon. The Sanhedrin, the governing legal body for Jews, was active for centuries before it was brought to France by Napoleon Bonaparte.

As individuals, Jewish people were given rights in France in 1791, when they became citizens of France. This was the first time in France that Jews were thought of not just as a community, but as individuals, and their religion was considered separate from their political conscience.

In 1807, Napoleon helped to organize the Grand Sanhedrin, which is the Supreme Council for Jews, which went back to the time of Moses.

There are three cities where Jews lived that are French today but were not originally part of France. The first, Avignon, called "The City of Popes," is in southern France. It has a Pope's palace and it was the residence of popes in the fourteenth century, as this small city became a Christian capital, and for most of the fourteenth century was ruled by Rome. The first synagogue there was built in 1221 and today there is still a sign which states "Rue de la Veille Juiverie," which means "Street of the Old Jewish Quarter."

With the popes in power in Avignon, Jews had a protected status, different from the rest of Europe—although there were still restrictions, including that they had to live in their own area. The Jews have continued to live in Avignon, and today there are still about 500 Jewish families, mostly Sephardic, residing there. It was not until 1791, after the French Revolution, that Avignon's citizens voted to be a part of France.

Another community now a part of France with a long Jewish history is Cavaillon, whose synagogue goes back to 1499. Today, there is a museum which houses a circumcision cloth with a boy's name and birth date sewn into it. There is also a map that shows Cavaillon as a protected city for Jews, as well as an ordinance from the bishop of Cavaillon from 1781 which gave Jews permission to live outside the Jewish quarter. The synagogue there is no longer used.

Carpentras, the third city that now belongs to France, has a synagogue that was built in 1367, and today is still open for Shabbat services to be conducted for the approximately 650 Jews who live there. In the synagogue there are Oriental carpets, a large seventeenth-century menorah, and a beautifully carved ark. Under Christian rule, the Jews were told that their synagogue was too tall, as it was higher than the town's church. In 1807, the Jews lowered it and painted the synagogue ceiling blue and put stars in to symbolize that it was still reaching towards God and heaven.

When the Nazis came into France during World War II, citizens were rounded up and deported, mostly to death camps. Today there are approximately 600,000 Jews who live in France, and much anti-Semitic sentiment is still expressed in the newspapers, by various organizations, as well as by many individuals.

The Ottoman Empire and Safed

When Jews were expelled from Spain in 1492, it was the Ottoman Empire, under the Sultan Bayazid II, who welcomed them. He supposedly also said of the Spanish King Ferdinand, "Can you call such a king intelligent? He is impoverishing his kingdom and enriching my kingdom." The Jewish people settled in Constantinople, Galata, Salonika, Adrianople, and Nicopolis, as well as in many smaller towns. In time many synagogues existed in the Ottoman Empire. The Jews thrived economically, bringing their talents as physicians, bankers, diplomats, and scientists. Many Jews were involved in commerce and crafts, including the manufacture of weapons and gunpowder, and they also prospered as port financiers and musicians.

In 1516–1517, under the Sultan Selim I, the Ottoman Empire took over Egypt, Syria, Palestine, and the Arabian Peninsula. Many Jews came to settle in Palestine, some of whom had been forced to convert to Christianity but wanted to come back to Judaism. Nearly 10,000

THE ARK IN SAFED SYNAGOGUE. *This synagogue in Safed, Israel, where, after the Jewish expulsion from Spain, the mystical Kabbalah continued to be studied, is still in existence today.*

Jews were living in Palestine by 1550. The Jews settled mostly in Safed, in the Galilean Hills. Safed was an important textile center, but Jews who came there also were involved in agriculture, shopkeeping, peddling, and international trade. Safed was important, spiritually, as near to it, sages from the Talmudic period are buried, including Rabbi Shimon Bar Yochai, considered the author of the Zohar. Joseph Karo, there in 1488–1579, wrote the *Shulhan Arukh* which established the code of Rabbinic Jewish Law. Hence the intellectual study of Jewish literature continued to be pursued in Safed.

For example, poetry was written there by Isaac Luria and Solomon Alkabez. Mystical devotion, known collectively as Kabbalah, was the main reason, however, that Safed was important in Jewish history, as the ability to practice mystical devotion to promote harmony in the world and to be closer to God became available for everyone, not just for a small restricted group of people. By the end of the sixteenth century, Safed as a center of study of mysticism began to decline. Today Safed is a beautiful enclave with ancient synagogues and much history of Jews who tried to find answers as to why the Inquisition and expulsion existed at all. By 1950, approximately 37,000 Jewish people emigrated to Israel after it became a state in 1948, including many people who came from what had been the Ottoman Empire.

MOSES HAMON AT THE COURT OF SULEIMAN THE MAGNIFICENT. This Jewish doctor, Moses Hamon, was welcomed by the Turkish rulers, who wrote that Spain was stupid for ridding itself of the Jews, who were doctors, merchants, scientists, and teachers.

Today, ninety-five percent of the Jews in Turkey (formerly the Ottoman Empire) are Sephardic, and only five percent are Ashkenazic. Around 20,000 Jews live in Istanbul, 1,500 in Izmir, 200 in Bursa, 100 in Ankara, and Edirne has 80 Jews. The community is upper-middle-class and mostly self-employed.

The sultans protected the Jews and forbade, with laws called *fatwas*, the blood libels that took place in Spain, Portugal, and Italy. The sultans chose Sephardim as their personal physicians.

The first printing presses in the Ottoman Empire were established by the Sephardic population and the first book in the empire was printed by Sephardic Jews.

There was a second welcoming of the Jews under Kemal Atatürk, the President of Turkey. When the Nazis in Germany refused work to Jewish professors, scientists, and architects, Atatürk invited those professionals to come and work in Turkey. Turkish diplomats worked to save as many Jews as possible from the German-occupied areas. Turkey, in staying neutral, was again, as in 1492, a haven for the persecuted Jewish communities of Europe.

FUNCHAL, MADEIRA. Many Jewish and Marrano families came to Madeira to escape the Portuguese Inquisition.

Madeira, the Azores, Bermuda, and Hawaii

Some historians believe that the first Jews on the island of Madeira, off the coast of Spain, were the original settlers who came from Portugal in the seventeenth century as Nuevos Cristos. As early as 1631, 1780, and 1820, Jews accused of being false Christians were taken from Madeira back to Coimbra to the Inquisition on the mainland of Portugal.

For centuries, Jews on Madeira continued to be persecuted and forced to practice Judaism in secret, while working mostly in the vineyards and in other types of agricultural jobs, especially raising sugar cane. Still today, there are descendants of the Crypto Jews living on the island of Madeira.

During the middle of the nineteenth century, there were droughts on Madeira, and jobs for Portuguese, including Crypto Jews, became scarce. Many were forced to move in order to earn a living for their families. Some went to the island of Bermuda in 1839, and others to the islands of Hawaii in 1849. In both parts of the world, they worked in agriculture, and many still do. However, the Portuguese also have assumed jobs in many other areas of work, and some even own their own businesses today. The Nuevos Cristos in Bermuda and Hawaii all have names of objects in nature and many are interested in finding out about the traditions in their homes that lead back to having Jewish roots from the Inquisition.

One important Nuevo Cristo Madeiran from the early years was Maoel Dias Soeiro, as he was known with a Christian name; his name as a functioning Jew was Manasseh ben Israel (1604–1657). He was the son of parents who were persecuted during the Inquisition. The family ran from Portugal to Madeira to France, and finally to Holland, where they were not Judaized. It was there that they were allowed to live as Jews, that the family changed from Christian names to Hebrew ones.

Manasseh ben Israel was a rabbi, writer, philosopher, and scholar. He ordered Hebrew fonts made to print and to publish Hebrew texts in Amsterdam, and because of his efforts, Holland became a major area for Hebrew printing of books and manuscripts.

Manasseh ben Israel's most important accomplishment was to gain the support of England's Lord Protector, Oliver Cromwell, in re-admitting Jews to England. Jews had not been allowed to live in England since 1290. Manasseh never lived to see the actual Jewish return, as it took place six years after his death.

More recently, coming from Madeira to Hawaii in the nineteenth century, was the family of Phil Pasquini, whose book *Indentured Immigrants* tells of all the trials, abuse, and persecution his family has had to endure because of the Inquisition, followed by the forced working indentures that they had to fulfill in the Hawaiian Islands. Finding out about his Jewish roots, Phil Pasquini has taken back his Jewish religion and practices today in Ignacio, California (see his interview).

There is still today a Jewish presence on Madeira, as some Crypto Jews are beginning to publicly acknowledge their Jewish roots. The tag on a bag for a Crypto-Jewish family's Madeiran lace product is in the form of a Jewish star. In 1996, President Jorge Sampaio of Portugal, which still owns Madeira, formally renounced the expulsion of the Jews as "an iniquitous act."

The Azorean Islands, a thousand miles west of Portugal, were discovered around 1429 by Portuguese navigators. The Azores, an archipelago composed of nine islands, are situated in the middle of the Atlantic Ocean, within a surface located between the parallels 39°43' and 36°55' and the meridians 24°33' and 31°17', an area of 181,500 square kilometers, approximately twice the area of Portugal itself.

At a distance of 1,500 kilometers from the European continent and approximately 3,900 kilometers from the closest coast of the United States of America, the Azores, since their discovery and settlement, has been one of the more controversial issues in the history of the Portuguese discoveries.

Some historians believe that the archipelago was not geographically known until the second half of the fifteenth century, whereas others affirm that they were discovered in the first half of the fifteenth century by Henry the Navigator's sailors, and still others state that Baccario's map, dated 1534, showed already the major part of the Azorean islands as *"insulos de nuovo roperte,"* which means "islands recently discovered." It is also known from what can be read in the king's letter of July 2, 1439, in the reign of Afonso V, that these islands had already been discovered.

The Portuguese, including Nuevos Cristos on the Azorean Islands, worked in agriculture, including sugar plantations. It is thought that Jews came to the Azores as Nuevo Cristos in the late fifteenth century, after their expulsion by the Inquisitors from Spain and the forced conversion of Jews in Portugal. The Jews of the fifteenth-century Azores were also forced to convert to Christianity, as the Azores were part of the parent country of Portugal.

After 1818, there were actual Jewish communities on the islands, with the most important Jewish community in Ponta Delgada. The practicing Jewish communities were on the islands of Terceira and São Miguel. In 1848 the Jewish total population there was about 250. Most of the Jewish population was engaged in commerce, shipping, and agriculture.

According to Francisco Dos Reis Maduro Dias, Director of the Department of Culture and History on the island of Terceira, some of the habits of the earlier Jewish religious presence persisted among the Nuevos Cristos and still do to this day. It is believed today that perhaps there was some connection between the Jews of that time and the evolution of the "cult of the Holy Spirit."

Maduro Dias specifically spoke of a unique Azorean festival that takes place in a series of little chapels in the countryside and in little villages each year on the seven Sundays following Easter, a time that corresponds to the period between Passover and Shavuot or the counting of the Omar in the Jewish calendar year. The rest of the year the little chapels are closed. Having nothing to do with the Church, these ceremonies, says Maduro Dias, were developed by Nuevos Cristos Jews as a means of staying together to preserve some form of their heritage that was stolen from them. He also says a flat bread made without yeast, which is stamped with a seal of the crown of the Holy Spirit is used. At this time of year, during the holiday of Passover, in the Jewish tradition, the baking of unleavened flat bread is associated with Jews fleeing from the Pharoahs in Egypt without time for their breads to rise. Hence, their unleavened breads were referred to as flat, or matzah, just like that of the Communion wafer, or the Host. Of course there is no documentation of this unleavened bread being only for or about Nuevos Cristos, especially with the Inquisition looming over the Nuevos Cristos' society.

In the nineteenth century, the Portuguese, including the Nuevos Cristos, faced droughts in the Azores. As in Madeira, the people affected were mostly in agriculture, and when given a chance they moved to Bermuda. In 1839, Portuguese farmers came to work in Bermuda—first from the islands of Madeira and then from the Azores. By the early nineteenth century many Bermudian families became successful economically in cultivating crops to be exported to the east coast of the United States. Lilies, tomatoes, potatoes, and Bermuda onions were among the exports in 1923–1924. Many more Azoreans came to have better lives as they worked in Bermuda, in jobs other than in agriculture, including owning their own businesses. They, like other Nuevos Cristos too, have the names of things in nature and are also interested in explanations of some of the familial traditions that lead them back to having Jewish roots.

Today there are approximately 8,000 Bermudians of Portuguese descent. The names of these families include: Amaral, Botelho, Pacheco, Pereira (pear tree),

CLUB VASCO DA GAMA. This building housed the beneficent society for the Portuguese Vasco da Gama Society in Bermuda. The building also contained a school where the Portuguese language and culture were taught to young and old alike.

Silva, Sousa, Varao, Cordeiro, Costa, Cabral, Araujo, Cardoso, Vieira, Rodrigues, Lopes, Correia, Ferreira, Andrade, Medeiros, Paiva, Paulos, Oliveira (olive tree), and Pauao.

With the efforts of the Portuguese in Hawaii through the Portuguese Genealogical Society, headed by Doris Naumu, and with the Portuguese in Bermuda at the Portuguese Cultural Society, many of the persistent Jewish traditions are finally being uncovered and explained. Although there are many Portuguese there who have suspected that they might be connected to Judaism, others, who did not suspect, are also surprised to learn the reasons for many of their traditions and rituals.

According to Doris Naumu, they realize that they should learn of the roots that they were denied, and pass this knowledge on to their children because it is their right.

PORTUGUESE HAWAIIAN SOCIETY. The Lusitana Beneficent Society was started by the Portuguese in Hawaii to help take care of the sick, orphaned, and widowed members of their community.

Mexico, Central, and South America

South America, Central America, and Mexico have Jewish populations in many parts of their landscape of Ashkenazic origins, with many Jewish people coming after the Holocaust, at the end of the 1940s and the beginning of the 1950s. In addition, today, many Catholic and Christian families are beginning to suspect and then learn that many of their traditions and names lead them back to Jewish roots from ancestors who were forcibly converted to Catholicism by the acts of the Inquisition.

In Peru, for example, there are about 26,111,110 people, and only 3,000 counted as Jews. Less than half of one percent are known Sephardim; the rest are Ashenazim. There is a Sefaradi Israelita in Lima, the capital of Peru, at Enrique Villar 581, S. Beatriz. This organization has a beneficent society that takes care of the needs of the Jewish community there.

In Argentina there are 250,000 Jewish people. Most of these people came, as in most of Central and South America and Mexico, at the end of the nineteenth century from central Europe and after World War II as survivors or descendants of the Holocaust. They are, again, of Ashkenazic descent; only a tiny percent are known as Jews of Sephardic origin. In the capital of Argentina, Buenos Aires, there are three synagogues: Beit Jabad, which is Orthodox, Chasidic, and Beit Jabad Belgrano, also Orthodox. In Concordia there is one synagogue, called the Jewish Community of Concordia, which is also Orthodox. The third one is Jabad Lubavitch Rosario, which is Orthodox Ashkenazi.

Juan Lindo, a doctor whose father, Don Joagain Fernandez Lindo, was recognized as having Jewish roots, was President of the Republic of El Salvador in 1841-1852. He was also the President of the Republic of Honduras between 1847–1852. He was considered a great scholar, educator, and jurist. President Lindo built schools in every village in El Salvador with a population of at least 150 people. In 1841, he founded the National University of El Salvador.

This Sephardic family, originally from Spain, and then from Portugal, also had a historic presence in Panama, with Don Joshua Lindo, a banker who helped his country purchase the French shares of the Panama Canal.

In Mexico, there are 40,700 Jewish people, again mostly Ashkenazic in background. The old palace where the Inquisition was held is still standing in Mexico City. There are many descendants of Marrano Jews in the area called Merida, with Jewish traditions, although they do not acknowledge their Jewish roots readily. In the Pachuca area, just outside Mexico City, many Jewish escapees from the Inquisition are known to have lived. Today, there are also pockets of people where local Indians say that they are practicing Jews. There are other indigenous Indians with Jewish traditions who don't call themselves Jews, as in the Oaxaca area. It is known today that 300 years of Spanish Catholic domination left Mexico with an ingrained suspicion and hatred for anything Jewish. Jews were considered to be heretics. Today in Mexico City, most Jewish people keep a low profile, and many live in guard-gated communities and employ armed drivers for fear of being kidnapped.

CHILE SYNAGOGUE. *This synagogue in Santiago, Chile, is still in use today.*

Approximate numbers of Jews in Central and South America

Venezuela	35,000	Guatemala	1,200
Uruguay	32,500	Paraguay	1,200
Chile	15,000	Cuba	1,000
Colombia	5,650	Ecuador	1,000
Costa Rica	2,500	Bolivia	380

In the Spanish Latin countries today, denial of Jewish roots still attests to the fears instilled in Jewish families 500 years ago by the Inquisition. For those who are learning about the Jewish traditions that they are still practicing after all these years, the people are often still afraid to admit that these traditions indicate Jewish roots. Others are now coming forward to claim what was and is rightfully theirs today, and are not as fearful.

In Brazil, the Portuguese part of Latin America, there are 130,000 Jews, most of whom also came there at the end of the nineteenth century and during and after the Holocaust and are Ashkenazic in background. Dr. Tania Kaufman of the University of Pernambuco has stated that there are hundreds of thousands of Jews living as Catholics in Brazil today, with Jewish traditions that range from not eating pork, to burying their dead in twenty-four hours, to having the names of things in nature. Dr. Kaufman states that pockets of Brazilians are learning, today, that their practices are Jewish in origin and many are recognizing that their roots are taking them back to their Jewish religion.

Sugar cane, still grown in Brazil, was first brought by New Christians from the Island of Madeira. By 1579 the New Christian settlement from Portugal was very successful in Brazil, and in that year the Bishop of Salvador was given Inquisition powers there. An Edict of Faith was published in Rio de Janeiro in 1618 and many arrests were made, along with the seizing of goods and fines of 200,000 pesos. Many Portuguese fled to Spanish territories where the Inquisitors were preoccupied and not concentrating on Nuevos Cristos.

When the Dutch conquered Recife, Pernambuco, in the seventeenth century, those remaining Nuevos Cristos aligned with the Dutch Jews to form a large practicing Jewish community. Supposedly the taking by the Dutch of Recife, Pernambuco, was financed by Jews from Amsterdam, the primary one being Antonio Vaez Henriques.

Although the Inquisition functioned in Brazil, all of those suspected were sent to mainland Portugal for trial and punishment. In 1654, after the Portuguese reclaimed Pernambuco from the Dutch, the Court of the Inquisition demanded that

Synagogue in Recife. This photo shows the interior of the reconstructed synagogue in Recife, Pernambuco, Brazil. The original synagogue was destroyed in 1654 by the Portuguese, when the Jewish population was forced to convert, leave, or die.

the Jews convert to Christianity, leave, or die. Some Jews went back to Amsterdam. A group on one ship sent by the Dutch was pirated and the passengers left to die. Fortunately, a French ship, the *Sainte Catherine,* picked up the stranded passengers and eventually brought them penniless to New Amsterdam. Among them were twenty-three Jews who helped to form the first permanent Jewish presence in what is now the United States. In 1664 the English took over in a bloodless coup and New Amsterdam became New York.

Although the Inquisition has not existed for almost 200 years, the stigma of its punishments has been passed down to the generations of lost Jewish heritage in the Latin American countries, including Cuba.

Although mostly Ashkenazic, there are Jewish people today in other Latin countries as well. But the families of Nuevos Cristos in these countries are beginning to find that there is Judaism in their history.

Holland

Jews have been in the Netherlands since the fourteenth century, when groups arrived there having been expelled from England and France. In 1536 Spanish and Portuguese Jewish refugees from the Inquisition were granted rights to settle there. Holland for centuries became a place for Jews to be able to live, practice their religion (the Portuguese-Israelite Synagogue in Amsterdam, built in 1671–1675, was the largest synagogue in Europe at that time), conduct business (Jews owned over forty percent of the Dutch West India Company), colonize (as in Recife, Brazil in 1637), and live in relative peace.

THE ARK OF THE PORTUGUESE-ISRAELITE SYNAGOGUE IN AMSTERDAM. *This drawing by Elizabeth Malamed shows the ark that holds the Torahs in the Portuguese-Israelite Synagogue. The synagogue was used in the 1650s and is still in use today.*

The Portuguese-Israelite Synagogue in Amsterdam became the parent synagogue of the first six synagogues in America. Based on details of the original Temple in Jerusalem, the Sephardic style of Spanish and Portuguese synagogues, and the influence of the Dutch architectural and decorative arts, the Portuguese-Israelite Synagogue still stands today in the old part of Amsterdam. It is in the same area where the artist Rembrandt van Rijn lived when he painted many of the Jews in his neighborhood. "The Jewish Bride" is one of the many represented by Rembrandt, as is his "Jeremiah Lamenting the Destruction of Jerusalem."

The French artist Bernard Picart drew pictures of not only the Jewish synagogue in Amsterdam, but many of the religious celebrations and traditions and rituals both of the synagogue and domestic Jewish life, as well.

In the cemetery at Ouderkirk, which functioned from 1614 to 1850, the gravestones have scenes etched into them that point to the liberal ways in which Jews in Holland could portray their biblical stories, angels, and skeletons. These images were part of their Spanish heritage, to remind the viewer that eventually death comes to all. Jews in Amsterdam were allowed to be artists, as was Joseph Mendes da Costa, who painted "The Old Women Gossiping."

The Protestant painter Emanuel de Witte put on canvas the interior of the Portuguese synagogue in Amsterdam in 1654, which shows that

GRAVESTONE IN AMSTERDAM. *This drawing by Elizabeth Malamed depicts one of the elegant designs on cemetery stones in the burial ground for the Portuguese-Israelite Synagogue members.*

THE PORTUGUESE-ISRAELITE SYNAGOGUE. *This drawing of the Portuguese-Israelite Synagogue in Amsterdam is by Bernard Picart, a French artist who made many pictures of the Dutch Jews during their religious holiday celebrations.*

ISAAC ABOAB DE FONSECA. *Rabbi Isaac Aboab da Fonseca was from Holland and served as the first rabbi in the Americas, in Recife, Pernambuco, Brazil.*

the building has changed little since that time. Portuguese Jewish people, such as Isaac da Costas, built beautiful homes on the canals of Amsterdam, where the Star of David can be seen on his first-floor ceiling.

The Portuguese register of names of Jewish marriages that were just for the Sephardi lists 6,000 Dutch-Portuguese Jews from 1550 to 1850.

In 1642, when the Jews of Recife (Pernambuco) in Brazil established a synagogue, they sent for Rabbi Isaac Aboab da Fonseca (1605–1693) of the Portuguese-Israelite Synagogue in Amsterdam, to serve as their spiritual leader. His family had come originally from Portugal. He became the first congregational rabbi in the New World.

When the Dutch took Pernambuco, Brazil, away from the Portuguese in 1637, many Sephardic families came to settle and join with the Nuevos Cristos from Portugal who had already begun to regain their Sephardic Jewish roots there. Approximately 1,500 people with Jewish traditions came to Recife and many of them owned sugar plantations and mills in 1642. All went well until 1654, when the Portuguese regained Recife and the practicing Jews were ordered to convert to Christianity, leave, or die. Many left, but many stayed, and today there are literally many thousands of people with Jewish roots still living in Brazil, according to Dr. Tania Kaufman, professor at the University of Pernambuco in Recife. Many of those descendants of Nuevos Cristos are today discovering that many of their traditions lead them back to having Jewish roots.

Today in Holland there are approximately 30,000 Jewish people, many other Jews having been killed during the Holocaust in the twentieth century.

The Portuguese-Israelite Synagogue is still used for services today and is open to the public. The cemetery at Ouderkirk can also be visited, but the arrangements to do so have to be made in advance through the synagogue in Amsterdam.

The Caribbean Islands

During the first half of the seventeenth century, many of the Jews who belonged to the Sephardic communities of Holland and England began to come to the areas of the Caribbean that were not owned by either Spain or Portugal and were, therefore, free of the Inquisition. The majority of these Jews settled in what were to become the Dutch colonies of Suriname, Curaçao, St. Eustatius; in Jamaica, Barbados, and Nevis, which were English; in St. Thomas, which was Danish; in the French colonies of Haiti and Guadeloupe; and in Panama and Costa Rica in Central America, after they gained independence from Spain.

The history of the larger Jewish communities of the Caribbean started in 1654 when the Portuguese regained the area called Recife, Pernambuco, from the Dutch, who had been in control there since 1637. When the Portuguese gave the Jews three months' time to convert, leave, or die, some of the Jews sailed north to the Caribbean. Encouraged by England and Holland to settle in the West Indies in 1654, the organized Jewish communities eventually flourished on many islands, including Barbados, Jamaica, and Martinique. Only on the island of Martinique were Jews expelled by the Jesuits in 1685. According to tax lists in 1680, there were forty-five Jewish families in Barbados.

It has been thought that the first Jews to come to Cuba came with Christopher Columbus. They were Luis de Torres, Juan de Cabrera, and Rodrigo de Triana. They were all New Christians, having been forced to convert during the Inquisition.

When arriving in what we today call the island of Cuba, Christopher Columbus dispatched his interpreter, a Nuevo Cristo named Luis de Torres, to search the island. De Torres decided to stay on the island, and the King of Spain gave him a pension and named him a royal agent. He formed many relationships with the natives by marrying the daughters of some of the chiefs.

One New Christian who came after Columbus, Francisco Gomez de León, was accused in a trial in Havana of practicing Jewish rituals and then executed in Cartagena, Colombia, after which his fortune was taken by the Catholic Church.

During the sixteenth and seventeenth centuries, many Jews came to Cuba, some from Brazil after the Dutch lost their lands in 1654 to the Portuguese and the Inquisition forced Jews to leave Brazil.

From Cuba, Jews traded with the communities of both Amsterdam and Hamburg, Germany, although there was much harassment of them by local Christians, and many simply slipped into the Cuban environment, abandoning formal Jewish traditions. Today, however, many of those families are beginning to recognize the traditions that they had not abandoned as bringing them back to recognition of their Jewish roots.

Many Jews from Turkey came to Cuba in 1910–1920 on their way to the United States, where they found the doors closed to them. They then settled into Cuba and were referred to as *Polacos* (Polish). They built two synagogues in Camagüey, including Tiferet Israel for those Jews with Sephardic roots.

In 1924, there was a Sephardic synagogue in Santiago, Cuba. Havana had a Sephardic synagogue in 1914 and four Ashkenazic ones. By 1959, there were 15,000 Jews in Cuba. After Fulgencio Batista was overthrown by Fidel Castro, ninety-four percent of Cuba's Jews fled, as all religious groups, including Christians, were suspect. Many Christians left as well.

Fidel Castro was anti-Israel during his long leadership of Cuba, but he allowed 1,500 Jews to reside there. There is no rabbi in Cuba, although there are visiting rabbis who come from Santiago, Chile. There are three synagogues in Havana, including one Sephardic. Ninety percent of the Cuban Jews reside in Havana. The others are in Santiago, with ninety Jews, and Caibarien, Camagüey, Guantanamo, Santa Clara, and Sancti Spiritus, each with small numbers of Jews present.

By 1735 there were approximately 600 Jewish residents in Jamaica, mostly in the cities of Kingston, Port Royal, and Spanish Town.

Most of the early Jews on both Barbados and Jamaica were familiar with the sugar industry, the slave trade, merchant shipping, and shopkeeping from living experiences in Brazil and Europe, according to author Abraham Sachar. Because of their mercantile experience the Jewish residents were afforded religious tolerance and freedom there. This is also true of Jews on the English Island of Nevis; the Dutch Islands of Curaçao, St. Eustatius (now called Statia), Suriname, Bonaire, and Aruba; and the Danish islands of St. Thomas and St. Croix.

Those Jews who went to the Spanish islands of Trinidad, Cuba, Puerto Rico, and Hispaniola (Santo Domingo) did not get the same opportunity to live as Jews, since the Inquisition had caused them to convert to Catholicism to survive. Some of their descendants, however, know and today still tell the stories of their ancestors and their Jewish roots, since Sephardic Marrano communities did form on the Spanish islands as well. There are descriptions today of all of the synagogues of the Caribbean Diaspora except for those of Nevis and St. Eustatius. Those descriptions that are left tell of synagogues in the Sephardic form, each with the Torah in a large ark at the front of the building and the *tevah* or reader's desk in the middle of the room. As in the American colonies, the outsides of the buildings were left to the discretion of the local architects, so they would conform to the look of the community in which they functioned.

Although each of the Caribbean and West Indian islands has its own particular history, what tied them together were two distinct subjects: the raising of sugar (the white gold) and the trading of goods, including rum, slaves, and gunpowder. The people of the island of St. Eustatius, once Dutch, gave the first official cannon salute to the Betsy Ross flag during the American Revolution. When the British realized that the Dutch St. Eustatius residents were providing the American colonies the much-needed provisions that were being withheld by the British, the British took over the island and punished the citizens, including the very successful Jewish community. The Jewish merchant Moses Myers, for example, was forced into bankruptcy; he eventually moved to Norfolk, Virginia, where today his home and furnishings are still preserved by the Chrysler Museum.

The ruins of the Honen Dalim synagogue can be seen in St. Eustatius today. There are only about 300 permanent residents there today. There are signs to lead to the Jewish cemetery, where there are tombstones with the names of Paz, Benvuste, Henriques, and many other Sephardic families. There are the ruins of the mikveh (ritual bath), which no longer holds water.

In 1655, the Jews in Suriname received autonomy in education and justice and armed guards in their area of living called "Joden Savanne," whose capital was called "Jerusalem on the River." Some of the Sephardic inhabitants had the names of Nassy, Da Costa, Perera, and Nunes. These important families owned plantations where they developed methods for refining sugar, for extracting vanilla, and for producing both cocoa and indigo. Their synagogue was called Baracha Neve Shalom.

The Neve Shalom synagogue is located today on one of the most important streets of the capital, Paramarimbo. Founded in 1736, the synagogue is made of wood, its floor is covered with sand, and the furniture is from another synagogue from 1685. In 1985 the government helped to preserve the synagogue.

The synagogue of St. Thomas was rebuilt in 1833 after a fire destroyed the older building from the seventeenth century. There is a sand-covered floor to quiet people's footsteps as a reminder of the time when Marranos had to be so quiet when they were celebrating, in secret, their Jewish rituals.

Nevis's synagogue is thought to have been built in 1688. A cemetery has stones dating to 1680. Alexander Hamilton, the first Secretary of the United States Treasury, attended the Jewish day school on Nevis and studied Hebrew there, when no other school would accept him as a student because of questions about his illegitimate birth.

The synagogue on Curaçao, Mikve Israel (Hope of Israel), was established in 1651. In 1681 a new, larger synagogue was built.

Ceiling of the Syna- gogue in St. Thomas. The synagogue on the Caribbean island of St. Thomas still has the sand floors to remind its members of the quiet neces- sary to keep Jewish traditions alive in private homes during the Inquisition.

Tombstone in Curaçao. Jews fleeing the Inqui- sition in Spain came in the seventeenth, eigh- teenth, and nineteenth centuries to work on this Dutch island.

BATHERS OF THE DEAD IN AMSTERDAM. *The Chevra Kadesha, the Society of Brotherhood, took care of the burial of the deceased members of the Jewish community in Amsterdam, as it does today there and in other areas of the world, including Curaçao.*

The Jews of Dutch Curaçao became merchants, trading with Spanish and English colonies and Europe. Still today, the Jewish residents are loyal to their Dutch monarchy. In November 1992, Queen Beatrix of Holland attended a service in the historic Mikve Israel-Emanuel Synagogue.

From the seventeenth to the nineteenth centuries, Jews occupied many of the islands of the Caribbean, with a significant amount of liberty and religious freedom compared to what they had experienced in Europe, even though there were some civil laws that disallowed their complete freedom. Jews fought to be allowed to own land, farm, sit on juries, vote, and bear arms to defend their own property and lives.

Today, after hundreds of years, most of the Jewish religious sites are not in use, but the Dutch, British, French, Spanish, and Danish islands still tell a rich story of their Jewish occupation, from the time of the Inquisition until the present.

Italy

The Jewish community of Rome, the oldest in Italy, began in 161 B.C.E. Jewish people came into the Mediterranean area because the sea there was needed for their trading. In 70 C.E., the Roman Emperor Titus destroyed the second Temple in Jerusalem and brought back to Rome many Jews as slaves. The slaves developed their own particular rites of celebrating Judaism—known as the Italian Rite—with the Jews who were already living in the Trastevere area of Rome. There were between thirty and fifty thousand Jews then. This community lived in relative peace until the Pope's edict of 313 C.E., which gave to Christianity the power to persecute the Jews.

In the Middle Ages, as Rome declined, Jews moved into southern Italy, into Sicily, where under Byzantine and Moslem rule, they earned their livelihoods as merchants, farmers, silk weavers, and dyers. In the seventh century, there was a Golden

Age of Jews in Sicily. For the most part, at that time Jews did not live north of Rome.

By 1300 C.E., as city-states grew stronger in northern Italy as well, the possibility of prosperity was noticed by the Jews, they then moved into the cities of Ancona, Urbino, Perugia, Padua, Bologna, Verona, Milan, Ferrara, and Venice. Here in these areas, Jews also became both bankers and loan officers.

In the thirteenth century, when Italian Sicily became a part of Spanish Aragon, Jews began to be treated as badly as they were at that time in Spain. In 1492, King Ferdinand's Edict of Expulsion of Jews from Spain was also in effect for the Spanish territories of Sicily and Sardinia, and the Jews were forced to leave these areas, never to return. Under the Spanish, Jews were also expelled from Naples in 1541.

In 1555, Pope Paul IV issued a bull condemning Jews to live in segregated areas (ghettos) with a restriction on the type of work they could do, which included selling old clothes and lending money.

The first ghetto was in Venice, which actually gave the ghetto its name as the Jews were forced to live on top of a fourteenth-century cannon factory, which in Italian is called a *geto*. There was a large open piazza in the ghetto (which is how the word became spelled), where Jewish moneylenders were told to run their "banks." The Jews were allowed to leave the ghetto during the day, but they had to wear armbands identifying them as Jews. It was because of the Spanish expulsion in 1492 and the Inquisition that the Sephardic Jews, and Ashkenazim as well, were forced to move into the ghetto, where they formed synagogues, such as the Spanish and the Levatine ones. At night the Jews had to remain locked in their ghetto.

Rome also had a much smaller ghetto, with five gates locked at night. Sephardic Jews also lived here and built their synagogue called Scola Castigliana.

VENICE TORAHS. These Torahs, containing the Five Books of Moses and the laws of the Jewish people, were used in the ghetto of Venice, Italy.

In Florence, because of the Medici family, Jewish residents were treated with favor, as were the Jews in Mantua by the Gonzagas, and in Ferrera by the Este family.

As Humanism and the Renaissance emerged, there were Jewish translators who brought their culture and scientific work from both Spain and Portugal. Humanists in Italy and throughout Europe sought Jewish teachers to introduce them also to the Kabbalah's mysteries.

There were Jewish poets, historians, and music composers, as well as biblical and Talmudic scholars. Printing in Hebrew was done in Italy, starting in Ferrara, Mantua, Naples, and Rome. There were Jewish scholars of mathematics, the sciences, and astronomy.

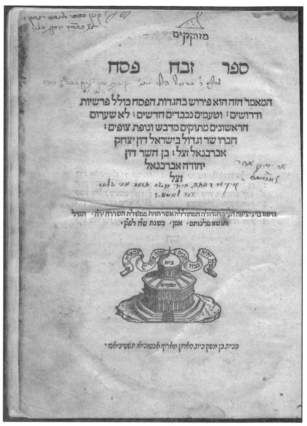

VENICE HAGGADAH. *Jews were forced to live in specific areas of Venice, called ghettos, where this Passover Haggadah was published to remind the Sephardic Jews of their traditions.*

It was not until after the French Revolution that the ghettos were abolished, when Napoleon opened the gates officially, and Jews were finally emancipated. Those Jews who live in the ghettos today do so by their own choice.

In the eighteenth century, Leghorn (Livorno), Italy, became a center for the coral industry and the diamond trade. The coral and diamond industries were owned, in many cases, by Sephardic Jews whose families had come out of Spain and Portugal because of the Inquisition. In 1769, eight out of the sixteen London Sephardic businesses dealt in coral and diamonds from Leghorn. One Jewish coral merchant from Leghorn, Abraham de Castro, stated in 1780 that "it is common for the coral fisheries to bring coral from the islands around Leghorn from six to eight thousand pounds of coral each boat—about three hundred of such boats are employed in collecting in each of the coral fishing seasons for the market of Leghorn." Coral was one of the principle commodities exported to India by the English East India Company during the seventeenth and eighteenth centuries. At one point, there was a two-way trade between Leghorn and India, with Indian pepper also sold as a commodity in Leghorn. (The original East India Company disbanded in 1858, and the new "Act for Better Government" was established for India. Benjamin Disraeli was in charge; Disraeli was instrumental in making Queen Victoria the Empress of India.)

Many merchants from Leghorn also emigrated to England to work as merchants, including Abraham and Jacob Franco, according to Cecil Roth, a historian of twentieth-century England.

The unification of Italy in 1870 gave Jews equal rights. Today, there are about 36,000 Jews in Italy, with 15,000 in Rome, 10,000 in Milan, 1,600 in Turin, 1,400 in Florence, and 1,000 in Leghorn (Livorno). There are also a few hundred in Bologna, Genoa, Trieste, and Venice. Jews also live in Alessandria, Ancona, Asti, Ferrara, Gorizia, Mantua, Merano, Modeno, Naples, Padua, Parma, Perugia, Pisa, Siena, La Spezia, Vercelli, Verona, Viareggio, and Casale Monferrato.

There are three Jewish museums, seventy ancient synagogues, and about 250 towns where Jews once lived, leaving traces that can still be found today. There is a rabbinical college in Rome, where students are taught about Jewish culture and identity, with two courses in Jewish studies that are accredited within the Italian college system.

England

Jews had been officially expelled from England in 1290 C.E. The location of the Jewish quarter of medieval London was on the northeast corner of "Old Jewry," but in 1272, the building was confiscated by the authorities. After that, there were supposed to be no more Jews in England, ever. It is known that Jewish physicians, called in by the English monarchs, and important Jewish traders, were allowed to practice their religion during the short periods of time that they were in England.

Coming as Christians after the Inquisitions in Spain and Portugal, some merchants of hidden Jewish descent began to settle in London. There are no exact numbers representing this group. These New Christians or Marranos began living in England starting from the end of the fifteenth century. They secretly held Jewish religious services and practiced Jewish rituals in both London and Bristol. However, Jews openly practicing in England were scarce until the resettlement of Jews, campaigned for starting in 1655 by Manasseh ben Israel (1604–1657), a rabbi, author, and printer of Marrano origin, who was from Amsterdam. His portrait, by the artist Rembrandt in the Jewish quarter of Amsterdam, hangs today in the Rijksmuseum in Amsterdam.

When in 1656 Manasseh ben Israel appealed to the English Lord Protector Oliver Cromwell to allow the Jews to return to England, Cromwell responded positively. Oliver Cromwell was tolerant of letting people of different religions settle as long as the security of the state was not endangered, and Manasseh argued for the enrichment of English society by Jewish citizens.

Rembrandt's Drawing of Manasseh ben Israel. *Rabbi Manasseh ben Israel from the Amsterdam Jewish community convinced Oliver Cromwell, the Lord Protector of England, to let a Jewish community return after it had been expelled centuries earlier.*

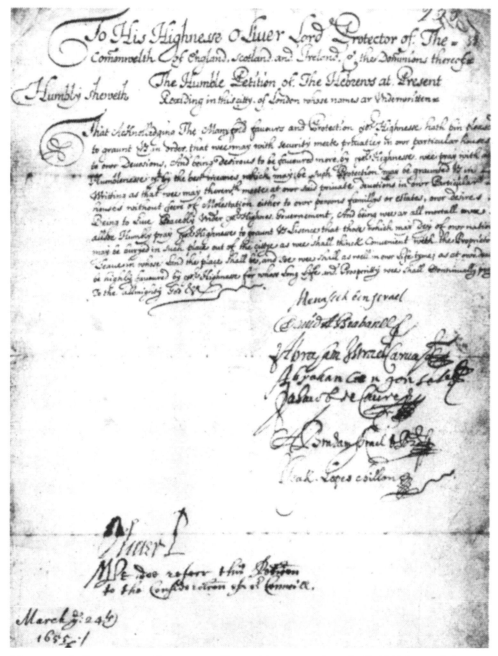

MANASSEH'S PETITION TO CROMWELL. *The petition was written by Rabbi Manasseh ben Israel to Oliver Cromwell, asking for permission for a Jewish community to come back and live in England.*

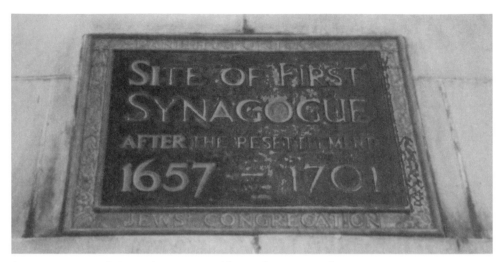

SITE OF ENGLAND'S FIRST SYNAGOGUE. The modern sign on the Portuguese synagogue, which was started in the seventeenth century in England after Lord Protector Oliver Cromwell allowed Jewish citizens to return to England. The Bevis Marks Synagogue is still in use today. Its parent synagogue is the Portuguese-Israelite Synagogue in Amsterdam.

In 1657, the Spanish and Portuguese Jews from Holland founded their congregation in England, the first since medieval times. In 1660 King Charles II of England officially recognized their Sephardic community, and in 1701, the Jews in London completed a magnificent synagogue, Bevis Marks, in the east end of London. Their rabbi was Haham David Nieto (1654–1728), who was a scholar fluent in Italian, Spanish, and Hebrew.

The Sephardic Jewish community was engaged in the business of buying and selling diamonds, gold, and coral with the countries of Portugal, Spain, Italy, Holland, Sweden, India, France, the Caribbean Islands (especially Jamaica), Brazil, South and Central America, and Mexico.

When it came to economics, it seemed that both Portugal and Spain had no prejudice against the profits made for them by the Marrano Jewish communities in the New World, and especially by those who lived in England, Holland, and Italy. For example, according to Cecil Roth in his *History of the Jews in England*, the city of Leghorn was the Italian headquarters for the products of the coral and diamond trades, which were owned mostly by the Portuguese Sephardic Marrano community. These products were exported to London via Amsterdam. London Sephardic Jewish merchants then exported the coral and diamonds to India, Spain, and Portugal, in exchange for precious stones and other goods. Most of the Jewish business owners of Portuguese descent spoke fluent Portuguese with their neighbors from Portugal. Diamonds from Brazil were also traded, after their discovery there in 1728. More than twenty-five percent of the gold imported into England was signed for by the Sephardic Jews, who received the gold from Portugal in trade. Seventy percent of the gold was for Jewish Sephardic Marrano merchant Francis Salvador.

By the middle of the eighteenth century, most of the major Jewish merchants of London had come from the Portuguese community. They or their fathers had come from Holland, Leghorn, or directly from Portugal. Portugal still considered these Sephardic merchants fugitives from the Portuguese Inquisition, even though they continued to trade with them. International trade declined in England in the middle of the eighteenth century, affecting the Jewish merchants and causing a social and cultural decline of the Sephardic communities. That, coupled with the assimilation and marriage of Sephardim with members of the English upper class, also caused the Sephardic community to dwindle. Those who remained loyal to the fold mixed socially with both Jews and non-Jews alike.

In 1774, when Empress Maria Theresa expelled the Jews of Prague, King George III and the British government demanded that the order be rescinded. It was the first time a European government acted in the interest of any minority. In the nineteenth century, the British government gave aid to persecuted Jews in foreign lands. Although there was intermittent anti-Semitism in England, artists such as Grace Aguilar (1816–1847), a writer of novels on Jewish subjects, brought Jewish ideals and morals to the British reading public. She wrote *Vale of Cedars,* which recounts the trials of the Spanish Marranos. Today there are 350 synagogues and about 300,000 Jewish residents in all of England, many of whom are of Sephardic descent.

India

Although there is much dispute as to the actual date that Jews arrived in India, ranging from the time of King Solomon to approximately 379 C.E., it has been accepted that they arrived in Cranganore, an ancient seaport on the Malabar and Kerala coasts in the southwestern part of India. Cranganore was known to the Greeks as Muzhiris and to the Jews as Shingly. The Moors and Portuguese eventually destroyed Cranganore, and the last Jewish prince of that area, Joseph Azar, had to swim to nearby Cochin carrying his wife on his shoulders, according to author Barbara Hansen. The Jews, known as the Pardesi, or the white Jews, were forced to leave Cranganore. They placed themselves under the rule of the Maharajah of Cochin and in 1344 built the first synagogue there. The Sephardic Jews arrived from Spain in 1514, and in 1568 built their synagogue for themselves. The Portuguese partly destroyed it in 1662, and in 1664 it was rebuilt with the aid of the Dutch. The synagogue is the oldest Jewish house of worship in the British Commonwealth. It is on Jew Street and Synagogue Lane in Jewtown, which is south of the Mattancheri Palace, which had been built by the Portuguese for the Rajah of Cochin, whom they controlled in 1555.

The synagogue is adorned with exquisite blue and white hand-painted Chinese floor tiles and is in the Sephardic form with its Ark at the front of the building and the *tevah* or reader's desk is in the middle. There is a 420-year-old brass pulpit from India. There were never more than 250 Jews in attendance, with the women worshiping upstairs in a gallery that is screened by brass latticework. The men were downstairs. Originally there were eight synagogues in Kerala, and today only one remains.

According to the caretaker, Jackie Cohen, Cochin Jews speak the language called Malayalam as well as English, but they use Hebrew for services. They follow strict Jewish dietary laws, including using a separate set of dishes for their Passover meals. They eat fish or chicken, and Mr. Cohen handles the kosher slaughter of the chickens.

The Sephardic migration to India came after 1492 from Spain and from Portugal in the sixteenth century, as Jews tried to escape the accusations, persecutions, and tortures of the Inquisition. But the Jewish people from Cochin had to suffer persecution from the Portuguese rule from 1502–1663. Only with the help of the local rajahs were Jews of Cochin able to survive the Portuguese introduction of the Inquisition into their lives. By appointing a Jewish chief, the rajah granted the Jews land adjoining his palace for a synagogue as he helped to foster the development of the Jewish community. In contrast to the Portuguese, the Dutch rule of Cochin from 1663–1795 brought an era of religious freedom and commercial prosperity for the Jews, according to Joan G. Roland, author of *Jews in British India*. Hebrew books were brought from Amsterdam, and in the nineteenth century Hebrew printing presses were functioning in Cochin. When the British took over in 1795, the economy began to decline for the Jews in Cochin.

There were two other Jewish communities in India, the Bene Israel in Bombay, and the Baghdadis in Calcutta. There were black Jews from Africa in India in the twelfth century, who claimed that their ancestors were part of the Lost Ten Tribes. Benjamin of Tudela, the Jewish traveler, mentioned that he saw them on a visit to India in 1167, and Marco Polo wrote of seeing them in 1293. The black Jews handled, dried, and ground spices while the white Jews did the trading of the aromatic tamarind, pepper, cinnamon, cloves, nutmeg, cardamom, ginger, and turmeric. The white Jews acted as middlemen, ship owners, and financiers, as stated in *The Book of Jewish Food*, by Claudia Roden.

Today, Jews still live mainly in Cochin, Bombay, and Calcutta, although the Cochin Jewish community now has fewer than thirty people. The Indian Jewish community is now about 5,000 people. The World Jewish Congress is working to strengthen India's Jewish community.

Iran

It is known that there have been Jews in the area now called Iran for about 2,600 years. They first came to Iran when the Babylonians conquered Jerusalem in 589 B.C.E., destroyed the Temple of David (built by his son, Solomon), and sent the Jews into a Diaspora or took them back to Babylonia as slaves.

In 539 B.C.E., when King Cyrus of Persia conquered the Babylonians, he not only freed the Jewish slaves, he allowed them to return to Jerusalem so that they could rebuild their Temple. Some of these Jews chose to settle in Persia (now called Iran).

JEWISH MEN OF IRAN. *Jews have lived in Iran since biblical times, and there are still some Jews living there.*

There the Jews became merchants and lived and worked in relative freedom, until the arrival of the Moslems in 642 C.E. Once the Moslems arrived, many restrictions were placed on the Jews, including restrictions against engaging in any business transactions with Moslems. Jews were prohibited from using public spaces, including the public baths, because under the Shiite Shahs, Jews were considered impure and unclean. The Jews were forced to live in poverty. There were forced conversions and harsh treatment for the Jews from the sixteenth to the twentieth centuries.

In 1906, there was a revolution and a new constitution that allowed Jews to become equals in Persian society. In 1925, the Shah Pahlavi gave Jews opportunities to be both economically and socially successful.

When the reign of the Shah ended in 1979, and the Ayatollah Khomeini began to rule in Iran, rampant anti-Semitic acts occurred, including the removal of the rights of Jews to own property and to run their own businesses. At that time, about 50,000 Jews left Iran. Many went to Israel, to Europe, and to the United States.

The laws have eased and today there are approximately 25,000 Jews in Iran, mostly in Tehran, which has eleven synagogues, two kosher restaurants, one hospital, one old-age facility, and one cemetery. Some of these Iranians are considered of Sephardic heritage. Hebrew is taught in some of the synagogues and a Jewish library is now open.

Iraq

Iraq was previously known as Babylonia. In Babylonia, the city of Ur produced Abraham, who is considered the first Jew. This country, located in what is called the Fertile Crescent, has had a Jewish presence since 722 B.C.E., when Jews from northern Israel, after being defeated by Assyria, were taken there. Then, when the Babylonians burned the first Temple in Jerusalem, the Temple of David that was built by his son Solomon in 586 B.C.E., many Jews were taken as slaves back to Babylonia.

When the Persian King Cyrus conquered Babylonia in 539 B.C.E., the Jewish slaves were freed. Many returned to Jerusalem, although some remained, and Jews resided there for centuries, until recently.

In 1922, after World War I, the British began to reform Iraq into a modern industrial country. In 1932 Iraq became an independent state. The Jewish people made major contributions to Iraq, including the establishment of medical facilities and schools. They were involved in music, playing with the Baghdad Orchestra.

When Israel became a Jewish state in 1948, there was much anti-Semitism in Iraq, and Zionism was considered a criminal act. Jews began to be persecuted, falsely accused of crimes, and many people were tortured and hung. By 1970, most of Iraq's Jews left Iraq for Israel and London. When Saddam Hussein was in power, he regularly railed against Israel and Zionism.

The center for Jewish culture in Bagdad is the Meir Taneig synagogue, the last Jewish working house of prayer in Iraq. In 1993, Tawfig Sofer was the oldest member of the synagogue of thirty-five members. He lived next to the synagogue. The interior of the synagogue there had white walls, a balcony for women, and 300 chandeliers.

As of 2004, there was another elderly Jew living there, protected, like Tawfig Sofer, by a Moslem, Muhammed Jassin. Ezra Levy, at eighty-five, can both read and understand Hebrew prayers. His son, Emad, thirty-eight, is the youngest member of the Jewish community there, and is a ritual slaughterer of their meat to keep it kosher.

There are now only a handful of old Jews who are constantly being forced to give the property belonging to the Jewish community back to the government. Although these Jews wish to leave, they don't have passports. Why the Iraqi government keeps them there at all is a mystery, since the government still refers to Jews in an anti-Semitic way with statements such as "descendants of monkeys and pigs."

Philippines

In the sixteenth century, the islands of the Philippines were under Islamic rule until the Spanish invaded and took over the government there. Included in the group when the Spanish came were Nuevos Cristos (Marranos or Conversos).

By 1590, two brothers, Jorge and Domingo Rodriguez, were living in the Philippines. Being of Jewish background, they were suspects of the governing Spanish rule there. In 1593, the brothers were sent to Mexico City and brought to trial by the Inquisition, where they were convicted of being practicing Jews, or Marranos. Both Jorge and Domingo had come with the Spanish *conquistadores* to colonize the islands of the Philippines as New Christians. Eventually, there were at least eight other New Christians sent to Mexico City to be tried and convicted. All were killed in autos da fé.

Under Moslem rule, an important rite was, as it is in Judaism, circumcision of all males. Under Islam, any male who refused this procedure was subject to death. When Christian Spain took over, the conquerors were unable to stop the locals from practicing circumcision, which under the Church and Catholic rule, was illegal in Spain or in any of her territories. Any Filipino Spanish citizen found practicing any form of Judaic or Islamic religious practice, including the act of circumcision, was to be tortured and burned at the stake in an auto da fé. This rule, of course, affected the Sephardic Nuevos Cristos (Conversos) of Jewish origin. The local Filipino citizens who were not Sephardic reasoned that circumcision had to be a Christian thing, because they said that Jesus Christ was Jewish and was circumcised himself, according to the Jewish Association of the Philippines. Today there is still a Feast of Circumcision in the Philippines on the third of January. Circumcision has continued to be practiced all these years in the Philippines in spite of the Catholic Church.

In the second half of the nineteenth century, Jewish traders came from France as well as from other countries to the Philippine Islands. Some Americans came before the United States occupation of the Philippines in 1898. Jews also came there from Turkey, Russia, and other parts of the Middle East. In 1924, the first synagogue was erected in the capital city of Manila. Many Jews later came running from both the Nazis and the Japanese during World War II, as the government was open to Jews being admitted. When the Japanese took over the Philippines during World War II, all Jews were interned, and much suffering ensued for them. The Japanese destroyed the Jewish synagogue, which was to be rebuilt after the war.

BETH YAAKOV SYNAGOGUE, THE PHILIPPINES. *Jews went to the Philippines in the eighteenth and nineteenth centuries. Today, there is still an active synagogue and small congregation in Manila.*

When America took control of the Philippines away from Spain, the Jewish population grew to approximately 500. The Ashkenazic synagogue in Manila is called Beth Yaakov. But there are still many Catholic people there who have Jewish roots and who are just discovering those roots today.

Today, the Jewish population numbers 250 to 300. There is a Jewish Association with between fifty and one hundred members and a community synagogue which opened in 1983 with a mikveh (ritual bath), and a rabbi who acts as a *mohel*, to do circumcisions, and as a *shochet*, to kill animals in the ritual kosher way. The synagogue is Syrian-Sephardic. There is also an orthodox Sephardic synagogue with a *mechitza* (a cloth to separate the men praying from the women) and also a mikveh. Kosher beef and chicken, killed by their rabbi, are available at the synagogue, as are kosher canned tuna fish and sacramental wine. Some packaged kosher foods come from the United States, Canada, and Australia, according to the Jewish Association of the Philippines. Services are held on both Friday nights and Saturday mornings.

Denmark

The Jewish community of Copenhagen was founded in the seventeenth century. In 1622, King Christian IV of Denmark signed a decree promising protection to the Sephardic Jews who would come to Copenhagen. In 1684, there were enough Jews to form a community. One of the famous Sephardic Jews of Copenhagen was Rodrigo de Castro from Lisbon, who was the King of Denmark's doctor. He is considered the father of modern gynecology. Alvaro Diniz, who became Samuel Yania, and his sons were financial advisors to the palace. Jorge Diaz, who became Samuel Abaz, was a literary and intellectual leader of Copenhagen.

China

The Chinese have known Jews as traveling merchants since the eighth century. The B'nei Menashe, a community of 5,000 Jews who still live in India and China today, claim that their ancestors escaped after Israel was divided into two kingdoms at the time of the first Temple in Israel. The Assyrians had invaded the northern kingdom and exiled and enslaved the Jews in Assyria. Their ancestors' escape took them through Afghanistan to Tibet, then on to Kaifeng, in Hunan Province, in 240 B.C.E., where there is still a Jewish community. The first synagogue was erected there in 1163 C.E., with Jews having come on "The Silk Road" between 960 and 1127 C.E. At that time, Kaifeng was one of the world's largest cities, and one of the seven ancient capitals of China. There were, according to W. Charles White in his *Chinese Jews,* Jewish communities in other parts of China, including Hangzhou, Guangzhou, Ningibo, Yanhzhou, and Cheng-Du. In the thirteenth century, Marco Polo, who traveled from Italy to China, remarked that he met and heard about Jews in China.

In the eighteenth century Jesuits wrote to Rome from Kaifeng describing the Jewish religious customs practiced there. Pictures drawn show a hall for the ritual slaughter of animals at the synagogue, and the holy Jewish writings. Lacking a

Kaifeng Synagogue, China. The Kaifeng synagogue in China, rebuilt in 1663, was in use as early as 1163.

Chinese Men Reading the Torah. The Torah in this synagogue is placed on a rosewood stand. Jews have lived and worshipped in China since the seventh or eighth century C.E.

rabbi, and as a result of assimilation and poverty, the community sold some of their Jewish papers and parts of the synagogue to Protestant missionaries in the nineteenth century. By 1866 the Kaifeng Synagogue was flooded and destroyed.

Today, there are still descendants in Kaifeng, the Song Dynasty capital, who think of themselves as Jews. Although they don't know much about their Jewish faith, they still don't eat pork. About 100 years ago they put up a sign in their neighborhood that reads "The lane of the sect that teaches the scriptures."

In the nineteenth century the city of Shanghai became a port center. Sephardic families from Baghdad, Bombay, and Cairo established a Jewish structure. Some of the families that came included the Kadoories, the Sassoons, and the Hardoons. In China today there are relics of Jewish culture in Shanghai and a small Jewish museum in Kaifeng. In 1922, China, as a member of the League of Nations, voted for a Jewish homeland. For over 2,000 years, Jews have never been persecuted in China.

The Ohel Rachel Synagogue Shanghai Jewish school is the most important Jewish community building still standing. It belonged to the Sephardic community in Shanghai and was used from 1920 to 1952. There are also houses belonging to Sephardic Jews, a cemetery, the Beth Aharon Synagogue, and an old market area, all in Shanghai and its environs. There is also a building decorated with Jewish stars.

To this day, Israel and China have close ties, with formal relations established in January 1992. The nations engage in trade and cultural exchanges. In 1998 the Shanghai municipal government provided funds for the renovation of the Ohel Rachel and Ohel Moishe Synagogues. In March 1992, the Israel–China Friendship Society was established, and in March 2002 it celebrated its tenth anniversary. It promotes travel between the two countries, as well as the restoration of Jewish artifacts and buildings in the historic Jewish areas of China.

The United States
Without the burden of having to live with all the horror of the Inquisition, and with a federal constitution to give them protection, Jewish citizens of the United States were able to establish communities where individuals and families could own their own businesses, own property, celebrate their Jewish traditions, and eventually participate in the governing bodies of the land in which they lived. On the national level, the Founding Fathers provided not only a Constitution to give Jewish citizens inalienable rights, but also a Bill of Rights that ensured an individual's private sphere of safety. As for the colonies, which in turn became states, each independently of the others provided rights to its citizens as it evolved.

The first Jewish community in America came to New Amsterdam in 1654 from Recife, Brazil. They formed the first synagogue in that area on what is Mill Street, called Shearith Israel. From there, synagogues were established in Newport, Rhode Island (Touro Synagogue); Charleston, South Carolina (Beth Elohim); Philadelphia, Pennsylvania (Mikveh Israel); Savannah, Georgia (Mickve Israel); and Rich-

TOURO SYNAGOGUE, NEWPORT, RHODE ISLAND. *Touro Synagogue, the oldest standing synagogue in America, is still in use. It was begun in 1759 and its architect was Peter Harrison.*

mond, Virginia (Beth Ahaba). All of the first six synagogues were in the Sephardic style, both architecturally inside as well as in the type of service celebrated. There were many Jews who were Ashkenazic in the colonies at that time, but the Sephardic people were considered more organized, educated, and able to integrate with the general society as well, and that is why the Sephardic style was chosen for the houses of worship. All of the six synagogues are still used today, and have active congregations.

Because of the freedom allowed to the Jewish people during the colonial period in America's history, there were many "firsts" for the Jewish citizens. Here is a list of just some important Sephardic contributors to early America, involved in the arts, literature, social reform, mercantilism, philanthropy, religion, medicine, education, agriculture, preservation, and heroism.

The first Jewish doctor in North America was Dr. Jacob Lumbrozo from

SKETCH
OF
PROCEEDINGS IN THE
Legislature of Maryland,
DECEMBER SESSION, 1818,
ON WHAT IS COMMONLY CALLED
The Jew Bill;
CONTAINING
THE REPORT OF THE COMMITTEE
APPOINTED BY THE HOUSE OF DELEGATES
" To consider the justice and expediency of extending to those persons professing the Jewish Religion, the same privileges that are enjoyed by Christians:"
TOGETHER WITH
The Bill reported by the Committee,
AND
THE SPEECHES
OF
THOMAS KENNEDY, Esq. OF WASHINGTON COUNTY,
AND
H. M. BRACKENRIDGE, Esq. OF BALTIMORE CITY.

Baltimore:
PRINTED BY JOSEPH ROBINSON,
Circulating Library, corner of Market and Belvidere-streets.
1819.

THE MARYLAND JEW BILL. *This bill gave rights to Jews in Maryland to participate in political forum.*

Portugal, who settled into the colony of Maryland on January 24, 1656, as the only Jew there. Dr. Lumbrozo was one of many prominent Sephardic men of medicine in early America. Dr. Samuel Nunez Ribiero, a native of Lisbon, Portugal, came to Savannah, Georgia in 1733 and was given great recognition by Governor Oglethorpe, for caring for very ill residents during an epidemic. Dr. Jacob de la Motta, as a native of Savannah, Georgia, practiced there and in Charleston, South Carolina, and served as an army surgeon during the War of 1812. He had correspondence with both Thomas Jefferson and James Madison. Dr. David Sarzedas practiced medicine in Charleston, South Carolina, in 1795, and Dr. Levi Myers was Apothecary General in South Carolina from 1799–1822.

Dr. John de Sequeyra in Williamsburg, Virginia, was first head physician of the hospital there, which was given to the colonies by George III. Dr. De Sequeyra treated mental health patients that he took out of prisons. He wrote treatises on diseases of the Commonwealth of Virginia, and he separated out diseases of both women and children. Educated in Holland, of Portuguese descent (he was tenth in a line of doctors from ten generations), Thomas Jefferson credits him with the introduction of the tomato to America as an edible vegetable. The pub-

Beth Elohim Synagogue, Charleston, South Carolina. This building was destroyed by fire, but the congregation still remains.

lic hospital has been recreated at Colonial Williamsburg in Virginia and is now a museum.

Dr. Daniel L.M. Peixotto was born in Amsterdam, Holland, July 18, 1800. He was educated in Curaçao and was a graduate of Columbia College in 1823. In 1819, he received a degree from the College of Physicians and Surgeons of New York City. He was a pioneer in the field of preventive medicine, including the use of vaccines. He also urged the identification of quacks, who assume unqualified medical positions and issue pharmaceuticals to unwary patients.

The first Jewish school in North America to combine both Hebrew and secular studies was formed in 1775 by the first Jewish congregation in America, Shearith Israel, in the Portuguese synagogue in New York City.

The first Jewish artist in America was Myer Myers, who resided in New York City in 1746. He was a silversmith who was eventually elected as the first president of the Silversmith's Society in New York. There were no guilds in America, as existed in England, and the society became America's equivalent to them.

The first indigo plant that was successful in America was put into the ground under the supervision of Moses Lindo, a Portuguese Jew in Charleston, South Carolina. He became Inspector General for indigo dyes and drugs for ten years in South Carolina and the Carolina provinces. Indigo became the major source of wealth for that colony.

Abraham de Lyon, a vintner from Portugal, and Isaac Nunes Henriques, originally from Lisbon, Portugal, developed plantations and ranches in Savannah, Georgia, until 1742, when the Spanish from Florida threatened to attack, bringing them reminders of the Inquisition and its horrors. They fled to the northern colonies, only to return after the Spanish threat was no longer a problem.

Isaac Miranda, from Portugal, had to pose as a Christian in the Conestoga Valley in order to receive a political appointment as a judge. He was accused of defrauding the Indians, although he claimed his innocence.

The first Jewish merchant who was recognized as a merchant prince was Aaron Lopez of Newport, Rhode Island. He came directly from Lisbon, Portugal, in 1752. He helped to bring to America the spermaceti industry, which converts whale oil into a lighting oil. According to Ezra Stiles, the seventh president of Yale College, Lopez was "a merchant of first eminence; for honor and extent of commerce probably surpassed by no merchant in America…without a single enemy and the most universally beloved by an extensive acquaintance of any man I ever knew." He owned all or part of thirty vessels at one point in his life, and he was a great patriot, contributing funds to fight against the British.

The first Jewish American-born clergyman, Gershom Mendes Seixas, was from New York's Shearith Israel congregation. Born in 1745, he was a fierce supporter of the colonies' efforts to rid themselves of Great Britain during the Revolutionary War and he became known as a "patriot rabbi." He also served congregation Mikveh Israel in Philadelphia. He was the first clergyman in America to be a trustee

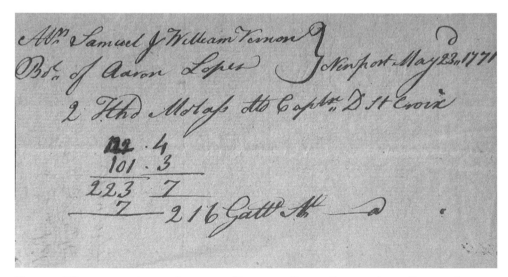

RECEIPT WRITTEN BY AARON LOPEZ, OF NEWPORT, RHODE ISLAND. *Aaron Lopez, who was considered a merchant prince, came from Portugal, where he was denied his Jewish rites. He chose to be circumcised as an adult in America, to fulfill the first covenant for a Jewish man.*

for Columbia University, and for twenty-five years he served in that capacity. He was one of the ministers who presided over the inauguration of President George Washington. His sermons were in English for the first time, not in Spanish. He preached the first Thanksgiving sermon ever by any Jewish clergyman in the thirteen colonies.

The first Jew to die for America during the Revolutionary War was Francis Salvador, a plantation owner from South Carolina, originally of Portuguese ancestry. He was elected to the General Assembly of South Carolina and he was a representative of the First and Second Provincial Congresses which revolted against the British. Today a plaque hangs behind the city hall in Charleston to commemorate Francis Salvador as a soldier and patriot for America.

Luis Moses Gomez and his son Daniel, of Portuguese descent, had a trading post in upper New York, eleven miles north of Newburgh. They traded with the Indians for furs and pelts. They were also active in the establishment of the first synagogue in America, Shearith Israel, in New York.

Another son of Luis Moses Gomez, Benjamin Gomez, was the first Jewish book dealer in America, who began his business in 1791. His family were originally Spanish Marranos who came from Madrid. His father was the merchant Luis Moses Gomez, whose fur trading with Indians along the Hudson River and his presidency of Shearith Israel in New York City brought much recognition from the Jewish community in the eighteenth century. His is the oldest standing house of a Jewish citizen in America. Benjamin Gomez sold important books dealing with either religious, historical, or scientific subjects, including the Bible and the works of Shakespeare. He eventually published books, including *Captain Cook's Third and Last Voyage* in 1795.

The first published Jewish woman poet in America was Penina Moise of Charleston, South Carolina. Her family was originally from Spain. A book of her poems was called *Fancy's Sketch Book,* published in 1835. She also wrote for other publications in Charleston, South Carolina, as well as hymns, the most famous being a volume of Hebrew hymns she wrote for Kahal Kadosh Beth Elohim, when this Charleston, South Carolina, Sephardic synagogue, one of the first six in America, became the first Reform congregation in America. Penina Moise was also a teacher. She never married. She lived to be eighty-three and was blind at the end of her life.

Judah Touro, born in Newport, Rhode Island, in 1775, was the first Jewish philanthropist on a large scale in America. He gained his wealth by being a merchant and ship owner in New Orleans. He built the Touro Infirmary, a hospital in New Orleans, and he organized the Shakespeare Alms House for the poor. In his will he left money to institutions of all denominations all over America.

The first Jewish commodore in America was Uriah Phillips Levy, whose family was of Portuguese descent, his mother being Rebecca Machado Phillips, whose family came to Savannah, Georgia, in 1733. Governor Oglethorpe of Georgia welcomed the Jews who came to Savannah because a young doctor from that ship helped to stop an epidemic from spreading there. That doctor was Uriah Levy's great-great-grandfather. Uriah Levy went to sea at ten years of age and then came home to prepare for his Bar Mitzvah in Philadelphia. When the War of 1812 started, he volunteered for service; and even with his excellent record, because he was a Jew, he was often beaten and hounded by false accusations. He eventually rose to the rank of commodore because of his absolute devotion to the United States Navy. He fought to have flogging (beating with a rod or whip) removed as a punishment and he helped to institute a better form of treatment for sailors. Today his statue stands in front of the Department of the Navy in Washington, D.C., and there is a naval chapel named for him. As an admirer of President Thomas Jefferson, he bought Jefferson's family house at Monticello in 1827 and restored it after it had fallen into disrepair. His family lived in it longer than Jefferson, before it was turned over to a group of people in Virginia who still care for it today. Uriah Levy is often today called America's First Preservationist, and the "Father of the Law for the Abolition of the Barbarous Practice of Corporeal Punishment in the Navy of the United States."

Mordecai Manuel Noah was appointed Consul to Tunisia by President James Madison, as the first Jew given an important diplomatic post in the foreign service.

Solomon Nunes Carvalho was a painter and daguerreotype photographer from a Portuguese family. He accompanied General John Frémont on his fourth trip across America to find a passage for the railway. Carvalho was to record the trip through the pictures he made for Frémont. Unfortunately, most of the pictures were lost by Frémont during a snowstorm and a bout with illness. Carvalho helped to start the first Jewish Benevolent Society in Los Angeles, California.

Early Jewish citizens of America were poets, industrialists, legislators, governors, judges, artists, businessmen, and scientists. They were the earliest social providers for the sick, the elderly, the poor, the widowed, and the orphaned, with their beneficent societies in each of the places where they resided. Jews became soldiers who served in the Revolutionary War (as did Francis Salvador), the War of 1812, (as did Isaac Franks), and also in the Civil War, with some Jews fighting for the North and some fighting for the South.

Jews established trading relations with Native Americans, including Luis Moses Gomez in New York, thus introducing the fur industry in America. He also helped John Jacob Astor begin his first fur-trading business. Jews were pioneers who surveyed the South, the East, the Midwest, and eventually the northwestern territories. It was a Jewish ship owned by Nathan Levy and David Franks that brought the symbol of our freedom, the Liberty Bell, to Philadelphia. Jews had even come as explorers with Columbus, such as Luis de Torres, who not only helped to finance the trip, but was the interpreter for it.

Jewish participants in the Buttonwood Agreement, including Ezekiel Hart and

Benjamin Seixas, helped to form the New York Stock Exchange. Many Jews formed the first banks in America, in Boston, Massachusetts (Moses Michael Hays), and in Richmond, Virginia (Jacob Cohen). Jews developed libraries, such as the Library Company of Philadelphia, founded by Benjamin Franklin and supported by the Barnard and Michael Gratz family, and personal libraries as in the Moses Myers House in Norfolk, Virginia.

In 1790, George Washington wrote to the Newport congregation. He stated: "The citizens of the United States have a right to applaud themselves for having given to mankind examples of an enlarged and liberal policy: a policy worthy of imitation. All possess a like liberty of conscience and immunities of citizenship. It is now no more that toleration is spoken of, as if it was by the indulgence of one class of people, that another enjoyed the exercise of their inherent national rights. For happily the Government of the United States, which gives to bigotry no sanction, to persecution no assistance requires only that they who live under its protection should demean themselves as good citizens, in giving it on all occasions their effectual support." These words, written by George Washington, gave the first official, national, governmental acceptance of Jews in America.

The United States of which Washington spoke was a smaller nation than it is today, and it was located primarily on what is now considered the East Coast. But also it must be stated that Jews were not only on the East Coast, but in the Southwest as well. These Jews came as Marranos or Crypto Jews into territories now called Texas, New Mexico, southern Colorado, California, and Arizona, as well as to Florida in the Southeast. They had fled the Inquisition in Spain and came to the New World often with forged papers and new names because of the expulsion decree when Ferdinand and Isabella stated that there would be no Jews allowed in Spanish territories. When the Marranos first settled on soil in the Southwest, the land was occupied by natives only, and they thought the land was a safe place to live. Today, many of the descendants of these Marranos are beginning to understand the origin and meaning of their Jewish traditions, such as lighting candles in basements on Friday night, not eating pork or shellfish, putting Hebrew letters on their gravestones, or not praying to Jesus Christ or the Trinity, but only praying to God.

Professor Stanley M. Hordes from the University of New Mexico is helping many of these families to identify their roots. Some of his clues are "...the gathering of nail clippings, sweeping to the center of the room, next day burial, mourning for a year, bathing after contact with the dead, covering the mirrors in a house of mourning, leaving pebbles on graves, and circumcision. Much is sometimes made of the presence of 'Star of David' motifs on gravestones and in churches..." Others include avoiding meat with milk, not eating eggs with blood-spots, salting and soaking meat, and covering the blood of slaughtered animals with dirt. Playing a gambling game with a top, sometimes called a *pon y saca* ("put in and take out") is said to resemble a Chanukah tradition, as is lighting one or more candles or a *luminaria* bonfire each night, starting over a week before Christmas, so that there are nine flames at Christmas, just as there are nine flames burning for the Chanukah lamp. The observance of a feast or fast in honor of Queen Esther is often cited. Baking of *pan de semita*, or "Semitic bread," is reported at Easter; *pan de semita* was like a heavy bread that, like the matzah eaten by Jews during Passover, did not rise.

Judah Monis (1683–1764), an Italian Jew of Portuguese descent, was the first Jewish man of letters in America, publishing a volume of religious discourses (*The Truth, the Whole Truth, and Nothing But the Truth*) in 1722, and *A Grammar of the Hebrew Tongue* in 1735. He was also the first Jewish faculty member at Harvard. His writings are evidence of his ability to quote the Bible, the Talmud, and various Kabbalistic texts. In order to teach at Harvard, it is assumed that he had to convert to Christianity, according to *The Cambridge Companion to Jewish American Literature*. Although he died a Christian, his gravestone refers to him as one of the Hebrew faith.

Just the opposite experience was had by Moses Lindo of Charleston, South Carolina. He served his colony as the chief inspector of indigo, which he helped to raise as a cash crop for England. Moses Lindo agreed to donate funds to the College of Rhode Island provided that Jewish students be admitted there and that they would not have to take exams on Saturday, their Sabbath, or any Jewish religious holidays. The college agreed to honor Moses Lindo's requirements, and so the donation was made. Today, we call the College of Rhode Island in Providence Brown University, and Moses Lindo's correspondence is still in their archives.

According to Rabbi Marc Angel of Shearith Israel, the oldest synagogue in America, Judeo-Spanish communities still read a Ladino text known as *Ketubah de Laley*, which describes a marriage contract between the Torah and the Jewish people. They also read a poetic rendition of the 613 *mitzvot* composed by Solomon ibn Gabirol, one of the great medieval Sephardic poets and thinkers.

Rabbi Angel also says that "Rabbi Moshe Almosnino wrote an important work in Spanish called *Regimiento de la vita*, which means 'rules of etiquette for governing one's life.' Every religious Jew was expected to be a model of gracefulness and good manners. Sephardic synagogues have been historically characterized by beauty and respect for detail. Since synagogues were built as sanctuaries of religious worship, the Sephardim felt they should reflect the dignity of the best standards of the community. The synagogue is a House of God, which should signify and requires our utmost respect."

Outside of Israel today, the United States has the greatest Jewish population, with the states of New York and California containing the largest Jewish presence. Although very small in amount, there is still some anti-Semitism in existence. Organizations like the Anti-Defamation League (ADL) work to protect Jews from discrimination, harassment, and violence. Many Jews have held very important roles in the United States government. Jewish judges like Benjamin Cardozo, who sat on the United States Supreme Court; Dianne Feinstein, who is the United States Senator from California, and representatives of Jewish persuasion from all levels of jurisprudence and legislature of states, counties, cities, and villages throughout the history of the United States have proven that Jewish people can function in any profession they choose. They can live anywhere they want and their freedoms are protected by the laws of the land, starting with the Constitution. For Jews, the highest form of freedom ever is in the United States of America.

A Partial List of Sephardic Communities and Synagogues Worldwide

Contact information may have changed. For a current and more complete list of resources, including other countries as well as a list of United States synagogues and communities by state, contact the American Sephardi Federation at http://www.americansephardifederation. org/sub/sources/synagogues_US.asp

Iberia

Spain

Comunidad Israelita de Barcelona
Avenir, 24
Barcelona 08021
Rabbi Jacob Carciente

Comunidad Israelita de Ceuta
Sargento Coriat, 8
Ceuta
Rabbi Isaac Benadiba Benayot

Synagogue of Maimonides *(not in use)*
Calle Judaeco
Córdoba
Inf. Antonio Perez

Arias-Montano Inst (Library-Jewish Seph Hist)
Calle Albansanz 26–28
Madrid 28037

Comunidad Israelita de Madrid
Balmes 3
Madrid 28010
Rabbi Moshe Bendahan

Museo Sefardi (Antigua Sinagoga de el Transito)
Calle de Samuel Levi
Toledo 45002
Director: Ana Maria Lopez Alvarez
Email: transito@mail.ddnet.es
Website: www.ddnet.es/sefardi

Portugal

Sinagogue Shaare Tikva
Rua Du York Direte
Lisboa 1200–280
Email: secretaria@cilisboa.org
Website: www.lisaboa.org

Comunidade Israelita Do Porto
Rua Guerra Junqueiro, 340
Porto 4100
Hazan Mordehai Aflalo

Gibraltar

K.K. Ets Haymin; Little Syn (Esnoga Chica)
91 Irishtown; P.O. Box 31
Hon. Minister Sammy Benaim

K.K. Nefusot Yehudah Synagogue
65 Line Wall Road
Pres. Isaac S. Benzaquen
Email: sbenzaquen@gibnynex.gi

K.K. Shaar Hashamayim
49 Engineer Lane; P.O. Box 174
Rev. Jacob M. Benzecry
Email: mebelilo@gibnynax.gi

Kahal Kadosh Abudarham
20 Parliament Lane (P.O. Box 190)
Pres. Solomon Levy MBE EDJP
Email: slevy@gibnet.gi

Gibraltar Jewish Community
10 Bomb House Lane
Rabbi Roni N.J. Hassid

The Rest of Europe

Greece

Beth Shalom
5 Melidoni Street
Athens (113)
Rabbi Jacob D. Arar
Email: isrkath@hellasnet.gr

Jewish Community of Rhodes
5 Polydorou Street
Rhodes
Inf. Maurice Soriano

Synagogue Shalom
Rue Symmiou
Rhodes
Inf. Lucia Modiano Soulam

Yad LeZikaron
24–26 Vassileous Irakliou St.
Thessaloniki 54624
Rabbi Dr. Itshak Dayan

Bosnia

Jewish Community of Banja Luka
Kordunaska Street 6
Banja Luka 78000
Pres. Daniel A. Romano

Jewish Community of Doboj
Kralja Petra Street 30/2
Doboj 74000
Pres. Mordehaj Atijas

Jewish Community of Sarajevo
Hamdjie Kresevljakovica 59
Sarajevo 71000
Hazzan David Kamhi

Croatia

Jewish Community of Dubrovnik
Zudioska Street 3
Dubrovnik 20000
Prof. Dr. Sabrina Horovic

Jewish Community of Rijeka
Filipoviceva Street 9
Rijeka 51000
Pres. Josip Engel

Jewish Community of Split
Zidovski Prolaz Street 1/1
Split 21000
Pres. Zoran Morpurgo

Zagreb Jewish Community
Palmoticeva Street 16
Zagreb 10000
Chief Rabbi Kotel Dadon
Email: scz@2g.hinet.hr

France

Communaute Israelite d'Aix-en-Provence
3 bis Rue de Jerusalem
Aix-en-Provence 13100
Harav Dr. Haim Harboun

Assoc. Cul Israelite d'Antibes Juan Les Pins
Villa La Monada-Ave. des Sables
Antibes 06600
Rabbin Marcel Zemour

Association Culturelle Israelite d'Avignon
2 Place Jerusalem
Avignon 84000
Rabbi Moshe Amar

Association Culturelle Israelite
213 Rue Sainte Catherine
Bordeaux 33000
Rabbin Claude Maman

Association Culturelle Israelite
20 Boulevard d'Alsace
Cannes 06400
Rabbis Lionel Drax, Jacob Gueds

Synagogue
Rue du Progres
Frejus-Plage 83600
Inf. G. Aymard

Synagogue
Chemin de la Ritorte
Hyeres

Synagogue
38 Rue Victor Hugo
Le Havre
Rabbin Alain Cohen

Communaute Israelite de Limoges
27 Rue Pierre Lerouns
Limoges
Rabbin Joseph Ohayon

Consistoire Israelite Sepharad de Lyon
317 Rue Dulguesalin
Lyon 69007
Rabbin Charles Perz

Consistoire Israelite de Marseille
117 Rue Breteuil
Marseille 13006
Grand Rabbin Jacques Ouaknin

Association Culturelle Israelite
5 Place Massena
Nice 06000
Grand Rabbin David Shooshana

Synagogue
15 Rue Notre-Dame de Nazareth
Paris 75003
Rabbi M. Haim Torjman

Synagogue
15 bis, Rue de Tourmellesreth
Paris 75004
Rabbi M. Roger Touitou

Synagogue
14 Place de Vosges
Paris 75004
Delegue Rabbinique M. Charles Liche

Vauquelin Synagogue
9 Rue Vauquelin
Paris 75005
Rabbin M. Jean Levy

Synagogue Berit Chalom (Algerian)
18 Rue Saint-Lazare
Paris 75009
Rabbin M. Salomon Malka

Synagogue Beth El
3 Rue Saulnier
Paris 75009

Synagogue Portuguaise
28 Rue Buffault
Paris 75009
Grand Rabbin J. Amar

Synagogue Don Isaac Abravanel
84–86 Rue de la Roquette
Paris 75011
Rabbin M. Claude Zaffran

WSF Social Committee
16 Avenue de Bouvines
Paris 75011
Pres. Jacques Abihssera

Synagogue Chivtei Israel
12–14 Cite Moynet
Paris 75012
Rabbin M. Aime Atlan

Synagogue
14 Rue Chasseloup-Laubat
Paris 75015
Rabbin M. Maurice Nezri

Synagogue
80 Rue Doudeauville
Paris 75018
Rabbin M. Mevorakh Jean-Pierre Zerbib

Synagogue de Montmarte
13 Rue Saint Isaure
Paris 75018
Rabbin M. Meyer Zini

Synagogue
120 Boulevard de Belleville
Paris 75020
Rabbin M. Guy Rahamim Hadjadj

Synagogue Rite Tunisien
75 Rue Julien-Lacroix
Paris 75020
Delegue Rabbinique M. Meir Ammar

Holland

Ets Haim Seminary
Mr. Visserplein 3
Amsterdam 1011 RD
Librarian A.W. Rosenberg
Email: biblio@etshaim.org
Website: www.etshaim.org

**Talmud Torah Portugees Israelietsch
Gemeente**
Mr. Visserplein 3
Amsterdam 1011 RD
Pres. Jacques Senior Coronel

**Santa Companha de Dotar Orphas e
Donzellas**
Eline Verestraat 33
Amsteelveen 1183 KX
Pres. Jaap B. Sondevan

**David Henriques de Castro
Foundation**
Kerkstraat 7
Ouderkerk Aan de Amstel
Dir. Dr. Cohen Paraira
Email: bethaim@wxs.nl
Website: www.bethaim.com

**Historic Jewish Cemeteries
Foundation**
Kerkstraat 7; 1191 JB
Ouderkerk Aan de Amstel
Rabbi H. Rodrigues Pereira
Email: bethaim@wxs.nl
Website: www.bethaim.com

Italy

Comunita Ebraica di Firenze
Via Luigi Carlo Farini, 4
Florence 50121
Rabbi Dr. Joseph Levi
Email: comeb2fi@tin.it
Website: www.firenzebraica.net

Comunita Israelitica de Genova
Via Bertora, 6
Genoa 16122
Rabbi Josef Momigliano
Email: comgenova@tin.it

Comunita Israelitica di Livorno
Via del Tempio 3
Leghorn
Rabbi Dr. Isidor Kahn

Comunita Israelitica di Milano
Via Guastalla, 19
Milan 28122
Rav Dott. G. Laras

Comunita Ebraica di Padova
Via San Martino & Solferino 9
Padua 35122
Rabbi Dr. Shimon Viterbo

Comunita Ebraica di Roma
Lungotevere Cenci
Rome 00186
Ch Rabbi: Dr. Shmuel Riccardo Di Segni
Email: rabbanut.roma@tiscalinet.it

Comunita Ebraica
Piazzetta Primo Levi 12
Torino 10125
Rabbi Dr. Alberto Moshe Somekh
Email: eff-rav.to@libero.it

Comunita Ebraica di Trieste
Via San Francesco, 19
Trieste 34133
Rabbi Avraham Piperno
Email: rav@triestebraica.it

Comunita Ebraica di Venezia
Cannaregio 1146
Venice 30121
Rabbi Eliahu E. Richetti
Email: chiefrabbivenice@virgilio.it

Comunita Israelitica Ebraica di Verona
Via Portici, 3
Verona
Rabbi Efraim Piatelli

England

Shaare Hashamaim (Bevis Marks Syn)
2 Heneage Lane
London EC3A5DQ
The Rev Halfon Benarroch
Hazzan
Email:bevismarks@first-step.demon.co.uk

Spanish & Portuguese Jews Cong.
2 Ashworth Road
Maida Vale
London W91JY
Rabbi Dr. Abraham Levy

Spanish & Portuguese Synagogue
8A St James Gardens Holland Park
London W11 4RB
Rev. Abraham Labi

The Exilarch's Foundation; Pblr "The Scribe"
Journal of Babylonian Jewry
4 Carlos Place
Mayfair
London W1K 3AW
Naim Dangoor, Exilarch
Website: www.scribe1.com

Manchester Congregation of Spanish & Portuguese Jews
18 Moor Lane
Kersal
Salford
Manchester M70 WX
Pres. David Salem

Sephardi Congregation of South Manchester
8 Queenston Road
Manchester M20 2WZ
Rabbi Shlomo Ellituv

Wembley Synagogue
46 Forty Avenue
Wembly
Middlesex
Dayan Pinhas Toledano

Africa

Temple Beth-El
61 Rue Taber Ben Hayane
Casablanca
Rabbi Israel Hazout

Communaute Israelite de Tanger
1 Rue de la Liberte
Tangier
Rabbi Jacob Tordjman

Sephardic Hebrew Congregation of Cape Town
P.O. Box 774, Sea Point 8060
Cape Town
Rabbi Ruben Suiza
Email: sephardicape@xsinet.co.sa

Sephardi Hebrew Congregation of Johannesburg
25 Main St. Rouxville 2192
Johannesburg
Rev. Joseph Matzner

Asia Minor

Turkey

Chief Rabbinate of Turkey
Yemenici Sokak 23 Tunel-Beyoglu
Istanbul 80050
Rabbi Izak Haleva
Email: jcommnty@atlas.net.tr

Karatas Musevi Sinagogu (Beth Israel)
Mithatpasa Cad. 265
Izmir
Rabbi Rafael Moron

Israel

Sephardi Communities Haifa
Ehad Ha'am 4–6
Haifa 33103
Inf. Haim Nadaf

The David Cardozo School
7 Cassuto Street
Jerusalem 96433
Rabbi Nathan T. Lopes-Cardozo
Email: nlc@internet-zahav.net
Website: www.cardozoschool.org

Congregation Shaare Ratzon (Istanbuli) Synagogue
Spanish & Portuguese Congregation
Rehov Bet El Jewish Quarter 18
Old City Jerusalem
Professor Isaac Benabu

Council of the Sephardi & Oriental Comm.
8 HaRav Kook P.O. Box 10
Jerusalem 91000
Dir: Yitzhak Armoza

Italian Syn Museum of Italian Jewish Art
27 Hillel Street
Jerusalem 94581
Hillel Sermoneta
Email: jija@netvision.net.il
Website: www.jija.org

Seph. Education Center in Jerusalem
Batei Machasseh 1; P.O. Box 14326
Old City
Jerusalem 91142
Dir Sal Nessim
Email: speheduc@netvision.net.il

Shehebar Sephardic Center
26 Galed Street
Jerusalem 97500
Rabbi Eliahou Shamaula
Email: sscjlm@netvision.net.il

Israeli Indian Federation
Hapalmach 10
Netanya 42249
Inf. Yaacov Benyamin

Hechal Yehuda Recanati Synagogue
Ben Saruq, 13
Tel Aviv 62969
Inf. Mr. Shemuel Recanati

Ohel Moed
3/5 Shodal Street
Tel Aviv
Chief Rabbi Haim D. Halevi

Israeli Moroccan Fed
176 Ibn Gevirol
Tel Aviv 62032
Inf. Aharon Nachmias

South America

Argentina

Asociacion Comunidad Israelita Sefaradi
Camargo 870
Buenos Aires, C1414AHR
Chief Rabbi Isaac A. Sacca
Email: acisba@continuidad.com.ar
Website: www.shabuatov.com

Comunidad Israelita de Flores—"Agudat Dodum"
Avellaneda 2874
Buenos Aires

Sociedad Hebraica Argentina
Sarmiento 2233
Buenos Aires 1044

Centro Educativo Sefaradi en Jerusalem
Tucuman 2153
Buenos Aires 1050
Email: csefar@einstein.com.ar

Congregacion Sefaradi
Lavalle 2449
Buenos Aires 1052
Rabbi Iosef H. Chehebar
Email: concregacion@pla.net.ar

Yeshiba/Colel "Shebet Ahim"
Pinzon 1261
Buenos Aires 1287
Rabbi Shlomo Yabra
Email: rabyabra@shabuatov.com

Brazil

Centro Israelita
Rua José de Hollanda 798
Recife
Inf. Marcel Kosminsky

Kahal Zur Israel (Predates 1654)
Rua do Bom Jesus, 197
Recife
Pres. Tania Kaufman, Dra.

Sinagoga Agudath Israel
Rua Nascimento Silva 109
Rio de Janeiro
Rabbi Gabriel Abov Tboul

Sinagoga Bene Sidon
Rua Conde de Bonfim 521
Rio de Janeiro
Hazan Simon Nigri

Sinagoga Maghen David
Rua Visconde de Cabo Frio 29
Tijuca 20510
Rio de Janeiro
Hazan Marcos Balassiano

Templo Union Israel
Rua José Hygino 375
Rio de Janeiro
Hazan José Cohen

Uniao Israelita Shel Guemilut Hassadim
Rua Rodrigo de Brito, 37, Botafogo
Rio de Janeiro
Rabbi Abraham Anidjar

Museu Judaico de Rio de Janeiro
Rua Mexico, 90sata110; 20031
141 Centro
Rio de Janeiro
Pres: Max Nahmias
Email: museujudaico@uol.com.br
Website: www.museujudaico.org.br

Congregacao Religiosa Israelita "Beth El"
Rua Barata Ribeiro, 489
Rio de Janeiro
GB ZC–07
Rabbi Abraham Anidgar

Congregacao Mekor Haim
Rua São Vicente de Paula, 254
São Paolo 01229
Rabbi Itschak Dichi

Fed Sefaradi Latino Americana
Inhambu 902
Apto 122
São Paolo 04520–013
Pres. Claudio Leon

Chile

Fed Sefardi Latino Americana
Avenida Ricardo Lyon 812
Santiago
Rabbi José Gabbai

Colombia

Com. Ebrea Sefaradi, Maguen Obadia
Calle 79, No. 9–66
Bogota
Rabbi Shelomo Elharar

Paraguay

Fed Sefaradi Latino Americana
Caballero 896
Asuncion
Inf. Dr. Jacob Cohenco

Peru

Soc. de Benef. Israelita Sefaradi
Enrique Villar 581; S Beatriz
Lima 1
Rabbi Abraham Benhamu
Email: abenhamu@terra.com.pe

Fed Sefaradi Latino Americana
Juan de Arona 701; 2 Piso San Isidro
Lima 27
Inf. Dr. Yakir Dannon Levy

Uruguay

Circulo Israelita Sefaradi del Uruguay
Lauro Muller 1769/302
Buenos Aires 282
Montevideo
Inf. Nessin Nelson Canias
Email: nelsonc@netgate.com.uy

Uruguay Sephardic Community
21 de Septiembre 3111
Montevideo
Rabbi Aharon Ribco

Comunidad Isrelita Sefaradi del Uruguay
Calle Buenos Aires 234
Montevideo 11000
Rabbi José Gabay

Venezuela

Fed Sefaradi Latino Americana
Apartado 3861
Caracas 1010
Inf:.Amram Cohen Pariente
Email: amram@kosher.com

Central America, Mexico, and the Caribbean

Panama

Fed Sefaradi Latino Americana
P.O. Box 4219
Panama 5
Inf. David Bassan

Costa Rica

Canapi
Box 8–6540 (1000)
San José

Mexico

Congregacion Maguen David A.C.
Horacio 1528
Colonia Los Morales
Rabbi Meir Antebi

Alianza Monte Sinai
Tennyson 134
Mexico, D.F. 11560
Rabino Salvador (Yeoshua) Hilu
Email: msinaiprensa@prodigy.net.mx

Fed Sefaradi Latino Americana
Tehuantepec No 118 Col. Roma
Mexico, D.F.
Inf. Isaac Salinas

Comunidad Sefaradi
Prol. Ave. de los Bosques 292
Tecamachalco
Rabbi Abraham Palti

Cong. Monte Sinai
Fuente de la Huerte 22
Tecamachalco
Rabbi Abraham Tobal

Comunidad Israelita de Baja California
Avendida 16 de Septiembre, #3000
Tijuana, B.C.
Rabbi Mendel J. Polichenco
Email: Rabino@telror.net
Website: www.bajajai.com

Caribbean Islands

Jewish Community of the Cayman Islands
P.O. Box 72
Grand Cayman, Cayman Islands
    KY1–1102
Inf. Harvey de Souza

Centro Hebrero Sepharadi
Calle 17, No. 462 Vedado
Habana, Cuba 10400
Pres. José Levy Tyr

Congregation Mikve Israel-Emanuel
(P.O. Box 322) Hanchi de Snoa #29
Curaçao
Rabbi Hazzan Avery Tracht
Email: directive@snoa.com
Website: www.snoa.com

South Central Asia

India

Magen Hassidim Synagogue
8 Mohamed Shahid Marg
Agripada, Bombay
Hon Sec. Jacob Shmoel Garsukar

Magen Abraham Synagogue
Bukhara Moholla; Opp Parsee Agiary
Ahmedabad 380001
Rabbi Joshua Kolet

Council of Indian Jewry;
The Jewish Club
Jeroo Bldg. 137 M.G. Road
Bombay 400 023
Sec. J. Bhattacharya

Indian Sephardi Fed
63 Belle View; 85 Warden Rd
Bombay 400 026
Salomon F. Sopher

Magen David Synagogue
340 Sir J.J. Road
Byculla
Bombay 400008

Beth El Synagogue
26/1 Pollock Street
Calcutta 700001
Pres. M.D.E. Nahoum

Cochin Synagogue (1568)
Synagogue Lane
Cochin 2
Warden S. H. Hallegua

Keneseth Eliyahoo Synagogue
43 Dr. V. B. Gandhi Marg
Fort Bombay 400023

Kurla Bene-Israel Prayer Hall
275 C.S.T. Rd. Jewish Colony
Kurla (W) Bombay 400070

Gates of Mercy Synagogue (1796)
254 Samuel Street
Mandvi
Bombay 400 003

Judah Hyam Synagogue
2 Humayun Road (near Taj Mahal Hotel)
New Delhi 110003
Hon. Sec. Ezekiel Isaac Malekar
Email: shulanoel@hotmail.com

Beth El Synagogue (1849)
909 Mahatma Gandhi Rd
Panevel Maharashtra 410206
Sec. Simon Samson Dighodkar

Shaar Hashamaim (Gates of Heaven)
Synagogue
Jamsetji Maneckji Road
Tembhi
Thane 400601
Sec. Ezra Moses

The Far East

China

Ohel Leah Synagogue
70 Robinson Road
Hong Kong, SAR
Rabbi Yaakov Kermaier
Email: Pauline@ohelleah.org
Website: www.ohelleah.org

PART FOUR

Teshuva, or the Return to Judaism

For those descendants who desire to come back to Judaism and drop their Christian identity, there is in Judaism the concept of Teshuva (return).

According to Rabbi Adin Steinsaltz, a scholar, "Teshuvah is a spiritual reawakening, a desire to strengthen the connection between oneself and the sacred [shivah], not only to the past [one's own or one's ancestors'], but to the Divine Source of all being.... You shall return [shavta] to the Lord your God."

This then encompasses "a return to ancestral Jews, to Jewish roots, and to God." During the Inquisition, the belief in a unitary God was often used as evidence of blasphemy by those accused of Judaizing, among converts who referred to God in the Spanish singular "el Dio" instead of "el Dios," which would represent the three-part divinity of "the Father, the Son, and the Holy Ghost."

One clue to contemporary descendants is the response of mothers and grandmothers, aunts and uncles all referring to God only as "el Dio," which is not what the Catholic Church teaches—the tripartite God.

In addition to using the term for only one God, Marranos (Crypto Jews) kept many of their other Jewish rituals in secret. Today there are many descendants of Crypto Jews who still practice their Jewish traditions, in secret, in parts of what used to be the Spanish or Portuguese Christian colonies.

CHAPTER EIGHT

Secret Names of Portuguese and Names of Spanish Jews

TODAY, WITHOUT THE FEAR OF REPRISALS by the Catholic Church, many people are looking into their religious roots if they suspect those roots are different from the religious customs they've practiced all these years.

One clue to the identity of people descended from Marranos can often be found in their names. Most Jewish men were originally referred to by their first names plus "Ben" (son of) and then their father's and sometimes their mother's first name— e.g., Kenneth ben Daniel.

In 1497, when the Jews were rounded up and brought into Lisbon, Portugal, by King Manuel, in addition to forcing a conversion on the Jews to Christianity, King Manuel forced the Jews to take new names. Most prevalent among the names taken were ones that meant something in nature. Some examples are Coelho (rabbit), Pinto (spotted horse), Pereira (pear tree), and Da Silva (of the blackberry plant). There are hundreds of names that were taken by Jewish people at that time. Today, these names remain one of the many clues to Jewish identity, and they indicate how families have stayed together when an interviewee lists many of those names as his or her relatives.

Also, when the people I interviewed referred to their spouses and relatives who had many of those names—and when I would ask if they found any similarities among names—most often, the answer was one of surprise, but also an enlightened understanding of other similar traditions and values they shared with other descendants of Marranos.

In the Spanish tradition, some of the names are Rodriguez, Riveira, Nunes, Montenegro, Miranda, Lopez, Ribeira, and Gómez. These names often surprise people who don't think of them in connection with Judaism.

Many times I am asked about the possibility of Jewish roots because someone has found out that their name is similar to one whose roots are Jewish—or in the case of the Portuguese, that the name means something in nature, which they've heard could indicate Jewish roots.

One particularly interesting name indicating Jewish identity is Henriques, which means "son of Henry." This name refers to the Portuguese king called "Henry the

Navigator," who helped Portugal become a maritime success. Some Jews took this name as a deterrent to being suspected of being Jews. One could do worse than be identified with King Henry.

Surnames of Spanish and Portuguese Marranos and Their Descendants

One clue to the identity of people descended from Marranos can often be found in their names. These lists are of known Jewish individuals, and are presented here as a reference for today's descendants to use as a possible guide to their own heritage, whether the heritage comes from Spain, Portugal, Gibraltar, southern France, or wherever their Marrano ancestors lived.

1. Marrano Family Names

Note: Some of these names have variants, e.g. d'Costa; de Costa; de la Costa; la Costa, etc.

Abravanel	Fonseca	Ramos
Abulafia	Furtado	Ravaya
Aguilar	Gonsales/Gonzalez	Ribero
Alconstantini	Gutierres/Gutierrez	Rocamora
Alonso/Alonzo	Herrera	Rodrigues/Rodriguez
Alvares/Alvarez	Kogadouro	Rousso/Russo/Rossi
Anazelotti	Lopes/Lopez	Sanches/Sanchez
Arellano	Lumbroso/Lumbrozo	Santa Maria
Barbanel	Luna	Santangel
Belasco	Maleha	Saraubo
Belmonte	Maldonado	Silva
Benveniste	Manna	Sobremonte
Bernal	Martines/Martinez	Solis/Soliz
Blasca	Medina	Spinosa/Spinoza/Espinosa
Caballeria	Melito	Teixeira
Caceres	Mendes/Mendez	Terongi
Calle/La Calle	Mendosa/Mendoza	Teruagi
Cardoso/Cardozo	Mosca	Trevino
Carillo	Nasi	Vaez
Carvalho	Neito	Vargas
Castro	Nunes/Nunez	Villahermosa
Chaves/Chavez	Oliveira	Villareal
Coronel	Orobio	Vottoria
Corsetto/Corzetto	Panarelli	Zacuto
Costa/Acosta	Pas/Paz	Zalmedina
Coutinho	Pena/Penha	Zaporta
Dias/Diaz	Pereira	Zemerro
Dormido	Peres/Perez	Zolli
Duarte	Picho	
Enriques/Enriquez	Pinto	
Fernandes/Fernandez	Porta	

2. Sephardic Surnames from Portugal and Gibraltar

From the Portuguese and Gibraltarean communities registry books

Abaob	Bendahan	Cansino
Abeasis	Bendelack	Cardoso
Abecassis	Bendran	Carseni
Abensur	Benedito	Castel
Abitbol	Benelisha	Cazes
Abohbot	Bendugo	Cohen
Abaidid	Beneluz	Conquy
Abquia	Benhayon	Coriat
Abudarham	Beniso	Cubi
Acris	Benitah	Danan
Adrehi	Benjamin	Davis
Aflalo	Benjo	Delmar
Albo	Benmergui	Diesendruck
Alkaim	Benmiyara	Elmaleh
Aloof	Benmuyal	Eaaguy
Amar	Benoalid	Eanaty
Amram	Benoliel	Farache
Amselem	Benrimoj	Ferares
Amzalak	Benros	Finsi
Anahory	Bensabat	Foinquinos
Asayol	Bensadon	Fresco
Askenazi	Bensaloha	Gabay
Assayag	Bensaude	Gabizon
Athias	Benselum	Garson
Atruel	Bensheton	Hadida
Auday	Bensimon	Hansan
Azancot	Bensliman	Hatchuel
Azavey	Bensusan	Israel
Azerad	Bentata	Kadosh
Azelos	Bentubo	Katzan
Azulay	Benudis	Labos
Balensi	Benyuli	Laluff
Banon	Benyunes	Laredo
Barcilom	Benzacar	Lasry
Baruel	Benzaquen	Lengui
Belilo	Benzecry	Levy
Benabu	Benzimra	Lezameta
Benady	Bergel	Magueres
Benaim	Bibas	Malia
Benamor	Blum	Maman
Benarus	Bohudana	Marques
Benatav	Brigham	Marrache
Benbunan	Brudo	Martins
Benchaya	Buzaglo	Massias
Benchetrit	Bytton	Matano
Benchimol	Cagi	Melul

Mor-José	Roffe	Sztuden
Mucznik	Ruah	Tangi
Muginstein	Rygor	Tapiero
Muller	Sabath	Taregano
Nahon	Salama	Tanrel
Namias	Sananes	Tedesqui
Nathan	Saragga	Tobelem
Navaro	Schocron	Toledano
Obadia	Sebag	Tuati
Ohana	Segal	Uziel
Oliveira	Sequerra	Varicas
Pacifico	Serfaty	Wahnon
Pallache	Seriqui	Waknin
Pariente	Serrafe	Wolfinsohn
Pimenta	Seruya	Zaffranay
Pinto	Sicsu	Zagury
Querub	Stock	

3. Sephardic Jews in Bayonne and Southwestern France During the Inquisition

Jews in southwestern France, 1492, from Bordeaux to Bayonne
Gabriel Soarez
Jacob Rodriguiez Périere
David Silveyra
Michel Calvo de Silva
Jean Baptiste Silva 1682–1742 (doctor to King Louis XV)
Madame Pereyra-Brandon 1780 (built a family synagogue)
Isaac Nunès Tavarez 1690–1770

The following people went to France during the Portuguese Inquisition of 1536
Fernan Nunes
Jacob Franco Castello Mendo
Duarte Nuñes Victoria (AKA Abraham Curiel)
Fernando Mendes da Costa
Alvaro Louis
Andres Lopez Villaréal
Diego Rodriguez Cardoso
d'Isaac-Israel de Avila
d'Isaque Alvares (married to Raquel Alvares do Almo)
Gonzalo Baez de Paiva
Rabbi Abraham Vaez
Rabbi Yshak de Acosta
Rabbi Isaac Abarbanel de Souza
Abraham de Paz
David Lindo
Abraham Lopes Caloso
Benjamin Lopez Caloso (son)
David Lappes de Pas
Aaron (Jacob ben) Sasportes
Raphael Meldola
Ester Gomes Ravelo

Members of a Portuguese community in Loden
Soloman Lopes Duber
Abraham Furtado
Mr. & Mrs. Azevedo Airè
David Grodis
Soloman Furtado
Benjamin Nuñes Tavarez
Mardochèe Lopes Fonseca

4. Sephardics of Livorno, Italy

Rodrigues

Alvares

Pereira

Mendes

Peixotte

Fonesca

Decosta

Aaron Lopes

Ribca Souza

Mordekai Mendes—France

Jacob Rodriguez-Periera

Pedro Aaron

Maria Abigail

David Pereyra-Suarès

Henriques Nunés family

Josef Henriques de Castro

Pereyra—Brandon

M. Aaron Salvedo

Azoulay

Isaac Nunés Tavaraz

Henry Léon

Samuel Abraham Nunes

B. Louis Noures

Mardoelée Fonséque

Antoinette Lopés

Rogel Lopes da Fonesca

Yshak da Silva Cardoso

Daniel Henriques de Sousa

Jayacob Pereira—Brandon

Selmomah de Olivera

Isaac Abarbanel Souza

Isaac de Medina

Jacob de Maize Nunès

M. Peixotto

Abraham Andrade Navio

Moise Carvalho

Isaac Oxeda

Francesco Carvalho

Antonio Rodriguez Silva

Louis Mendes d'Acosta

Manuel Vaes Oliveria

Gabriel Ferreira

Manuel Gomès

Fernando Mendes d'Acosta

Jacob Pereyre Brandon

N. Jacob Lopes Silva

N. Lopes Gomès Brito

Alvaro Louis

Isaac Carvaillo

George Rodriguez Gardoze

Manuel Louis

Samuel Louis Nunés

Moyshe Flores de Peyrehorade (France)

N. Mendes

Francisco Rodriguez Flores

Jahacab de Silva

Abraham Andrade Navio

Jacob da Silva Mendes

Diego Gomez de Salazar

Francois da Silva

Isabel de Salazar

Gabriel da Silva

George Cardoze

Gonzelo Mendez

    was Cuidad Rodrigo from Portugal

Gabriel Henriquez

Chevalier Fonsèque

Monsieur Pinède

Juan Abraham Rodriguez Pereira—1674

Abraham Abvod Fonsèque

Raphael ben Eleazar Meldola

    (Amsterdam)

5. Meanings of Names Used by Marrano Families

The following is a brief list of surnames and Christian names which appear to verify the explanation of the origin of some names.

Aguiar *to play knavish tricks*
Almelda *municipal sweeper*
Amaral *variety of Portuguese vine*
Anjos *angel*
Arruda *rue, herb, grace*
Avelar *wood of hazel trees*

Baptista *name given to St. John the Baptist*
Barata *black beetle*
Barrito *an elephant's cry*
Barro *earthenware, pottery*
Benito *holy, consecrated*
Bento *holy, consecrated*
Bernardo *Cistercian monk*
Bianco *white, blank*
Blanco *white, blank*
Botelho *small ancient measure of corn*
Braga *wall in ancient forts*
Branco *white, blank*

Camara *chamber, room, cabin*
Candido *candid, frank, sincere*
Carreira *way, road, race, route*
Carvalho *oak, oak tree*
Castro *old castle (Roman or pre-Roman origins)*
Chaves *keys, spanners*
Coelho *rabbit*
Cordeiro *lamb*
Correia *leather strap, belt*
Costa *coast, shore, bank*
Couto *enclosure*
Cunha *wedge, intercession*
Custodio *custodian, guardian*

Estevo *kind of shrub found in Douro and the Algarve*
Estrela *star, destiny, fate*

Fagundes *rascal*
Ferreira *sea-bream, ironworker*
Figueira *fig tree*
Figueiredo *fig grove*
Fonte *fountain, source*
Franco *frank, open, sincere*
Furtado *stolen, robbed*

Jacinto *hyacinth, precious stone*
Jesús *Jesus*
José *Joseph*

Leal *loyal, faithful*
Leite *milk*
Lima *lime*
Luis *Louis d'or (French gold coin)*
Luz *light, brightness*

Machado *axe*
Madeira *wood, timber, lumber*
Madeiro *wood, timber*
Maia *May Day*
Marques *marquis, marquess*
Massa *dough, mass of people*
Mato *brushwood, undergrowth*
Monteiro *huntsman, forest warden*
Moreira *mulberry bush*
Mota *mound of Earth*

Nascimento *birth, nativity*
Neves *snows*
Nunes *odd, odd number*

Oliveira *olive tree*
Oliveria *olive tree*

Pavao *peacock*
Pedro *stone, rock*
Pereira *pear tree*
Pimental *pepper plantation*
Pinheiro *pine tree*
Pires *saucer*
Ponte *bridge*

Raposo *fox, cunning man*
Rego *furrow, channel*

Santos *saints, holy, sacred*
Sequeira *dryness, drought*
Serra *saw (tool), ridge of mountains*
Silva *bramble, blackberry bush, gold lace*
Silveira *bramble, blackberry thicket*

Terceira *third, mediatrix*
Terra *Earth, world, land*
Toste *drinking to a toast*
Trindade *Trinity*

Varga *marshy plain*
Ventura *fortune, luck, destiny*
Vieira *scallop, scallop shell*
Vital *vital, essential*
Viveiros *nurseries, garden*

6. Portuguese Surnames and Variants

The surnames listed below are based on the spellings of the Portuguese surnames as found in the 1987–1988 telephones books of the Azores, Madeira, and Lisbon. Each of the following surnames was subject to variations. The adopted Anglicized spelling and evolved names have been placed in parenthesis. There is no intention on behalf of the author to change or to correct a family's preference of spelling. When in doubt, the author resorted to the Portuguese spelling.

Abreu (Aubrey)
Agrela (De Grilla)
Aguiar
Almeida
Amaral
Andrade (Andrews)
Anjos
Arruda
Avilla

Barios (Burrows)
Baptists (Baptiste)
Barbosa (Barboza)
Benevides
Borges (Burgess)
Botelho (Bothello)
Brum (Brown)

Carreiro
Carvalho
Chaves
Cordeiro (Corday)
Correia
Custodio

De Couto (De Coute)
De Fontes
De Luis (Dallas)
De Silva
Dias
Domingos
Durta
Duvalder

Enos

Farias (Faries)
Farpellia
Faustino
Ferreira
Figueira
Figueiredo
Flasidada
Freitas

Garcia
Gomes (Gomez)
Goncalves (Gonsalves)
Gouveia

Jacinto
Jesús
Joaquím (King)
Jorge (George)
José (Joseph)

Machado (Marshall)
Madeiros
Malaquias
Marques (Marks)
Martins (Martin)
Matias (Matthews)
Massa
Melo (Mello)
Moniz
Moreira (Marirea)
Mota
Moura

Oliveira

Pacheco
Paula (Paul)
Pavao
Pereira
Pimentel (Pimental)
Pires
Perry, Parry, Paris
Ponte

Raposo (Repose)
Rebelo (Rebello)
Rego
Reis (Ray)
Resendes
Revis
Ribeiro
Rodrigues (Rodriguez)
Rosa (Roza)

Santos (Saints)
Sequeira (Skater)
Silveira
Simao (Simon)
Simas
Simones (Simons, Simmons)
Soares
Sofrino
Sousa (Souza)

Tavares
Teixeira (Terceira)
Trindade (Trinidad)

Vicente (Vincent)
Vieira (Viera)
Vitance

CHAPTER NINE

Examples of Those Who
Continue to Return to Judaism

ALTHOUGH SOME MARRANO FAMILIES still practice what they know to be Jewish beliefs in secret, others don't practice any particular Jewish traditions, but are fully aware of their families' histories.

To be able to identify oneself as being of Jewish ancestry is like coming out of the closet, and this is happening in many parts of the world.

In Recife, Pernambuco, university professor Tania Kaufman works with doctoral students who go out to the surrounding communities to work with groups of people, helping them to identify traditions they practice as being a part of a Jewish heritage. In many cities in America, individuals are beginning to examine their beliefs and customs which seem similar to those of their Jewish neighbors, to see if they have Jewish roots as well. In Mexico, Hawaii, Bermuda, and other places, the questioning goes on. Are we of Jewish blood? And if so, to what degree are we going to acknowledge that fact? Would we simply state it? We might incorporate some Jewish holidays into the year, or we might completely celebrate and become full-time members of the Jewish community. *"Somos Judías"* ("We are Jews") is proclaimed, and once again, a Jewish lineage once taken away continues to exist in the world, from generation to generation.

What is done with the information garnered is always very personal to the person or family involved. Often information gathered by one member of a family is shared with some or all members of that family. Not always is the information welcomed by family, because older people don't necessarily want their lives to change and are not interested in delving into their past. Often, even siblings and cousins don't want to rock the boat of their existence, or upset the ways in which their own family units function.

Here are some of the families who have been interested in reclaiming some or part of their Jewish roots:

Barbara, who lives in Honolulu, Hawaii, has begun to think of the Jewish New Year (Rosh Hashanah) and the Festival of Lights (Chanukah) as part of her family's celebrations. Making brisket and serving potato pancakes are now included in her holiday preparations, as she continues to learn more about Jewish life's passages. She lives in today's world.

But others, such as Aaron Lopez and Jacob Rodriguez Riviera, both residents of Newport, Rhode Island, in the eighteenth century, in order to recapture their Jewish roots that had been denied them in their native country of Portugal, had to be circumcised as adults. Aaron even changed his name from the Latin (Duarte) to the biblical Hebrew (Aaron). When Aaron Lopez's son was born in Newport and there was no one to perform the ritual circumcision necessary as a Jewish son's first Covenant with God, Aaron and his wife rode to New York to have the rite performed.

According to Professor Hordes of the University of New Mexico in Albuquerque, there are some families there who lit candles in cellars or darkened rooms on Friday night as a tradition, until they learned that they were really celebrating the beginning of the Jewish Sabbath (Shabbat) by that act.

In Brazil, the members of the D'Oliviera family refrain from eating either pork or shellfish, both forbidden by Jewish dietary laws of kosher (*kashrut*), because those foods are deemed to be unclean and therefore unhealthy. For this family, finding out that their traditional eating habits were tied to a religion was a surprise.

In Bermuda, there are families with separate pots for meat and separate pots for milk products, and milk and meat are never put on the table at the same time or eaten together. They thought that it was just a quirky family tradition until they learned that according to Jewish ritual law, it is disrespectful to eat a calf in its mother's milk. (This dietary law serves as a signpost that one should always show respect in every circumstance.)

All of those rituals over the past 500 years Jews were forced to do in secret in order to appear loyal to the Church, as the families had to show the world outside of their houses a Catholic face. Because of this, often the meanings of the rituals were forgotten, and only the acts of the rituals remained. Now, at last, explanation is given as to why the rituals exist and are important to the Jewish religion.

At another level of identification, according to Alan Tigay in his letter from Jerusalem, one woman knew that her mother's family had Jewish origins in Spain. She said, "We practiced Jewish traditions as much as we knew."

Another woman who has Jewish roots on both sides of her family says that her mother's family came from a village in the Mexican state of Michoacan, where most of the inhabitants don't mix milk and meat, don't work on Saturday, and leave pebbles on tombstones, all examples of Jewish customs.

Some Catholic families kiss the doorposts of their homes, stating that they do it because it helps to separate the inside from the outside. Actually, they are kissing what would normally be a mezuzah on the door of Jewish homes.

Other Catholic or Christian families, as in Hawaii or Bermuda, thoroughly clean their houses on Friday but either put the dirt under a corner of a carpet or put it in a bag, tie it up, store it in a closet, and throw it out on Monday. They do this because "Grandma said it was bad luck to throw dirt out of the house on Friday." The bad luck, actually, would have been if their family had been observed cleaning their home on Friday during the time of the Inquisition; they would have been suspected of Judaizing so they learned to clean but to not throw the dirt out until it was "safe." Today, having lost the reason why, they are still doing it.

In the Shinto cemetery in Honolulu, Hawaii, in the early twentieth century, one Portuguese Catholic family was buried. On their gravestones are squiggled the Hebrew letters for God. According to the community there, these people knew that they had Jewish roots, but wanted to hide them from their neighbors. But they wanted to make sure that God knew they were of Jewish blood.

In the southwestern United States, many Hispanics have been formally converting to Judaism in recent years, according to Simon Romero in *The New York Times*. In addition to recognizing and learning about Jewish customs their families had practiced for centuries, some have researched their Jewish ancestry through genealogical research and even DNA testing. As a result, they are returning to Judaism. "I've had to go beyond my comfort level in something I would call a reversion rather than a conversion," said El Paso lawyer John Garcia. "There were an intervening 400 years when my family had become Catholic, but something about Judaism, I don't know exactly what it was, was kept alive."

In Belmonte, Portugal, Jewish ritual has been practiced in secret for 500-plus years. Unleavened bread has continued to be baked, and ritual cleansing of people has taken place in the waters around the town. Descendants of Jews, with no books or rabbis to refer to, have one Hebrew word left, *Adonai,* the word for God. Coming out to the community finally unafraid, as Jewish people, the older generation prefers to keep their rituals as they have celebrated them for more than 500 years, whereas the new generation of thirty-to-forty-year-olds have learned all about Jewish practices and today embrace more Jewish traditions in their daily lives.

In Toronto, Ontario, Canada, some of the Catholic families bake unleavened breads, called "undelev," in April, as did their families in the Azores Islands of Portugal. These families still don't recognize that they are really celebrating the Jewish holiday of Passover, commemorating when Jewish residents of Egypt ran from the Pharaoh Ramses, across the Red Sea, to leave the horrors of slavery in Egypt. In their haste, they baked bread but did not have time to wait for their bread to rise. So today, during the week of Passover, Jewish people are to eat only unleavened products, as are these Azorean families of Toronto.

Many of those who have discovered that they have a Jewish origin, have become "anusim," which means "to return." These people have embraced Judaism and become devoted to its many rituals and laws in order to live, finally, a Jewish life. They don't feel that the last 500 years of not celebrating Judaism has made them any less Jewish; they only need to educate themselves on how to live as Jews. Many justly feel insulted when told that they really need to convert back to Judaism, for they feel having been deprived of their rightful heritage for 500 years is being devalued, and that a sincere desire to return should be sufficient for acceptance.

Many communities in the world, including those of Majorca in Spain; Recife,

Pernambuco, in Brazil; and Belmonte, Portugal; now have both rabbis and Jewish studies centers to help Jewish descendants to return.

Some universities and societies are involved with these projects to help to identify individuals and whole communities of Jewish descendants, as does Professor Hordes at the University of New Mexico in Albuquerque.

Societies such as the Portuguese Genealogical Society, under the direction of Doris Naumu, are open to having lectures, and they maintain files and books to help the members of the society to recognize and identify their Jewish origins.

Some of the clues to the Jewish identity that keep appearing in those communities include birth rites, marriage rites, and death rites; relating to community by services to the sick, poor, and elderly, etc.; celebrating holidays and festivals with fragments of rites and traditions; the ways in which a house is cleaned and its inhabitants are dressed; work habits, including the insistence on Saturdays with no work; reading the Old Testament but not the New Testament; and praying only to God.

Having interviewed seventy people, I now realize that there are hundreds of thousands of Latin people in the world who have some or many of the same Jewish traditions as the people I've met. It is noteworthy that in many locations around the world evidence of hidden Jewish traditions has been discovered. In addition, the history of the Sephardic Diaspora can be seen in traces and tracks worldwide. Here are some examples.

A secret synagogue hidden behind a false wall was uncovered during construction in a house in the city of Porto, north of Lisbon.

Luis Moses Gomez, who fled to escape the wrath of the Spanish Inquisition, came in 1703 to New York and practiced openly as a Jew. In 1705 he was granted a certificate of denization by Queen Anne of England. It gave him rights to own property, run a business, and live as a free man without pledging his oath to England's Church. He eventually became important in New York, economically, and was the first president of the oldest congregation in the United States, Shearith Israel, in 1708. His home is still available to been seen in Marlboro, Ulster County, New York, up the Hudson River.

Izmir, a city in Turkey, had dozens of synagogues, some dating back to the sixteenth century. The Geveret Señora Synagogue, founded in 1660, is named for Gracia Mendes Nasi, a Converso secret stateswoman and patron who came to Constantinople in 1553 and paid for many synagogues and lands in and out of the Ottoman Empire.

In the ancient city of Ephesus, there are to be found images of a menorah, Lulav, and Etrog on the steps of the library.

During the 1730s in Lisbon, Portugal, there were puppet operas of the Barrio Alto Theater written by Antonio José da Silva, a New Christian by birth and a lawyer by profession. The operas were a satire of Portuguese society. In an auto da fé, Da Silva was put to death at the stake in 1739.

There is a Sephardic Hebrew center in Cuba, today.

The Inquisition building where trials and autos da fé took place is still standing in Cartagena, Colombia.

In the *New York Times* of May 1948, it was reported that there were 30,000 Spanish Jews in Morocco and Tangiers who were in grave danger because of their Moslem neighbors.

Today, there are only handful of Jews in Iraq, which used to be called Babylonia and where thousands of Jews once lived. Many Sephardic Jews also emigrated there after the expulsion from Spain in 1492.

For Mexicans who are Catholic, but descended from Judaism, the Inquisition is recent history, since, as in the rest of Latin America, in Mexico the Inquisition Courts existed from the 1500s until late in the 1800s. Judaism had to be practiced in secret for fear of harassment, torture, or death. For this reason, Marrano women covered their eyes with their hands when they prayed. But Judaism did survive, as evidenced by the presence of returning Jews there today.

Today in Mexicali, Mexico, Rabbi Daniel Mehlman goes to the home of Alfredo and Lupe Mendrano to help celebrate Shabbat. The families in Mexicali were born into Catholic families but, like Dr. Mario Espinoza, an obstetrician-gynecologist, are certain they are descended from Jews who were forcibly converted to Christianity centuries ago. Rabbi Stephen León of El Paso, Texas, across the border from Ciudad Juarez, Mexico, has worked with forty families who have memories of Crypto-Jewish practices. Dr. Espinoza of Mexicali, Mexico, whose family live as Crypto Jews, has studied Hebrew and Judaic practices.

To celebrate the holiday known as Chanukah, dough is fried in oil for Sephardic Jews and people with Jewish roots. In Spain, the dough is called *banuelos*, in Hawaii it's called *malassadas*, and in Holland, *oliebollen*.

A clue to Nuevo Cristo heritage is found in Sephardic cooking, which included the use of pomegranate, limes, tamarind, coconuts, rose and orange water, black pepper, ginger, cloves, cinnamon, cardamom, olive oil, sesame, turmeric, cumin, nutmeg, almonds, oranges, tomatoes, cocoa, lemon, pine nuts, and honey.

After 1492 many Sephardic Jews went to Amsterdam and Rotterdam in Holland; Antwerp, Belgium; and Hamburg, Germany. In 1593, Ferdinand II, Grand Duke of Tuscany (Italy) invited New Christians (Marranos) to settle in Pisa and Livorno, allowing them to return to Judaism. France also invited New Christians to settle in Bayonne, Toulouse, Bordeaux, Marseilles, Avignon, Carpentras, and Cavaillon—all of which became important Marrano centers. Marranos lived in England in secret until Oliver Cromwell allowed Jews to come back to England to live freely in 1656, having been banished from England in 1290. Some Marranos emigrated to the regions around Sarajevo and Bosnia. Marranos also migrated to the East Indies, India, America, North Africa (Tunisia and Morocco), and to the Ottoman lands that centered in Turkey, Greece, and Palestine. Eventually Marranos lived in most of the Spanish and Portuguese colonies. The Medicis accepted Marranos in Florence, and eventually Mantua, Genoa, and Venice accepted them also.

In Spain and Portugal secret Jews (Marranos) were noticed and identified by what was referred to as "Jewish habits," which included not lighting fires from Friday night to Saturday night, cleaning houses on Friday, cooking on Friday for Saturday meals, and women lighting candles on Friday night. Marranos were also spotted when the families put on clean clothes on Saturday. They were suspected if they did not eat pork or shellfish, if they didn't mix milk and meat, if they made flat breads in March or April, or if they fasted on a day in September or October.

Among the many ways Jews and Marranos were identified during the Inquisition were a number of Jewish traditional practices involving food preparation and dietary laws and customs. They included making *adafina*, a lamb stew with onions and garbanzo beans; making *almondrote de berenjena*, which includes eggplants baked with egg and cheese and served cold; preparing meats with onions and garlic and frying them in vegetable oils instead of pork fat; and soaking meats in salt water to drain the blood out. When Crypto Jews were forced to eat pork, the pig was prepared with ingredients used by Jews when they ate lamb or beef, such as onions and garlic.

Jews had traditional forms of macaroons, almond cakes, and sponge cakes. Dietary laws required that animals for food be killed with a sharp knife, in a single cut of both the trachea and jugular vein, to cause the least pain. To be eaten, fish had to have both scales and fins. And there were special foods—and special dress—for Jewish festivals such as Sabbath, Passover, Rosh Hashanah, Yom Kippur, Chanukah, Sukkot, and Purim.

Pan de semita, or Semitic bread, is a secret Jewish matzah that is eaten today in the Mexico–Texas border area. It is made from vegetable oil, flour, raisins, pecans, and water. *Capirotada* is a Passover food made from wheat flour, raw sugar, cinnamon, cheese, butter, pecans, peanuts, and raisins. These ingredients were used by secret Spanish Jews and are still recorded in the Holy Office Archives of the Inquisition today.

The secret Jews of Mexico decapitated chickens in the 1640s and hung them on a clothesline so the blood would drain out. Today, rural Mexican-Americans in Texas drink tea, fruit juices, or chocolate during Easter week. There's much evidence to be found in the foods that these people were also observing Passover in addition to Lent and Easter, although many didn't know it until it was pointed out that they were eating traditional sixteenth-century Sephardic foods, especially the bitter herbs added to the meal.

Mexican-Americans in Texas cast the first piece of the *masa* dough into the fire, before cooking up a batch of corn tortillas or bread. These same people also do not eat pork on Fridays. Some Mexican-Americans don't eat pork after six P.M. or sundown on Friday.

Many Sephardic families still recite a blessing after meals in the Ladino language, a combination of both Spanish and Hebrew, which was used by Jews in Spain. Here is that blessing in the original Ladino: *"Ya comimos bevimos, y al Dio santo Barukh*

Hu u-vouch Chemo bendishimos; que mos dio y mos dara pan para comer y panyos vestir, y anyos muchos y buenos para bivir, el Padre el grande que mande al chico asegun tenemos de menester para muestras cazas y para maestros hijos. El Dio mos oiga y mos aresponda y mos apiade por su nombre el grande, que somos almicas sin pecado. Hodu L'Adonai ki tov ki le-olam hasdo. Hodu L'Adonai ki tov ke le-olam hasdo. Siempre major, nunca peor, nunca mos manke la meza del Criador. Amen."

Here is the blessing translated into English: "We have eaten and drunk, and we bless the Holy One. Blessed be He and His holy Name, Who has given us and gives us bread to eat, and clothes to wear, and many good years to live. The Almighty Father Who provides for the littlest one, so may He provide that we have the necessities for our homes and for our children. May God hear us and respond to us, and have pity on us for the sake of His great Name; for we are little souls without sin. Praise the Lord for He is good, for His kindness is everlasting. May things always be better, never worse; may the Creator's table never be lacking for us. Amen."

According to the cookbook *Savoring Spain and Portugal,* by Joyce Goldstein, *alheira,* a highly seasoned Portuguese sausage, was created by Marranos to feign loyalty to Christianity. These sausages were made from a mixture of poultry and bread, which was then disguised with garlic, paprika, and chilies to resemble pork. Today, pork is used in most *alheiras,* except for the ones eaten by observant Jews.

Like stews, the *cocido* in Spain or *cozido* in Portugal is a soup that is derived from the *adafina* or Sephardic Jewish soup that sat warming to be served on the Sabbath. Originally, before the Inquisition, the Jews made this from vegetables, beef or chicken, and eggs. After the Inquisition began, and Jews had to show their loyalty to the Church and to Catholicism, pork was added. Today, observant Sephardic Jews, once again eliminate the pork, although today pork is loved in Portugal and Spain and eaten by most families there who don't know of their Jewish ancestry.

There are many families who, because of the Jewish tradition in their homes for 500 years, still refrain from eating any pork product. Of course most of the time, the Jewish reason is forgotten and only the tradition, passed down from one generation to the next, remains. The same is true of many other Jewish traditions for the descendants of the Marranos, Nuevos Cristos, or New Christians.

CHAPTER TEN

In Conclusion

FRAGMENTS OF A JEWISH CIVILIZATION that was so great and beautiful are being pieced together every day by individuals, whole families, and in some cases, whole communities. Many questions are being asked so quietly that they are almost in the form of whispers, and others are being asked in a loud, demanding voice. The goal: to find answers.

The memory of the Inquisition and the ingrained fears of reprisal are still very real today for some descendants of the Nuevo Cristo families. The warnings that they still receive, from their families, their neighbors, their communities, and the Catholic Church in some parts of the world, make it difficult to use the words "I think I have Jewish roots." Fears of being ostracized at many levels of society still echo as a deterrent to finding out the truth that is so rightfully theirs. So the people whisper their questions about their family secrets, gossip, and information that is often tangible in the form of letters, diaries, bibles, marriage and death certificates, birth papers, and even marks and words squiggled on the design of cemetery stones and art. Often a telltale hint is one's name, which can become a part of the Jewish family's original history; Portuguese names that mean something in terms of animals, plants, trees, and other forms in nature often reveal a family's Jewish roots.

Many resources are available for these inquiring descendants of Nuevos Cristos today. Much research has been done by individuals, universities, and organizations of various types; and even the Spanish government has worked to find out as much information as possible concerning the Inquisition and all of its consequences.

Inquisition records have been translated into various languages and have been read over and over again in an effort to understand each individual case, each supposed crime involved, and each punishment delivered by the Inquisition. Bit by bit, pieces are being put together, like a huge puzzle, that will tell the story and answer frequently asked questions, such as "Where did it happen? To whom? And most importantly, why did it happen to my family?"

The genealogies of individuals and of whole families, like the DaCosta and Salvador families, have been researched and assembled for their descendants to read and to learn, that they may know and be proud of their heritage. In addition to individual papers, there are books, such as *Gente da Nação* (People of the Nation), by José Antonio Gonsalves de Mello, and films like *The Last Jews of Portugal in Belmonte*, which was made as a local film by the people of Belmonte and is distributed by the National Center for Jewish Film. Today, there is also the Internet, which can help uncover facts and histories for those who seek information. Like a widening circle, the Internet can lead the user to other people, to talk with and share information. The Museum of the Diaspora in Israel and the Mormon Church also have valuable information for people whose families came originally from Spain and Portugal.

More often than not, families are ready to learn. They are accepting of new facts about their genealogy and history, and are helpful in sharing whatever they can remember that would also add clues of Jewish identity. It becomes a sensitive issue for a family to decide what, if anything, they are going to do with the newly found recognition of Jewish roots.

Groups of interested people are being formed; seminars and whole conferences are being dedicated to the exploration of the events and history of the Inquisition, expulsions, punishments, and the trials of migrations. These forums are also able to give people the facts that will help them to do their own private investigative work to find their own family history and to finally come back to the roots that are rightfully theirs.

This quest for personal and family identity, and for facts that could confirm Jewish roots, was the purpose for this book. The gratifying results are seen in the answers to the questions I asked as I interviewed people about their traditions and feelings. The questions were about birth, death, and marriage rites; foods eaten and holidays observed; education's place in the family and the family's disposition toward charity; how prayers are recited—where, when, and to whom. Interviewees told about their superstitions, amulets, family habits, and other traditions, such as games they played and the ways they prepared their food.

The people I interviewed were like sponges, soaking up the explanations I gave for the traditions they observed. They wanted to know why each tradition exists and they were forthcoming with everything they could think of about their family's history.

Most expressed joy at being a part of an old religion that has survived in spite of much suffering throughout history. Jewish people are still here, contributing to the world because of their intelligence and hard work.

It has been a most enjoyable experience for me to meet and get to know the interviewees, many of whom have become personal friends. I hope that after reading this book—especially the interviews—other people who know or suspect that their families go back to the Iberian Peninsula, to Spain or to Portugal, will look into to their own families' traditions and histories. Perhaps they too will find that their families have traditions, passed down through the generations. And perhaps those traditions, after a rewarding closer look, will lead those people back to having Jewish roots.

Afterword

ALTHOUGH THE INQUISITION ENTITIES HAVE been disbanded by Spain, Portugal, and all of their colonies, it seems that a specter of the Inquisition continues to exist today.

On a recent trip to do research at the American Hispanic Society in New York, I discovered that within the structure of the Catholic Church, operating from the Vatican City in Rome, there is today an organization with the same precepts that formed the Inquisition. That organization, founded in 1542 by Pope Paul III, is known as the Congregation for the Doctrine of the Faith. It was originally called the Supreme Sacred Congregation of the Roman and Universal Inquisition, and its purpose was to defend the Church from heresy.

The Congregation for the Doctrine of the Faith is led currently by Prefect Cardinal William Joseph Levada, who came to Rome from the Diocese of Los Angeles, California. Prefect Cardinal Levada assumed this position only when the previous leader, the then Cardinal Joseph Ratzinger, became the current leader of the Catholic Church, Pope Benedict XVI.

The congregation's official function, or *raison d'être,* is to promote "in a collegial fashion encounters and initiatives to *spread sound doctrine and defend these points of Christian tradition which seem in danger because of new and unacceptable doctrines.*"

What are these "new and unacceptable doctrines"? That question is not addressed by the Catholic Church on its website, nor did I receive any explanations in response to my emails to Prefect Levada and to Pope Benedict XVI.

In order to help define the congregation's purpose, or *raison d'être*, I sent first an email to Cardinal Levada with a set of questions. When, after four weeks, no response came, I then wrote a more detailed email to both Prefect Cardinal Levada and Pope Benedict XVI:

> Dear Cardinal Levada,
> I am Sandra Cumings Malamed. I am a curator, lecturer, and a published
> author. My newest book that is going to be published is about the Inquisi-
> tion—its horrors and results for the descendants of the persecuted Jewish

families who are, as members of other religions today, only now beginning to recognize that many of the traditions of their lives bring them back to Jewish roots that were denied them by the Inquisition's Court and Tribunal 500-plus years ago.

The countries of Spain and Portugal have ceased to have Inquisition laws and organizations left in their societies. I recently heard about the Catholic Church's organization called the Tribunal de la Fé (or Court of the Faith) which I believe is now called the Congregation of the Doctrine of the Faith. According to the Hispanic Society of America your organization still protects the precepts of Inquisition philosophy. Is this true?

As a concluding chapter of my new book, since I have only heard of your organization within the last month, I will write about what you tell me you represent in terms of attitudes toward both Judaism and the State of Israel.

This new chapter will be added to my book by the time it goes to the publisher. I hope to hear from you about my questions as well as to the purpose of what your organization is today and what it does. The answers you provide will be written in the last chapter; if I do not get a response I will state that also, which will leave questions in themselves as to why and what is being hidden from me and the world.

I thank you in advance and I remain,

Sincerely,

Sandra Cumings Malamed

I never received an answer.

This silent treatment is alarming. If there is nothing for the Catholic Church to hide, why is there not more transparency about the goals of the Congregation of the Doctrine of the Faith? As Warren Bennis, Daniel Goleman, James O'Toole, and Patricia Ward Biederman, authors of *Transparency: How Leaders Create a Culture of Candor,* point out, "trust and transparency are linked," and "transparency is one evidence of an organization's moral health." In view of the apparent "no information available to the public" attitude of the Catholic Church concerning this matter, we can only assume that there is something to hide. Because the doctrine founded by Pope Paul III led directly to the threats, persecution, and punishment inflicted by the Inquisition in Spain, Portugal, and their colonies all over the world, we must question why the organization in Rome in 1542 still exists today. And we must insist that questions such as the ones I posed in my email be addressed, answered, and finally explained.

Without explanation, we must worry that the Inquisition is not really abolished but is only on hold. If seeds of another Inquisition have been put in place for the future, once again, any people, person, culture, or religion could become the

Church's target of accusations of heresy. Will heretics once again become subject to the Church's acts of punishment, including autos da fé and death?

If Spain and Portugal could eliminate all vestiges of the Inquisition in their cultures and their laws, why hasn't the Catholic Church done the same? Is it not ashamed of the damage done to so many individuals and families for centuries? If it is not, it should be! And now is as good a time as any to eliminate the specter of the Inquisition once and for all.

Appendix A
Timelines for Spain, Portugal, and the World

These timelines give a chronological overview of the history of Jews in Iberia and in Spanish and Portuguese colonies in other parts of the world, during the period from 1600 B.C.E. to 1996 C.E.

Spain

1600 B.C.E. Immigration into the area now called Spain (Espania, the hidden land).

586 B.C.E. Babylonians seize Jerusalem and destroy the Temple of Solomon and David. Jews taken captive and brought to Babylonia. Some Jews flee across Africa and settle in the area now called Spain.

534 B.C.E. Persian King Cyrus conquers Babylonia and helps Jews return to Jerusalem.

6th cent. B.C.E. Phoenician colonies established in the Iberian Peninsula.

300 B.C.E. Jewish traders already in Iberian Peninsula, according to legend.

30 C.E. (approx.) Crucifixion of Jewish rabbi known as Jesus Christ.

1–400 C.E. Christianity is a grassroots, non-hierarchical popular movement.

2nd cent. C.E. Important Spanish cities in Roman Empire: Augusta Emerita (Mérida), Córdoba, Seville (Hispalis), Zaragoza (Caesar Augusta), Lugo, Cádiz (Gades), and Tarragona.

2nd cent. C.E. During the reigns of Roman Emperor Hadrian and the Antonines (Antoninus Pius, Marcus Aurelius, Verus, and Commodus), more Jews move into what is now Spain, enjoying greater freedom throughout the empire.

280–500 C.E. Compilation of the Talmuds.

359 C.E. Hillel II fixes the Jewish calendar.

400 C.E. Christians severely persecuted by the Romans.

409 C.E. Iberian Peninsula invaded by three Germanic tribes, the Suevi, the Vandals, and the Alani.

450 C.E. Official signs of Spanish anti-Semitism appear at a meeting of the Council of Elvira, and the Roman Empire, now Christian, implements anti-Jewish laws.

476 C.E. End of the Roman Empire.

5th cent. C.E. Visigoths, another Germanic tribe, invade Spain and overcome earlier invaders.

480–711 C.E. Visigoths accuse Jews of plotting against the kingdom and declare, "only Catholics live in Spain."

567–586 c.e. King Leovigild decides Spain should be Catholic, in an effort to unify the Iberian Peninsula.

586 c.e. King Recarred converts to Catholicism and adopts the Nicene Creed. Thus begins a period of persecution of the Jews.

589 c.e. At the Third Council of Toledo, the first anti-Jewish laws are passed, ruling that children of a mixed Jewish–Christian marriage should be baptized, leading to a policy of forced conversion of the Jews.

612 c.e. Ten years after Reccared's death, Sisebut ascends the throne. Anti-Jewish laws no longer being enforced at this time.

early 7th cent. c.e. Visigothic King Sisebut persecutes Jews, passing edicts forcing Jews to convert and receive baptism. Those who refuse are tortured, their property is confiscated, and their families are scattered.

7th cent. c.e. Visigoths in Western Europe rely on a council called Aula Regia. This group of advisors to the court includes Catholic bishops, strengthening ties between Church and State.

627 c.e. Council of Clichy forbids sales of Christian slaves to Jews, fearing Jews will try to convert these Christians to Judaism.

631 c.e. Sisenand seizes the Visigothic throne and holds power for six years. As a Unionist, he seeks to have both Jewish and Christian converts surrender their faith under repressive rule.

633 c.e. Fourth Council of Toledo declares that forced conversions (as practiced by King Sisebut) are ineffective and in violation of "the full form of justice." However, the Council orders the separation of Jewish husbands from their Christian wives, unless the Jews convert to Christianity, and orders the separation of children from their converted parents to prevent them from learning Jewish customs.

638 c.e. The Sixth Council of Toledo, in which Sisenand's successor, Chintila, will not permit non-Catholics to live in Spain. Kings of Spain are required to enforce laws against Judaism.

642 c.e. Chindaswinth ascends the throne. He is more tolerant of Judaism, and many converts return to their faith during his reign.

653 c.e. Recceswinth assumes complete control of the throne, having ruled jointly with his father. Recceswinth is more zealous than all his predecessors in oppressing the Jews. At the Eighth Council of Toledo he proposes that converts who continue with their Jewish observances be put to death at the hands of converts, as well as other laws to deny unconverted Jews the practice of their religion and to limit their civil rights.

672–680 c.e. The reign of Wamba, who relaxes persecution of the Jews, concentrating instead on building monarchic control through a strong army.

680–687 c.e. Wamba's successor, Erwig, regresses to persecuting the Jews in his realm, changing legislation affecting Jews and recent Christian converts.

702–710 C.E. Witiza changes legislation concerning Jews and converts. His legislation abolishes forced conversion, but orders Jews to sell their property acquired from Christians at a fixed price to the treasury, forbids Jews to trade with Christians, and removes their small children, seven and under, to be raised as Christians.

709 C.E. Late in Witiza's reign, Jews join forces to protest his harsh policies.

710 C.E. Witiza's rule ends, just before the Moorish invasion of the Iberian Peninsula.

711 C.E. Moslem commander Tariq bin Ziyad, acting on behalf of Caliph Walid I of Damascus, leads a small force across the strait from North Africa to Gibraltar. Visigothic resistance is weak, the Moslem forces capture Córdoba and the Visigothic capital of Toledo, and Tariq defeats Roderic, the last Visigothic king. Within three years most of the Iberian Peninsula is under Moslem control.

717–720 C.E. Spain under Moslem rule is far more hospitable to the Jews, ushering in what is now called the Golden Age for the Jews in Spain. Known as "the people of the book," the Jews become administrators of cities and towns. Jews develop their arts and sciences, their mercantile skills, their literature and music, and the language of Ladino.

718 C.E. Pelayo (Pelagius) stops the Moors at Covadonga and becomes king of Asturias. He is credited with the beginning of the Reconquista, a long campaign on the part of the kings of Asturia, in concert with the Catholic Church, to reclaim Iberia from the Moslems. Early in the Christian reconquest, the kings of Asturias gain control over León.

719 C.E. Narbonne, part of Spain under the Visigoths, is captured by the Moslems. The location of the city makes it ideal for trade. It lies at the end of the trade route stretching from the East, through Spain, to the border of the Christian West.

751–763 C.E. Galicia joins Asturias.

759 C.E. Narbonne taken by Pepin I. Jews had a strong presence in Narbonne during the Visigothic rule, and enjoyed relative freedom from the more extreme persecutions elsewhere in the Visigothic realm.

768–814 C.E. The reign of Charles the Great (Charlemagne). During this period Jewish merchants are able to acquire wares and products from Charles's domains and transport them to remote markets. They make contact with suppliers in the East, having kept ties with Moslem Spain. Radhanites, a group of international Jewish merchants, prosper as well. Jews are very important in the area of world trade.

810 C.E. King Alfonso II, "The Chaste," moves his capital to Oviedo.

891–960 C.E. Fernán González, appointed Count of Castile by the King of León, makes himself virtually independent.

930 c.e. Abd-al-Rahman III, emir and Caliph of Córdoba, maintains pressure on the Christian north. Castile becomes important in the struggle between the Moslems and the Christians.

932 c.e. King Ramiro II of León crosses the Sierra de Guadarrama to sack Madrid, then a Moslem fortress.

939 c.e. Abd-al-Rahman marches with an army to destroy León in what he calls his "campaign of omnipotence." King Ramiro of León, Fernán González of Castile, and Toda, Queen Mother of Navarre, rally in defense and prevail on August 1, 939.

961 c.e. Hakam succeeds Abd-al-Rahman III. He follows a policy of alternating diplomacy and force, dealing with the Christian rulers.

976 c.e. Hisham, at the age of eleven, succeeds Hakam when Hakam is killed by his wife and the boy's tutor, Al-Mansur, who acts as Regent.

981 c.e. Al-Mansur eliminates all rivals and seizes control as Prime Minister and dictator.

997 c.e. Al-Mansur sacks Santiago de Compostela, where Christians are taken captive and paraded through the city carrying cathedral bells.

1000 c.e. Rabbi Gershom ben Judah issues an edict prohibiting polygamy.

1002 c.e. Al-Mansur dies, leaving the leadership of the Caliphate of Córdoba in disarray, with rivalry between the heirs of Hisham II and the heirs of Al-Mansur.

1031 c.e. The Caliphate of Córdoba ceases to exist. Moslem Spain splinters into some thirty *taifas*, or faction states, each with its own ruler.

1021–1058 c.e. Solomon Ibn Gabirol, born in Malaga, considered the first Jewish philosopher of Spain.

1035 c.e. Sancho III of Navarre dies, leaving his lands and properties to his sons, Garcia, Fernando, and Ramiro. Ramiro, who is illegitimate, inherits Aragon, and his domain extends southward at the expense of the Moorish emirate of Zaragoza.

1037 c.e. León is conquered by Ferdinand I of Castile.

1044 c.e. The blood libel fable is started.

1055 c.e. Solomon Ibn Gabirol composes an extensive metaphysical work in Arabic, which is translated into Hebrew as *The Source of Life* and into Latin as *The Fountain of Life*.

1063 c.e. Rodrigo in battle alongside Sancho, aiding the Emir of Zaragoza against King Ramiro of Aragón. Ramiro is fatally wounded.

1065 c.e. After King Fernando I dies, Sancho becomes King of Castile. Fernando's second son, Alfonso, becomes King of Galicia.

1071 c.e. After murdering Sancho, Alfonso IV claims both Castile and León.

1072–1109 C.E. Alfonso VI proves to be a successful king.

1075–1141 C.E. Judah Ha-Levi is considered the greatest Jewish poet in Spain.

1076 C.E. Aragon annexes Navarre.

1085 C.E. Alfonso VI occupies Toledo. The fall of this *taifa* capital alarms other *taifa* rulers who send for help from the Almoravids of North Africa.

1086 C.E. Yusef, the Almoravid chief of Marrakech, arrives in Spain with an army of African and desert warriors. Conflict between Moslem and Christian Spain intensifies. Jewish freedom and achievements begin to decline.

1092–1167 C.E. Abraham Ibn Ezra is the first Jewish scholar in Spain. He is also a poet, mathematician, astronomer, religious philosopher, and Hebrew grammarian.

1096 C.E. Pogroms of the First Crusade.

1107 C.E. Jews of Moslem Spain suffer religious persecution from their new rulers, the fanatical Almoravides, who demand conversion of Christians and Jews to Islam or face exile.

1109–1158 C.E. Continued struggle on the part of Christian Spanish royalty to hold on to and reclaim their territory. Principal players include Alfonso VI of Toledo, his daughter Queen Urraca (1109–1126), and her son Alfonso VII. Alfonso the Emperor, Spanish king of Castile and León gains supremacy over other Christian states in Spain, and becomes emperor in 1135.

1110 C.E. Abraham bar Hiyya, Jewish astronomer, mathematician, and philosopher in Barcelona, composes the first Jewish encyclopedia, *The Foundations of Understanding and the Tower of Faith*.

1135–1204 C.E. Moses Maimonides was a Jewish philosopher and physician and the author of the *Guide for the Perplexed*. His family, originally from Córdoba, were forced to leave because of Almoravid intolerance.

1139 C.E. After a successful battle with the Moors at Ourique, Afonso Henriques is declared King of Portugal, thus establishing Portugal as a kingdom separate from León.

1139 C.E. Judah Ha-Levi completes his classic and influential philosophy of Judaism, called the *Book of Argument and Proof in Defense of the Despised Faith*. It takes the form of a series of dialogues between the king of the Khazars and an Aristotelian philosopher, a Christian, a Moslem, and a Jew.

1147 C.E. Pogroms of the Second Crusade.

1157 C.E. Alfonso VII of León divides his inheritance and bestows Castile upon his son Sancho III and León on his son Ferdinand II.

1158–1157 C.E. Sancho III dies and is succeeded by Alfonso VIII. Alfonso meets with other Spanish rulers to discuss and make plans concerning the reconquest of Moorish Spain, dividing the territory they hope to reclaim.

1168–1171 c.e. Spanish Sephardic Rabbi Benjamin of Tudela visits Jewish communities in Greece and writes about them in his account, *The Travels of Benjamin of Tudela.*

1173 c.e. Benjamin of Tudela returns after eight years of travel through Europe, Africa, and Asia.

1188 c.e. Alfonso IX succeeds Fernando to the throne of León at the age of eighteen. He summons rival factions, clergy, nobles, and townsmen to an assembly called the Cortes, which is the name still used for Spain's parliament. This meeting was arguably the first parliament in Europe.

1190 c.e. Rise of the Kabbalah.

1190 c.e. Pogroms in England.

1195 c.e. Alfonso IX of León and Alfonso VIII of Castile have territorial differences, but papal pressure forces them to unite in the crusade against the Almohades. The Castilians suffer crushing defeat at Alarcos, when the Leonese fail to appear.

1197 c.e. The Pope intervenes in the feud between the two Alfonsos. Alfonso IX marries Alfonso III's eldest daughter.

13th cent. c.e. Jews treated badly in Sicily when it becomes a part of Spanish Aragon. During this century Girona is a center of Jewish learning in Spain.

1212 c.e. Alfonso VIII, joined by Pedro II of Aragon and Afonso II of Portugal, leads Spain's crusade to victory against the Almohades at Las Navas de Tolosa.

1213 c.e. Pedro of Aragon's son and heir, Jaime I, is born

1215 c.e. The Pope orders the separation of Jews and Christians.

1215 c.e. Fourth Council of the Lateran orders Jews to wear badges.

1229 c.e. Jaime I, Pedro's son, comes of age. He will be known as "The Conqueror" for his successful campaigns against the Moslems in Majorca and Valencia.

1230 c.e. Ferdinand III, also called Fernando III the Saint, accomplishes final reunion of León and Castile.

1234 c.e. Books of Maimonides are burned at Montpellier.

1236 c.e. Ferdinand conquers Córdoba.

1238 c.e. Papal Inquisitions established in Aragon.

1239 c.e. Pope Gregory IX orders the kings and bishops of France, England, Spain, and Portugal to confiscate Hebrew books. The Talmud is condemned and burned in France and Rome.

1243 c.e. Ferdinand conquers Muricia.

1246 c.e. Ferdinand conquers Jaen.

1248 c.e. Ferdinand conquers Seville.

1250 C.E. The first blood libel accusations against the Jews on Spanish soil occurs in Saragossa.

1250 C.E. A Papal bull requires that Jews not associate with Christians.

1252–1284 C.E. Alfonso the Learned (or the Wise) presides over the medieval Castilian culture from Seville.

1262 C.E. Alfonso the Learned takes Cádiz.

1263 C.E. Rabbi Ben Nahman of Catalonia defends Jewish practices and laws at the royal palace in Barcelona, in a debate with Pablo Christiani, a Jewish convert to Catholicism.

1263 C.E. Moslem peasants in Valencia rebel and are expelled.

1266 C.E. Las Siete Partidas of Alfonso X denies Jews the right to hold public office and forbids Christians from accepting medical treatment from Jews, but it also encourages some humane treatment of Jews, orders respect for Jewish holidays, and forbids robbing synagogues.

1267 C.E. Pope Clement IV gives the Inquisition the freedom to pursue converted Jews.

1273 C.E. When Don Solomon Ibn Zadok of Toledo, a wealthy Jew, dies, Alfonso X seizes all his property in Seville, Carmona, and Eoja, and gives it to the Cathedral of Seville.

1284 C.E. On Alfonso the Learned's death, Sancho IV is crowned. Civil war with his brothers and nephews erupts.

1286 C.E. Rabbi Moses de León, a mystic in Guadalajara, Spain, completes the Zohar, a major text of Jewish mystical thought. A commentary on the Torah, it deals with the nature of God and the destiny of the human soul.

1290 C.E. Jews are expelled from England.

1296 C.E. Jewish population in Spain (Castile, Aragon, and Navarre) is estimated to be 150,000, the largest Jewish population in western and central Europe.

1300 C.E. Christians now control all of Spain except for Granada. Sephardic Jews are under pressure to defend Judaism in arguments with Christians.

1300s C.E. The Alhambra, a Moslem fortress, is built in Granada during the fourteenth century.

1306 C.E. Jews are expelled from France.

1309 C.E. Spanish take control of Gibraltar away from Moors.

1310–1320 C.E. *The Golden Haggadah*, the earliest illuminated Sephardic Haggadah, is believed to have been created in Barcelona.

1312 C.E. A Spanish ecclesiastical council in Zamora prohibits Jews from holding public office, building new synagogues, or associating with Christians, and requires Jews to wear distinctive clothing.

1320 C.E. King Don Pedro's Jewish treasurer, born Samuel Levi Abulafia, helps to lessen anti-Semitism in Spain.

1321 C.E. Abner of Burgos converts to Christianity and begins writing polemics against Judaism.

1325 C.E. Alfonso XI comes of age and restores effective government.

1333 C.E. Spain loses control of Gibraltar to the Moslems.

1340 C.E. Alfonso XI ends the last major Moorish invasion of Spain from North Africa.

1348 C.E. The Black Death is blamed on Jews, who are accused of poisoning the wells. Despite attempts by Pope Clement VI in Avignon, King Pedro IV of Aragon, and other European rulers to defend the Jews from mobs, many perish.

1350 C.E. Alfonso XI dies from the plague. Pedro succeeds to the throne.

1354 C.E. 12,000 Jews are executed in Toledo.

1356 C.E. First record of Jews in Gibraltar.

1378 C.E. Ferrant Martinez, archdeacon of Ecija, preaches anti-Jewish sermons in Seville, calling for destruction of synagogues and isolation of the Jews.

1391 C.E. Massacres in Spain claim the lives of 15,000 to 20,000 Jews, including many wealthy doctors, scientists, astronomers, merchants, bankers, and advisors to the courts of Spanish states.

1397 C.E. Profiat Duran, also known as Isaac ben Moses Ha-Levi, completes *Shame of the Gentiles,* a popular work defending Judaism. Duran had converted to Christianity after the persecutions of 1391, but later returned to Judaism.

1408 C.E. Castile and Aragon require Jews to live within restricted areas and to wear distinctive marks on their clothing.

1412 C.E. Fray Vicente Ferrer preaches conversion of the Spanish Jews. Valladolid laws require Jews to live only within the *aljamas,* designated quarters.

1413–1414 C.E. The Disputations of Tortosa are held. They are a series of debates between Christian and Jewish theologians.

1415 C.E. Bull of antipope Benedict XIII supports the conversion of the Jews.

1420 C.E. The birth of Tomás de Torquemada, who will become a prominent figure in the Spanish Inquisition.

1435 C.E. The death of Pablo de Santa Maria, a Converso who became Bishop of Burgos.

1435 C.E. The conversion of the Jews of Majorca.

1437 C.E. Birth of Don Isaac Abarbanel (died 1508), who became a Jewish biblical scholar, financier, royal treasurer, an advisor to King Alfonso V, and a financial advisor (fund-raiser) for Ferdinand and Isabella.

1449 c.e. A new wave of anti-Semitic sentiment in Toledo, including a tax reform focusing on Marranos. Anti-Semitic books are written, including *Limpieza de Sangre (The Blood Libel),* with the intent of keeping New Christians away from Old Christians, to maintain purity of Christian blood. Riots in Toledo and elsewhere destroy Jewish districts and lead to more conversions.

1451 c.e. The birth of Queen Isabella.

1452 c.e. The birth of Abraham Zacuto in Salamanca. He became an astronomer and mathematician.

1460 c.e. Fray Alonso de Espinas's *Fortalitium Fidel* urges conversion of the Jews.

1462 c.e. Spanish again take control of Gibraltar and force the Moslem community to leave.

1462 c.e. Anti-Converso riots in Carmona, Seville.

1467 c.e. Anti-Converso riots in Toledo.

1473 c.e. Riots in Andalucía. Persecution of the Jews in Valladolid. Marranos are massacred in Córdoba.

1474 c.e. An attack on Marranos of Segovia.

1474 c.e. Jews from Spain arrive in Gibraltar.

1474–1505 c.e. Isabella reigns as Queen of Castile.

1476 c.e. All Conversos are expelled from Gibraltar.

1478 c.e. Bull of Pope Sixtus IV establishes the Castilian Inquisition. Isabella and Ferdinand are given permission to appoint Inquisitors to investigate heretics, such as Moslems, Jews, and others who don't follow orthodox Catholicism.

1480 c.e. Castilian Cortes prohibits relations between Jews and Conversos.

1480 c.e. Courts in Toledo call for Jews to wear badges and live in their own districts.

1480–1488 c.e. In Seville, during this period 500 Jews were punished, in addition to 700 who were burned alive.

1481 c.e. The first auto da fé of the Spanish Inquisition takes place in Seville. Heretics are burned at the stake. First Edict of Grace is published in Seville, and thousands of Castilian Jews and Conversos come forward to testify.

1483 c.e. Tomás de Torquemada named Inquisitor General in Castile, charged with centralizing the Spanish Inquisition. An Inquisition tribunal established in Ciudad Real. Many New Christians complain to the Pope about their punishment and lack of freedom in their communities.

1484 c.e. Inquisition established in Valencia. Pedro de Arbues named provincial Inquisitor in Aragon.

1485 C.E. Arbues is assassinated. Conversos are implicated in the plot, causing a backlash of increased persecution of the Jews.

1486 C.E. Christopher Columbus meets with several Conversos, including Luis de Santangel, Comptroller General to Ferdinand and Isabella; Gabriel Sanchez, a treasurer of Aragon; and Abraham Zacuto, an influential astronomer and astrologer. Santangel influences the Spanish monarchs to support Columbus's explorations.

1487 C.E. Aragonese Inquisition established in Sicily.

1488 C.E. Spanish Inquisition established in Majorca.

1490 C.E. 330,000 Jews live in Spain, out of a general population of eight million.

1490–1491 C.E. The Infant of La Guardia blood libel. Six Conversos and two Jews accused, tried, convicted, and burned at the stake in Avila for allegedly murdering a Christian child for his blood. Jews of Avila request a document of protest, fearing riots as a result of the year-long trial and its outcome.

1492 C.E. War with Granada ends January 2 with the surrender of Boabdil, the last Moorish king.

1492 C.E. Ferdinand and Isabella issue the Edict of Expulsion on March 31, ordering all practicing Jews to leave Spain within four months or die. By July, there are no more Jewish communities left. This is the beginning of the Sephardic Diaspora from Spain, in which Jews will relocate throughout the world.

1492 C.E. Thousands of Conversos in Spain are interrogated, of whom thousands are punished, burned at the stake, and their property is confiscated by the Spanish Court. The monarchs use this money to wage wars and fund their explorations.

1492 C.E. Christopher Columbus sets sail August 3. On board is Luis de Torres, a Marrano of Jewish birth, who serves as an interpreter. He becomes the first European to set foot in the New World.

1493 C.E. Pope Alexander VI issues a Papal Bull on May 3, stating that all lands discovered or to be discovered and conquered by Columbus belong to Ferdinand and Isabella of Spain and to their successors to the throne.

1493 C.E. Columbus and his interpreter, Luis de Torres, find Hispaniola, now called Haiti and the Dominican Republic.

1494 C.E. Treaty of Tordesillas establishes territories to be claimed by Spain and Portugal.

1495 C.E. Isabella appoints Cardinal Francisco Ximenez de Cisneros, a pious learned Franciscan, to be chancellor and to oversee reforms. She encourages the establishment of printing presses in Spain.

1499 C.E. Expulsion of the Jews from Navarre.

16th cent. C.E. Jews migrate to Chile, Peru, and Argentina (Rio de la Plata, north of Buenos Aires).

1500 C.E. Thousands of New Christians are accused of practicing Jewish customs and being witches. Fewer than 100 cases result in executions.

1503 C.E. Christopher Columbus lands in Jamaica.

1507 C.E. Cardinal Ximenes de Cisneros appointed Inquisitor General.

1510 C.E. Catholic Church does not like the large numbers of New Christians migrating to Cuba. The bishops in Puerto Rico want the New Christians there to be removed.

1513 C.E. The Inquisition is established in Navarre.

1514 C.E. Jews from Spain settling in India.

1519 C.E. Hernán Cortés lands in the Yucatán.

1520–1521 C.E. Revolt of the Comuneros (*Guerra de la Comunidades)* in Castile involves many Conversos.

1528 C.E. Execution of first two men accused of Judaizing in New Spain (Mexico).

1530 C.E. Jews from Spain and Portugal make their first settlement in Jamaica. They come as Conversos.

1534 C.E. Garcia de Orta goes to India, where he writes *Coloquios dos Simples e Drogas he Cousas Medicinais da India,* an exhaustive study of oriental flora important to western medicine.

1541 C.E. Jews are expelled from Naples, which is under Spanish rule.

1550 C.E. Philip II of Spain tries to make the Netherlands a Spanish province and bring the Inquisition there.

1565 C.E. Spanish colonization of the Philippines begins.

1568 C.E. Jews in India, originally from Spain, build a synagogue in Cochin.

1568–1648 C.E. The Eighty Years War, resulting in Dutch independence from Spain.

1570 C.E. The Inquisition is established in Lima, Peru; Peru at this time includes what are now called Ecuador and Bolivia.

1571 C.E. The Inquisition is established in New Spain (Mexico). Many autos da fé take place in the plazas of Mexico City.

1572–1778 C.E. Twenty-six Judaizers tried in Nicaragua and Guatemala.

1574 C.E. Mexico's Inquisition of Nuevos Cristos begins.

1580 C.E. Spain's Philip II adds Portugal's empire to Spain's.

1580 C.E. Manila, in the Philippines, holds its first auto da fé.

1583 C.E. Fray Rodrigo de Yepes writes *Historia de la muerte y glorioso martirio del Sancto Innocente, que llaman de La Guardia,* the story of the "Holy Child of La Guardia." During the 17th century it will serve as the basis for a popular play by Lope de Vega, *El Nino Inocente de la Guardia,* and in the 18th century the story will be adapted by José de Canizares under the title *La Viva Imagen de Cristo.*

1588 C.E. The small synagogue in Córdoba, on Jews Street, is used as a shoemakers' church for an annual Mass.

1589 C.E. Luis de Carvajal y de la Cueva is arrested in March in Mexico.

1590 C.E. After months of imprisonment, Luis de Carvajal of Mexico ("El Mozo") becomes the spiritual leader of the Carvajal family. A posthumous punishment is imposed on Don Francisco, whose remains are exhumed and publicly burned.

1596 C.E. The Inquisition still functioning in Peru.

1601 C.E. Most Nuevos Cristos in the Inquisition of Mexico are removed by being either imprisoned, deported, or killed.

1603 C.E. In the Rio de la Plata region of Argentina, 25 Portuguese New Christians are expelled from Buenos Aires as a part of the Lima Inquisition.

1604 C.E. Papal pardon for Judaizing activity in Iberia is briefly in effect.

1610 C.E. An Inquisition in Cartagena, Colombia, accuses Nuevos Cristos of being witches.

1619 C.E. The Tribunal of the Inquisition is not allowed in Buenos Aires, because the Jews living there have made major contributions to Argentina's economy.

1639 C.E. Eighty-four accused Marranos die in autos da fé in Peru. In Rio de la Plata, Argentina, Francisco Maldanad da Silva is tried as a Judaizer.

1640 C.E. Portugal separates from Spain.

1640 C.E. Three Judaizers burned in Manila, the Philippines.

1648 C.E. The Netherlands take back control of their country, separating from Spanish rule.

1649 C.E. In Mexico, Antonio Vaez is executed, accused of having Passover Seders in his home.

1650 C.E. Most Nuevos Cristos in Mexico are not in Mexico City, but in smaller towns.

1655 C.E. English rule begins in Jamaica, allowing Conversos originally from Spain and Portugal to once again practice Judaism.

1664 C.E. Isaac Nunes Belmonte is Agent General for the King of Spain in the Netherlands.

1665 C.E. There is a marked change in the Inquisition's attitude towards Jews, resulting in less severe punishment inflicted on Jewish heretics.

1679 C.E. A violent persecution of Majorcan *Chuetas*. "*Chuetas*" is a Majorcan term for Marranos.

1680 C.E. The peak of Spanish Inquisition of Portuguese Jews.

1690 C.E. Joseph Tesuran Lobo is Spanish Consul to New Zealand.

1692–1776 C.E. Franciscan priests in New Mexico. Many of them were born in the Iberian Peninsula, and more than half of them are referred to as *"criollos"* because they were born in the New World.

1722–1725 C.E. Last major wave of Inquisition trials against Judaizers in Spain.

1730 C.E. Many persecutions, including autos da fé, take place in Madrid, Mallorca, Granada, and Seville.

1740 C.E. Joseph Manuel de Acosta is the Spanish consul to New Zealand.

1756 C.E. A grand auto da fé takes place in Toledo.

1782–1788 C.E. Discriminatory laws against the Majorcan *Chuetas* are eliminated.

1788 C.E. The last Crypto Jew, a Nuevo Cristo, is imprisoned for circumcising his son.

1808 C.E. The Inquisition is temporarily suppressed by the occupation of Spain by Napoleon of France.

1812 C.E. The Spanish Cortes suppresses the Inquisition in Spain and her colonies.

1814 C.E. Spanish King Fernando VII reestablishes the tribunals.

1819 C.E. Spain cedes the Floridas to the United States on February 22.

1820 C.E. Spanish Inquisition permanently suppressed. At this time, all of South America (except for Brazil), all of Central America, Mexico, and some Caribbean islands belong to Spain.

1821 C.E. Mexico wins independence from Spain. The Mexican Inquisition is abolished.

1834 C.E. The Spanish Inquisition is finally abolished.

1865 C.E. Isabel II of Spain abolishes purity of blood as a requirement for holding state positions.

1866 C.E. Spain abolishes all legal distinctions between Old and New Christians.

1869 C.E. Non-Catholics are given rights of residence and freedom to practice religion.

1880s C.E. Ashkenazim (Jews from middle Europe) settle in Spanish territories of South and Central America.

1924 C.E. King Alfonso, Dictador General Primo de Rivera, issues a decree that recognizes Sephardic Jews as Spanish citizens.

1940 C.E. The Arias Montano Institute for Sephardic Research is established in Madrid.

1964 C.E. General Franco signs an order establishing a Sephardic center and a Jewish Museum in Toledo.

1965 C.E. A bronze statue of Maimonides is placed in the plaza opposite the synagogue on the Street of the Jews in Córdoba.

1966 C.E. Spanish law guarantees religious freedom.

1968 C.E. The dedication of the first modern public synagogue in Madrid.

1968 C.E. The Edict of Expulsion is revoked.

1985 C.E. A mezuzah is placed with the bronze statue of Maimonides in Córdoba.

1992 C.E. 500 years after the Edict of Expulsion, when the Jewish community was expelled from Spain, King Carlos celebrates Sephardic culture and apologizes for the Spanish Inquisition.

1996 C.E. In Barcelona, the two-room Sinagoga Mayor, thought to be one of the oldest synagogues in Europe, is excavated.

Portugal

800 B.C.E.	Phoenicians begin trading along Portuguese coasts.
700 B.C.E.	Celts settle in Portugal, followed by Greeks.
600 B.C.E.	According to legends, Jews settle in the Iberian Peninsula, although they may have settled there as early as 900 B.C.E.
6th cent. B.C.E.	Phoenician colonies established in the Iberian Peninsula.
circa 5 C.E.	Lusitania, a Roman province in the Iberian Peninsula founded by Augustus, includes all of modern central Portugal as well as much of western Spain.
2nd cent. C.E.	Christianity is introduced. Pagan worship is still active in Lusitania.
306–337 C.E.	Persecution of Christians by Romans mostly ceases under the rule of Constantine, who becomes the first Christian emperor of Rome. Pagan beliefs are still tolerated.
612–620 C.E.	Visigoth invasion of the Iberian Peninsula. St. Isidore of Seville writes Sisebut's law decreeing the baptism of all Jews, leading to 90,000 conversions.
circa 672 C.E.	Collapse of the Visigothic state. Wamba is elected king on the death of Recceswinth. Ervigious succeeds Wamba. With help from Julian, the Metropolitan of Toledo (a converted Jew), Ervigius issues oppressive measures against the Jews.
687 C.E.	Egica comes to the throne.
710 C.E.	Rodrigo, the last of the Visigothic kings, ascends to the throne.
1095 C.E.	The country of Portucale (Portugal) is established.
12th cent. C.E.	Kingdom of Portugal formed.
1109 C.E.	Invasion of the Moors.
1109–1185 C.E.	Life of Afonso I, son of Henry of Burgundy. Afonso rules Portugal for almost 60 years.
1139 C.E.	Afonso defeats the Moors in the Battle of Ourique.
1143 C.E.	Dom Afonso Enriques founds the Kingdom of Portugal with the Treaty of Zamora, becoming its first king and the forebear of one of the main royal houses of Europe.
1147 C.E.	Afonso places his lands under Papal protection and secures Castilian recognition of his title. Afonso takes Lisbon from the Moors.
1143–1179 C.E.	Afonso extends his boundaries against both the Spanish Christians and the Moslem Moors.
1179 C.E.	Pope Alexander III addresses Afonso as king for the first time.
1223–1247 C.E.	During the reign of Sancho II, he gives Jews high public offices, causing resentment toward them from the lower- and middle-class Christians.

1247 c.e. Sancho II is deposed and succeeded by his brother, Afonso III.

1249 c.e. The last city in the Algarve is conquered by Afonso II, and Portugal attains its present shape.

1279–1325 c.e. King Dinis orders that all official documents be written in Portuguese, not Latin. He establishes the Jewish quarter of Santarém in Portugal.

1297 c.e. The line between Portugal and Castile in Spain is established. A synagogue is built of stone in the Tras-os-Montes region of northern Portugal.

1325–1357 c.e. During the reign of Afonso IV, Jews are forced to wear distinctive emblems.

1350 c.e. Castelo de Vide, Portugal, contains a Jewish quarter. Its synagogue is later restored as the castle Fonte da Vila.

1357–1367 c.e. During the reign of Pedro I, the gates to Jewish areas are closed at night to limit the Jews' movement. Pedro orders the execution of two of his servants because they robbed and killed a Jewish person.

1367–1382 c.e. The reign of King Fernando I of Portugal. Conflicts with Castile, Spain. War follows his death in 1382.

1373 c.e. British–Portuguese alliance.

1385 c.e. Portuguese victory against Castile.

1385–1432 c.e. During the reign of King Joao, decrees are again passed requiring Jews to wear special clothes with a distinctive emblem, and to obey curfews at night.

1394–1460 c.e. The life of Prince Henry the Navigator, an important maritime explorer, who helped establish the Portuguese colonial empire.

15th cent. c.e. Jews in the Azores are forced to convert to Christianity.

1415 c.e. Conquest of Cueta from the Moors, marking the beginning of Portuguese expansion.

1415–1427 c.e. Prince Henry the Navigator begins the series of sea explorations to Africa, Madeira, and the Azores.

1419 c.e. Portuguese discover Madeira, an island off the coast of Spain.

1427 c.e. Portuguese discover the Azores, islands 1,000 miles from Portugal.

1433–1438 c.e. During the reign of Dom Duarte, laws are introduced which prevent Jews from employing Christians.

1433–1481 c.e. Guedelha Negro, a rabbi, is astrologer and physician to King Duarte from 1433–1438 and to King Afonso V, from 1446–1481.

1446 c.e.   The Afonsine Ordinances, a set of rules dictating the behavior of Portuguese Jews. Jews must live in special districts called *Juderias*. Jews have their own courts and their own judges, but must obey Portuguese laws. They must wear special items of clothing. Social contact with Christians is forbidden. Jews may not visit the house of an unmarried woman. In response to these restrictions, many Jews become New Christians.

1449 c.e.   Many Jews are killed during riots in Lisbon.

1450 c.e.   Isaac Abravenael, a respected doctor and philosopher and a principal merchant during the second half of the 15th century, makes a loan to King Afonso V.

Circa 1450 c.e.   José Sapateiro, a Jew, goes on a voyage to the East and brings back news of the mythical kingdom of Prestes.

1450–1500 c.e.   The Church in Portugal opposes major persecution of Jews, but tries to influence Jews to convert to Christianity.

late 15th cent. c.e.   Jews move to the Azores.

1471 c.e.   Portuguese sail across the equator, using the Southern Cross for orientation.

1487 c.e.   Samuel Porteiria Gacon publishes the Five Books of Moses (the Pentateuch). It is the first book printed in Portugal using movable type.

1488 c.e.   Joao refuses to back Columbus. As a result Columbus goes to Castile, Spain, and receives backing from Ferdinand and Isabella.

1488 c.e.   Bartolomeu Dias rounds the Cape of Good Hope.

1489–1492 c.e.   Eliezer Toledano works in Lisbon. He publishes eight works in Hebrew.

1492 c.e.   Jews expelled from Spain ask for permission to enter Portugal. King Joao urges at a council at Cintra that Jews from Spain be temporarily admitted to Portugal, but that they pay a toll and entry fee. Some Jews are allowed to stay in Portugal, in exchange for a fee. Others are required to leave on Portuguese ships, and must pay for their passage. Some Jews are given important scientific and economic positions. Others are sold as slaves.

1493 c.e.   Christopher Columbus, returning from the West Indies, sails into the Tagus River in March, on his way to Spain.

1494 c.e.   The Treaty of Tordesillas divides the New World into two areas. Most of the New World is given to Spain, while territories in Africa and India are given to Portugal.

1495–1521 c.e.   The reign of King Manuel I, during which Portugal finds the sea route to India and discovers Brazil.

1496 c.e. King Manuel of Portugal signs a marriage contract with Isabella, daughter of Ferdinand and Isabella of Spain. He agrees to a clause that there will be no Jewish blood in Portugal. He submits to pressure from Spain and orders the expulsion of the Jews and Moors from Portugal, unless they convert to Christianity. About 20,000 Jews convert and are promised protection. Jews who choose to leave must embark from Lisbon. On December 25, 1496, Manuel orders all unbaptized Jews to leave within ten months.

1497 c.e. Vasco da Gama makes an epic voyage to India, using the solar declination tables of Abraham Zacuto, a Jew who was converted forcibly to Christianity.

1497 c.e. Manuel I decrees that all Jewish children under the age of 14 be taken from their parents, baptized, and educated in the Christian faith.

1498 c.e. Isabella, Manuel's wife, dies in childbirth.

1500 c.e. Pedro Alvarez Cabral discovers Brazil for the Portuguese.

1500 c.e. By the end of the 15th century, much of the individual wealth in Portugal is in the Jewish or New Christian community. One of the largest Jewish quarters in Portugal at this time is Evora.

16th cent. c.e. The Sephardic migration from Portugal to India.

16th cent. c.e. During the century approximately fifty autos da fé are held in Portugal.

1501 c.e. Portuguese explore the coast of North America and discover Newfoundland and Greenland.

1501–1568 c.e. The life of Garcia de Orta, a New Christian physician and naturalist born in Lisbon.

1502 c.e. New Christians are allowed to market wood from Brazil in Portugal.

1502–1663 c.e. Portuguese rule Cochin in India. Jews are persecuted there.

1502–1578 c.e. The life of Pedro Nunes, a mathematician and cosmographer, who teaches navigators how to follow the sea route to India.

1503 c.e. Expeditions by Amerigo Vespucci, under the patronage of King Manuel I, confirm Brazil as part of the South American continent.

1505 c.e. Riots against Nuevos Cristos.

1506–1534 c.e. Riots against Jews cause about 2,000 Nuevos Cristos to be killed.

1506–1534 c.e. Portugal establishes stockable trading posts (factories), trading with indigenous people in Brazil for exotic birds and animals, and for help in harvesting Brazilian wood, which is in demand in Europe.

1510 c.e. Portuguese conquer Goa in India.

1510–1569 c.e. The life of Gracia Nasi, a New Christian born in Portugal and christened Beatriz de Luna. While living in Holland, Venice, and Constantinople, she helps Portuguese Crypto Jews and fights against the Inquisition.

1515 C.E. Signs are posted in Lisbon in an effort to turn the population against the Jewish residents.

1519 C.E. Ferdinand Magellan sets off on the first voyage around the world. He is killed in the Philippines in 1521, and the voyage is completed in 1522 by Juan Sebastian del Cano.

1521 C.E. King Manuel I dies.

1521–1557 C.E. The reign of King João III. He attempts to establish the Inquisition in Portugal from 1521 to 1533.

1529–1531 C.E. French privateers and adventurers raid Portuguese ships and conduct trading while anchored off shore.

1531 C.E. King João III asks Pope Clement VII to issue a bull establishing the Inquisition perpetually in Portugal.

1531 C.E. A massive earthquake in Portugal is blamed on the acceptance of the Nuevos Cristos heretics.

1533–1535 C.E. King João III tries to free the Portuguese Inquisition from Papal interference.

1534–1540 C.E. The Portuguese Crown establishes 14 captaincies, land grants given to Portuguese nobles and courtiers in the New World, to establish colonial settlements to grow and process sugar.

1535 C.E. Solomon ben Moses Alkabetz (c. 1505–1576) arrives in Safed, where he writes mystical poetry, including "Lekhah Dodi" ("Come, My Beloved"), which gains immediate popularity and is integrated into the Kabbalah Shabbat (Friday evening) service.

1535–1539 C.E. King João III and the Pope dispute over the appointments of the Chief Inquisitor.

1536 C.E. New Christian José Vizinho, a doctor and astrologer to King João, translates his work into Latin.

1536 C.E. Pope Paul III gives his approval for the Portuguese Inquisition, and the Vatican issues proclamations for the Inquisition to begin in Portugal, through the offices of Holy Roman Emperor Charles V.

1539–1542 C.E. Conflict between the Portuguese Crown and the Pope concerning the Inquisition becomes more acrimonious. Portugal breaks ties with Rome.

1540 C.E. The first auto da fé occurs in Lisbon.

1541 C.E. Inquisition functions in six Portuguese cities: Oporto, Coimbra, Lamego, Tomar, Evora, and Lisbon.

1542–1543 C.E. King João III and the Pope continue to disagree on policy.

1543 C.E. Oporto's only auto da fé happens in February.

1543 C.E. Portuguese arrive in Japan, the first Westerners to experience Japanese culture.

1543–1544 C.E. The Pope intervenes in the Inquisition, calling it excessive.

1544–1547 C.E. Rome and Portugal renew relations.

1547 C.E. The Oporto Inquisition is suppressed.

1547 C.E. A Papal bull recognizes an independent Portuguese Inquisition. An Inquisition is established without restrictions.

1548–1550 C.E. Many Portuguese Judaizers are sent to Brazil.

1549 C.E. Portugal establishes a group of Judaizers and Franciscans, who, in the name of the Church, investigate the New Christians.

1550 C.E. São Paulo has the largest Jewish settlement in Brazil. Jews also live in Cananeia (named after the region of Canaan).

1553 C.E. Abraham Usque, a Marrano printer, publishes the Ferrara Bible, a Spanish translation from the Hebrew.

1555 C.E. The Portuguese control the Rajah of Cochin.

1557 C.E. Portugal receives Macao as compensation for clearing the China Sea of pirates.

1560 C.E. Inquisitions are set up in Goa, India.

1570 C.E. Brazil introduces laws against Nuevos Cristos.

1578 C.E. Many Portuguese noblemen travel to Morocco.

1579 C.E. The Bishop of Salvador grants Inquisitional investigations in Bahia, Brazil.

1580–1640 C.E. The crowns of Spain and Portugal are united under Kings Felipe II, III, and IV of Spain.

1591–1595 C.E. The Bishop of Salvador grants Inquisitional investigations in Pernambuco, Brazil.

1598–1621 C.E. New Christians in Portugal offer sums of 170,000 cruzados for permission to leave Portugal with all their goods and the dismissal of all charges against them. The government accepts the offer for those who can afford to pay the funds.

1599 C.E. The Bishop of Salvador grants Inquisitional investigations in Olinda, Brazil.

1600 C.E. Many of the sugar mills and plantations of Brazil are managed or owned by Nuevos Cristos.

1600–1650 C.E. Seventeen Judaizers are accused in Brazil and sent to Lisbon for trial.

1601 C.E. Portuguese discover Australia, according to some historians.

1604–1657 C.E. The life of Rabbi Manasseh ben Israel. Born in Madeira and christened Manoel Dias Soeiro, he lives part of his life in the Netherlands before settling temporarily in Brazil. He publishes many works on theology, grammar, philosophy, medicine, and economics.

1604 c.e. Portuguese Crypto Jews disperse throughout Hispanic world.

1610 c.e. Inquisitions established in Colombia and in Salvador, Brazil.

1613–1685 c.e. The life of Antonio Serrao de Castro, a New Christian pharmacist and writer. He is tried in 1672 before the Inquisition's Court of the Holy Office, and is forced to wear a penitential habit. He dies penniless.

1624 c.e. The Dutch seize Bahia, the capital of Brazil, in May.

1625 c.e. Portugal takes Bahia back from the Dutch.

1626 c.e. Inquisitions are established in Angola.

1628 c.e. Philip IV grants Portuguese Converso merchants the right to trade freely.

1630 c.e. Dutch West Indies Company begins the conquest of Brazil, led by John Maurice of Nassau. They overrun almost all of Brazil north of the São Francisco River. At this time approximately 1,000 Jews live in Recife, Pernambuco.

1631 c.e. Jews in Madeira accused of being false Christians are taken back to Coimbra to face the Inquisition.

1637 c.e. The Dutch capture Recife from the Portuguese.

1640 c.e. Portugal begins to establish independence from Spain.

1640 c.e. Approximately 5,000 Jews live in the Dutch colony of Pernambuco, Brazil. Jews control over 50 percent of the sugar industry there.

1642 c.e. Isaac Aboab da Fonseca (1605–1693) from Amsterdam is appointed Rabbi of the community of Recife. He is the first rabbi in the Western Hemisphere.

1642 c.e. Portugal takes money from Nuevo Cristo merchants in Brazil and Portugal.

1644 c.e. The Jews of Recife are offered amnesty by Portugal if they will not side with the Dutch. They side with the Dutch.

1645 c.e. Portugal begins to regain control over Recife.

1646 c.e. An Inquisition is held in Bahia for 118 people. It reveals that many do not eat pork, do not work on Saturday, meet secretly to perform ceremonies, and do not respect Christian images. Many are accused of having other names than their Christian names.

1647 c.e. The Brazilian Trading Company upholds its Nuevos Cristos' right to keep their money.

1650 c.e. Rabbi Manasseh ben Israel is instrumental in persuading Oliver Cromwell to allow Jews to come to England to live.

1650–1700 c.e. Nine Judaizers accused in Brazil are sent to trial in Portugal.

1654 c.e. Brazilian "New Holland" retaken by the Portuguese. Jews must leave.

1654 C.E. One of the ships leaving Brazil with Jews is captured by pirates and the passengers are left to die. The passengers are rescued and brought to New Amsterdam, a colony in America. Of them, 23 are Jews, who form the first Jewish community in North America.

1662 C.E. The Sephardic synagogue in Cochin is destroyed by the Portuguese.

1664 C.E. In a bloodless coup by the English, New Amsterdam becomes the colony of New York.

1665 C.E. There is a marked change in the Inquisition's attitude towards Jews, with a decrease in the severity of punishments for Jewish heretics.

1668 C.E. Spanish acknowledges that it no longer dominates Portugal, in the Treaty of Lisbon.

1680s C.E. The peak of the Inquisition's persecution of Portuguese Jews.

1691–1760 C.E. The life of Jacob Castro Sarmiento, a doctor, who was baptized with the name Henrique de Castro Sarmento. In 1721 he leaves Portugal and lives in London, taking his Jewish name, Jacob. His work is recognized at the Royal College of Medicine, and he is the author of important texts on the natural sciences.

1693 C.E. Catherine of Braganza, wife of King Charles II, returns to Portugal from England, with a retinue of 100 and a large supply of English furniture.

1695 C.E. Gold is discovered in Minas Gerais, Brazil. Over the next 75 years, native-born Brazilians as well as an estimated 600,000 people from Portugal and the Atlantic islands migrate to Minas Gerais.

18th cent. C.E. Portugal expands her colonies in Africa, Angola, and Mozambique.

1703 C.E. The Treaty of Methuen is signed between England and Portugal, allowing English commerce to become a dominant force in Portuguese life. The English set up a factory in Lisbon, while English wine merchants establish themselves in Nova Gaia, in Northern Portugal.

1705–1739 C.E. The life of Nuevo Cristo Antonio José da Silva, born to a wealthy colonial family in Rio de Janeiro, Brazil. He is one of the great Portuguese playwrights of the 18th century. He is imprisoned for his works and is condemned to die at the stake in an auto da fé in Lisbon.

1706–1750 C.E. The reign of King João V, the beneficiary of most of Brazil's gold. He uses his wealth to build the palace at Marfa, Portugal. He prohibits furniture imports from Portugal to Brazil.

1707–1713 C.E. The last major wave of Inquisition trials against Judaizers in Brazil.

1733 C.E. Samuel Nunez Riviero comes from Lisbon to Savannah, Georgia.

1739 C.E. The last public auto da fé takes place.

1740 C.E. The city of Vila Rica (now called Ouro Preto), in Minas Gerais, Brazil, is a significant town of 20,000.

1750–1777 c.e. The reign of King José I, son of João V. During his reign laws prohibiting furniture imports to Brazil and back lapse, replaced by laws prohibiting goldsmiths and oil painting other than for churches.

1752 c.e. Aaron Lopez arrives in Rhode Island from Lisbon.

1755 c.e. A severe earthquake destroys most of Lisbon.

1755 c.e. The Marquis of Pombal is made Prime Minister. Thanks to his enlightened policies, activities of the Inquisition in Portugal are suspended. He also instigates economic and social reforms to modernize the economy and right the balance of trade with England.

1760–1790 c.e. Coffee is a newly emerging cash crop, grown primarily on large plantations in the area known as the Paraiba Valley, Brazil.

1763 c.e. Rio de Janeiro, connected to Minas Gerais by the Royal Road in the early 18th century, replaces Salvador as the capital of Brazil, with a population of 30,000.

1773 c.e. King José I removes laws discriminating against Marranos or New Christians. In May, the Marquis de Pombal abolishes all legal differences between Old and New Christians.

1777 c.e. King José I dies and is replaced by Queen Maria I, with Pedro III as her consort.

1778 c.e. Neo-classicism replaces rococo style in Portugal.

1780 c.e. Jews accused of being false Christians in Madeira are tried by the Inquisition in Coimbra.

1780–1800 c.e. Descendants of Jews who fled from the Inquisition to Gibraltar and North Africa are invited back to Faro in the Algarve, to settle and to help the Portuguese economy revive. Approximately 60 families return.

19th cent. c.e. Jews from the Azores move to Bermuda and Hawaii, because of droughts.

1804 c.e. Jewish resettlement of Portugal begins. First Jewish tombstones appear in Lisbon cemetery.

1808 c.e. Anglo-Portuguese troops under Wellington defeat the French at Roica and Vimieiro.

1808 c.e. With the arrival of the Portuguese royal court in Rio de Janeiro, neo-classicism is adopted as the fashionable style in Brazil, with Sheraton, Adam, and Hepplewhite becoming the models for furniture design in the 19th century.

1810 c.e. Jews begin to return to Lisbon.

1818 c.e. Jewish communities begin to appear in the Azores.

1820 c.e. Jews accused of being false Christians in Madeira are tried by the Inquisition in Coimbra.

1821 c.e. The Court of the Inquisition is formally terminated.

1822 c.e. Brazil declares its independence from Portugal.

1830 c.e. Jews begin to return to Portugal from the Azores.

1839 c.e. Crypto Jews from Madeira move to Bermuda.

1848 c.e. Total Jewish population in the Azores is approximately 250 people.

1849 c.e. Crypto Jews from Madeira move to Hawaii.

1858 c.e. Slavery is abolished in Portugal.

1892 c.e. Portuguese decree affirms freedom of worship.

1900 c.e. Most Crypto Jews in Brazilian communities become very invisible in their practice of Judaic traditions.

1910 c.e. King Manuel II, the last King of Portugal, is deposed. A republic is established, providing separation of church and state.

1916 c.e. Portugal enters World War I on the side of the Allies.

1917 c.e. Samuel Schwartz discovers remnants of Crypto Jews still practicing Judaism in an area of Portugal that includes Belmonte, Beira Alta, and Covilha.

1921 c.e. The Sephardic synagogue in Tomar, Portugal, is declared a national monument.

1922 c.e. Gago Coutiho and Sacadura Cabfal fly from Portugal to Rio de Janeiro, in the first flight across the South Atlantic.

1923 c.e. Samuel Schwartz purchases the Sephardic synagogue in Tomar.

1926 c.e. With the National Revolution in May, a dictatorship is established. General Oscar Carmona becomes President of the Republic and Professor Antonio de Oliveira Salazar becomes Prime Minister.

1974 c.e. The Carnation Revolution overturns the dictatorship and restores democracy. This leads to the end of the Portuguese colonial empire.

1982 c.e. The town of Guarda, Portugal, is paired with the sister city of Safed, Israel.

1986 c.e. Portugal joins the European Union.

1989 c.e. Thirty-two men from Belmonte are circumcised by a *mohel* from Lisbon.

1991 c.e. Cabrito Neto, in the Algarve, receives permission from the British Library to reprint the Gacon Pentateuch, the Five Books of Moses. One thousand copies are printed.

1993 c.e. The reprinted Pentateuch is presented in Faro on May 21 to the President of Portugal.

1993 c.e. Yom Kippur services are held in the restored Sephardic temple in Tomar, 500 years after its forced closure.

1996 C.E. Portuguese President Jorge Sampaio formally renounces the Inquisition as an "iniquitous act."

1997 C.E. Belmonte has a new synagogue.

2002 C.E. Portugal is one of the first countries to adopt the single European currency, the euro.

2006 C.E. Approximately one thousand practicing Jews live in Portugal.

2006 C.E. In December, a 16th-century synagogue is discovered, hidden behind a wall in a house being renovated in Porto, Portugal. It has been authenticated by the Portuguese Institute of Architectural Heritage.

The World

40,000 B.C.E. Modern humans living in the Iberian Peninsula.

20,000–9,000 B.C.E. Prehistoric cave art exists in the Iberian Peninsula.

1000–0 B.C.E. Babylonian and Roman dispersions of Jews from Palestine.

722 B.C.E. Earliest known presence of Jews in Babylon.

589–586 B.C.E. Babylonians conquer Jerusalem and destroy the Temple of David.

539 B.C.E. King Cyrus of Persia conquers Babylon and frees the Jewish slaves, allowing them to return to Jerusalem.

323 B.C.E. Jews are living in Greece.

285–246 B.C.E. The reign of Ptolemy II, Macedonian king of Egypt. He hires 70 Jewish scholars to translate the Torah into Greek.

240 B.C.E. Jews escape Assyrians and travel through Afghanistan and Tibet, to eventually reach Kaifeng.

161 B.C.E. The beginning of the Jewish community in Rome.

118 B.C.E. The Roman colony of Narbonne is established in transalpine Gaul. Narbonne will become an important center for the Jews in the Middle Ages.

37–4 B.C.E. The reign of Herod the Great, in Jerusalem.

4 B.C.E. to 30 C.E. The life of Jesus Christ, a Jewish teacher and prophet, believed by Christians to be the Son of God and the Messiah. He is crucified after a brief public ministry during the rule of Pontius Pilate, because his preaching alienated both Roman and Jewish authorities and he was considered a dangerous messianic pretender.

27 B.C.E. to 476 C.E. The Roman Empire, beginning with the first emperor, Augustus.

20 B.C.E. to 50 B.C.E. The life of Jewish philosopher Philo of Alexandria.

79 C.E. Roman Emperor Titus destroys the Second Temple in Jerusalem and brings back many Jews as slaves.

100 C.E. Synagogues exist in many Greek cities.

117–138 C.E. The reign of Roman Emperor Hadrian. He excludes Jews from Jerusalem and introduces a general edict prohibiting circumcision.

218 C.E. Roman legions arrive in the Iberian Peninsula for the first time.

3rd cent. C.E. Before the Christianization of the Roman Empire, Jews are not seriously persecuted.

306 C.E. The Church Synod of Elvira bans marriage, sexual intercourse, and community contacts between Christians and Jews.

312 C.E. Emperor Constantine converts to Christianity, which becomes the official religion of the Roman Empire.

313 c.e. The Pope's edict gives power to Christians in Rome to persecute Jews.

321 c.e. Jews are living in Cologne, Germany.

331–1453 c.e. Eastern Roman emperors restrict the rights of Jews.

337 c.e. Emperor Constantine creates a law making the marriage of a Jewish man to a Christian woman punishable by death.

379 c.e. By this time Jews have begun arriving in India.

388 c.e. Roman law prohibits marriage between Jews and Christians.

423 c.e. Roman law prohibits Jews from owning Christian slaves.

481 c.e. Clovis I succeeds his father, Childeric, as king of the Salian Franks, and becomes the first ruler of the Merovingian Dynasty.

493 c.e. Clovis I marries Clothilde, a Christian Burgundian princess.

496 c.e. Clovis I converts to Roman (Western) Catholic Christianity, strengthening the ties between his Roman subjects and the Germanic conquerors. By the close of the 5th century, Christianity is the official religion in Rome, and there are edicts combating the influence of heretics and Jews.

6th cent. c.e. Jews now inhabit Gaul, having accompanied the Roman Empire northward into western Europe as merchants and traders.

533 c.e. Two ecclesiastical councils in Gaul declare that there shall be no intermarriage between Christians and Jews, and any existing intermarriage "must be dissolved on pain of excommunication."

583 c.e. An edict declares the "Jews are not to enter the convent of nuns for any reason or any kind of business, or be familiar with them, whether secretly or otherwise." Jews were not to appear in public during the Easter season.

7th cent. c.e. The "Golden Age" of Jews in Sicily.

642 c.e. Moslems arrive in Iran.

711 c.e. The Moors of North Africa use Gibraltar as a stepping stone to conquer Spain.

800 c.e. Carolingian Empire is founded, with the crowning of Charlemagne as Emperor by Pope Leo III.

900–1400 c.e. The Catholic Church actively campaigns against Judaism, forcing Jews to debate publicly with friars. The intent is to induce Jewish conversions to Christianity and to wipe out remnants of Judaism.

960 c.e. Jews travel to China via the Silk Road.

962 c.e. The Holy Roman Empire is founded, with the crowning of Otto I. The Holy Roman Empire succeeds the Carolingian Empire.

12th cent. c.e. Black Jews in India, originally from Africa, claim their ancestors were part of the Lost Ten Tribes.

1163 C.E. First synagogue erected in Kaifeng.

1167 C.E. Benjamin of Tudela mentions seeing black Jews in India

1189 C.E. Jews are persecuted in England. The Crown claims all Jewish possessions and most of their houses are burned.

13th cent. C.E. Jews begin to be treated badly in Sicily, when it becomes part of Spanish Aragon.

13th cent. C.E. Marco Polo, traveling for Portugal, meets Jews in China.

13th cent. C.E. The Zohar, or the Book of Splendor, also called the Kabbalistic Bible, is written. It appears in Avila about 1300 B.C.E.

1221 C.E. The first French synagogue is built in Avignon.

1242 C.E. The Talmud is burned in Paris.

1260 C.E. When Jews in France obtain a royal patent facilitating the collection of their debts, their quarter is invaded by armed Christians. The Jews are defended by the Knights Templar.

1272 C.E. The building holding the Jewish quarter in London is confiscated by authorities.

1290 C.E. The expulsion of the Jews from England; 1,600 leave the country.

1293 C.E. Marco Polo mentions seeing black Jews in India.

1298 C.E. Jews are persecuted in Austria, Bavaria, and Franconia; 100,000 are killed.

1300 C.E. Jews move into the Italian cities of Ancona, Urbino, Perugia, Padua, Bologna, Verona, Milan, Ferrara, and Naples.

14th cent. C.E. Jews arrive in the Netherlands.

1306 C.E. Expulsion of the Jews from kingdoms of France; 100,000 exiled. Many go to Spain.

1344 C.E. The Pardesi Jews who left Cranganore place themselves under the rule of the Maharajah of Cochin and build their first synagogue.

1367 C.E. A synagogue is built in Carpentras, France.

1391 C.E. Ferrand Martinez, Archdeacon of Ecija, incites riots against the Jews throughout Spain. The massacres claim the lives of 15,000–20,000 Jews. Many of those who survive convert to Christianity, at least outwardly.

15th–19th cent. C.E. The Diaspora plays a major role in spreading Jewish values and the Jewish religion to other parts of the world.

1431 C.E. The Council of Basel, Switzerland, requires Jews to attend church and forbids them to attend university.

1453 C.E. The Ottoman Empire recaptures Constantinople from the crusaders and advances to Greece. The Ottoman Empire is more tolerant of the Jewish religion.

1453 c.e. Franciscan monk Capistrano persuades the King of Poland to terminate all civil rights of the Jews.

1474 c.e. The first Jews arrive in Gibraltar from Spain.

1475 c.e. Jewish printing presses come to Italy.

1476 c.e. All Conversos are expelled from Gibraltar.

1479 c.e. Jewish population of Gibraltar is approximately 600.

1487 c.e. Aragonese Inquisition is established in Sicily.

1488 c.e. A new Spanish Inquisition begins work in Majorca.

1488–1579 c.e. The life of Joseph Karo, who was born in Spain, moved to Turkey, and lived in Safed, Israel, where he writes the *Shulhan Arukh*, establishing the code of Rabbinic Jewish Law.

1492 c.e. Columbus sets sail, eventually to discover the New World. Some Conversos accompany him. This year there is also a Sephardic migration to India.

1492–1650 c.e. Many Nuevos Cristos leave Spain and Portugal for North Africa, the Italian communities, Holland, Turkey, England, Gibraltar, and islands in the Atlantic, including Gibraltar, the Azores, Madeira, and the Caribbean, and to the New World continents. These migrations are motivated by a desire to escape persecution, and also by economic opportunities in new lands.

1493 c.e. Jews are forced to leave Sicily and Sardinia, both under Spanish rule.

1497 c.e. Jews in Portugal (many of whom came recently from Spain) are required to convert to Christianity or face expulsion.

1499 c.e. The founding of a synagogue in Cavaillon, France.

16th cent. By the end of the 15th century, New Christians are living in England. During the 16th century, there is a Sephardic migration from Portugal to India, and many Jews go to Cuba. The Philippines are under Islamic rule, and Marranos live in Antwerp, where the practice of Judaism is restricted.

16th–20th cent. c.e. Jews in Iran suffer forced conversions and harsh treatment.

1500 c.e. Explorer Pedro Alvarez Cabral finds Brazil, accompanied by Gaspar da Gama, a Jew who was forced to convert to Christianity in 1497.

1502–1663 c.e. Portuguese rule Cochin, India; Jews are persecuted.

1504 c.e. A group of 24 Conversos led by Fernando de Noronha receives permission from King Manuel I to colonize and develop the Portuguese colonial possession in Brazil.

1504 c.e. Inquisition is established in the Canary Islands.

1510 C.E. The Spanish government tries to establish the Inquisition in all its dominions; but the local offices in the Netherlands do not cooperate, and the Inquisitors are chased out of Naples, with the approval of the Pope.

1514 C.E. More Jews arrive in India from Spain.

1516 C.E. The governor of the Republic of Venice orders Jews to live in only one area of the city. Called Ghetto Novo, this is the first ghetto in Europe.

1516–1517 C.E. The Ottoman Empire takes over Egypt, Syria, Palestine, and the Arabian Peninsula.

1517 C.E. The Protestant Reformation begins when Martin Luther posts his "95 Theses" on the church door at Wittenberg, Germany.

1521 C.E. Several New Christians accompany Hernán Cortés in his conquest of Mexico.

1523 C.E. It is decreed that only those who can prove Catholic lineage to the fourth generation may settle in Mexico.

1527 C.E. Jewish expulsion from Venice begins.

1528 C.E. The execution of the first two men accused of Judaizing in New Spain (Mexico).

1536 C.E. Spanish and Portuguese Jewish refugees are granted rights to settle in the Netherlands.

1536 C.E. After the Portuguese Inquisition is instituted, Portuguese Sephardim migrate to Bayonne, France.

1537 C.E. The Portuguese Inquisition officially established. Many New Christians go to Brazil to avoid the Inquisition or because of deportation and exile.

1539–1595 C.E. The life of Luis de Carvajal y de la Cueva, a Converso, who served as Governor of Nuevo León, Mexico. He and members of his family are accused by the Mexican Inquisition of Judaizing. He dies in prison, and family members are burned at the stake.

1540 C.E. Portuguese settle in Italy, with many in Ferrara.

1540 C.E. Conversos play an important role in the colonization of Chile. Among those Spanish officers involved in the colonization of Chile are Rodrigo de Orgonos and Diego Garcia de Caceres, both of whom are believed to have been Conversos.

1541 C.E. Under Spanish rule, Jews are expelled from Naples.

1545–1563 C.E. In a series of 25 meetings, the Council of Trent discusses the purity of the Christian faith.

1550 C.E. There are more Spanish Conversos than Spanish original Catholics living in the capital of Chile.

1550 C.E. Physician and merchant Hector Nunes, a Portuguese-born Converso living in London, tries to be accepted into English Christian society and is rejected and despised as a Jew and a foreigner.

1550 c.e. Nearly 10,000 Jews are living in Palestine.

1550–1850 c.e. Holland keeps a register of Sephardic Jewish marriages, listing 6,000 Dutch Portuguese.

1555 c.e. Pope Paul IV issues a bull requiring Jews to live in ghettos.

1555 c.e. The Portuguese control the Rajah of Cochin.

1565 c.e. The Philippines are conquered by the Spanish.

1568 c.e. Jews build a synagogue in Cochin, India.

1568–1648 c.e. The Eighty Years War, establishing Dutch independence from Spanish rule.

1570 c.e. The Lima, Peru, Inquisitional Tribunal is established. Its jurisdiction includes present-day Chile.

1570–1689 c.e. During this period 191 Jews are accused as New Christians and brought before the Lima, Peru, Tribunal.

1571 c.e. The Inquisition is established in New Spain (Mexico).

1580 c.e. Philip II of Spain adds Portugal's colonial empire to Spain's empire. Portuguese of Jewish lineage start entering Argentina. In response, an Inquisitor is placed in the region.

1589 c.e. Isabel Rodriguez de Andrada, niece of Don Luis de Carvajal, is tortured by the Inquisition. The persecution of this family and their associates over the years is partially responsible for the flight of many original colonizers of northern Mexico. They move north into what is now the American Southwest.

1593 c.e. Cornelis de Jode (the Jew), a New Christian cartographer and engraver in Antwerp, publishes an atlas, *Speculum Orbis Terrae.*

1593 c.e. Jorge and Domingo Rodriguez are brought to Mexico from the Philippines and convicted of being practicing Jews.

1595 c.e. Portuguese New Christians settle in Hamburg.

1596 c.e. Forty-five Jews are burned in an auto da fé in Mexico City.

1596–1659 c.e. Crypto Jews are involved in almost every auto da fé in Spain and Portugal.

1600 c.e. By the end of the 16th century, Safed is declining as a center of the study of mysticism.

17th cent. c.e. Jews go to Cuba. A Jewish community is founded in Copenhagen, Denmark.

17th–18th cent. c.e. Coral is a principal commodity exported from India by the English East India Company.

17th–19th cent. c.e. Jews inhabit many of the Caribbean Islands.

1602 C.E. The Dutch East India Company is chartered with major investment from Sephardic Jewish community.

1604 C.E. Portuguese Crypto Jews disperse throughout the Hispanic world.

1604–1657 C.E. The life of Manasseh ben Israel, founder of the first Hebrew printing press in Holland.

1612 C.E. City officials of Hamburg, in Germany, recognize the Sephardic community.

1618 C.E. An Edict of Faith is published in Rio de Janeiro, and many arrests are made.

1619 C.E. The Tribunal of the Inquisition is not allowed in Buenos Aires, Argentina, because the Jews living there have contributed to Argentina's economy.

1621 C.E. The Dutch West India Company is chartered with major investment from Sephardic Jewish community. It starts operations in America and Africa.

1622 C.E. King Christian IV of Denmark signs a decree promising protection to Jews who move to Copenhagen.

1624 C.E. Approximately 50,000 former Europeans live in Brazil, many of whom are New Christians. They own sugar mills and engage in business, commerce, education, writing, and even the priesthood.

1624 C.E. The Dutch capture Bahia in Brazil.

1628 C.E. Filipe IV grants Portuguese Converso merchants the right to trade freely.

1630 C.E. The Dutch capture from Portugal the northeastern region, Brazil, including Recife, Pernambuco.

1634 C.E. The Dutch establish a colony, taken from Spain, on the Caribbean island of Curaçao.

1636 C.E. A number of Nuevos Cristos are arrested in Cartagena, Colombia, in an effort to destroy the Complicidad Grande (Great Conspiracy) of Lima, Peru.

1636 C.E. Rembrandt van Rijn in Amsterdam etches a portrait of Manasseh ben Israel.

1635 C.E. Kahal Zur Israel synagogue, the first Jewish community in the New World, is established in Recife, Brazil.

1639 C.E. An auto da fé takes place in Peru on January 23.

1640 C.E. A series of autos da fé in Peru, Mexico, and Colombia interrupt the business of New Christians in the Spanish colonies.

1642–1649 C.E. The period of greatest Inquisition activity in the New World, climaxed by the auto da fé in Peru in April 1649, from which only thirteen of one hundred Jews survived.

1648 c.e. Rembrandt van Rijn, living in the Jewish section of Amsterdam, creates the drypoint etching "Jews in a Synagogue."

1650 c.e. Abraham Israel Pereyra, a Crypto Jew, returns to Judaism in Amsterdam.

1650 c.e. Jewish public worship is legal in Hamburg, Germany.

1650 c.e. Gabriel Gomez is an agent of the King of Denmark.

1651 c.e. Mikvé Israel Emanuel Synagogue is established on Curaçao.

1654 c.e. Brazilian "New Holland" retaken by the Portuguese. Jews must leave. Twenty-three end up in New Amsterdam.

1654 c.e. Nuevo Cristos, in the wake of Inquisitions and expulsions, travel to Curaçao, Suriname, Jamaica, and Barbados.

1654 c.e. Emanuel de Witte paints the interior of the Portuguese synagogue in Amsterdam.

1655 c.e. Manasseh ben Israel goes from Amsterdam to London to persuade the English government to allow Jews to return to England.

1655 c.e. Jews in Suriname receive autonomy in education, justice, and armed guards in their living area, Jodensavanne.

1656 c.e. Dr. Jacob Lumbrozo from Portugal settles into the colony of Maryland. He is the only Jew there.

1656 c.e. Peter Stuyvesant, Governor of Dutch New Amsterdam, asks the Dutch West India Company directors to remove the Jews from his domain. His request is denied.

1656–1660 c.e. Jews return to London, granted protection by Oliver Cromwell. They are allowed to conduct business, establish a cemetery, and practice their religion. Manasseh ben Israel, who asked for permission for Jews to return to England, writes *Vindication of the Jews*.

1657 c.e. Sephardic Jews from Holland establish the first synagogue in England since medieval times, on Creechurch Lane.

1657 c.e. Manasseh ben Israel dies.

1658 c.e. Jacob Cohen, who helped establish Dutch rule in Recife, Pernambuco, Brazil, is an agent at Amsterdam for Prince Maurice of Nassau.

1662 c.e. Portuguese destroy the Sephardic synagogue in Cochin.

1663–1795 c.e. Dutch rule Cochin. Jews may practice their religion and trade freely.

1664 c.e. The Cochin synagogue is rebuilt, with the help of the Dutch.

1665 c.e. The Inquisition's attitude toward Jews changes, with a decrease in the severity of punishments given to Jewish heretics.

1668 c.e. Jewish people arrive in Newport, Rhode Island.

1670 C.E. David Bueno de Mesquita conducts missions for the Sultan of Morocco on behalf of the Margrave of Brandenburg.

1674 C.E. The English take New Amsterdam away from the Dutch and change the name to New York.

1679 C.E. Violent persecution of the Majorcan Conversos, or *Chuetas*.

1680 C.E. Forty-five Jewish families living in Barbados.

1681 C.E. A new synagogue is built in Curaçao, larger than the one built in 1651.

1684 C.E. Jews form a community in Copenhagen.

1684 C.E. Miguel Osorio represents the Queen of Sweden in Holland.

1684 C.E. David Salom d'Azevedo represents the Court of Algiers in Holland.

1685 C.E. Jews are expelled from Martinique by the Jesuits.

1688 C.E. The synagogue in the Caribbean island of Nevis is rebuilt.

1688 C.E. Joseph Penso de la Vega, a former Nuevo Cristo in Amsterdam, writes *Confusion de Confusiones,* the first book to describe the operation of the stock market.

1689 C.E. New Christians escaping the Great Conspiracy leave Peru for the West Indies or North America.

1690–1700 C.E. Daniel Abensur is minister of the King of Poland in Hamburg.

1692–1776 C.E. Franciscan priests in New Mexico. Many of them were born in the Iberian Peninsula, but more than half are called *Criollos*, because the were born in the New World.

1697 C.E. Four Jewish immigrants have settled in Charleston, South Carolina.

18th cent. C.E. Jesuits write to Rome about the Jewish religious customs practiced in Kaifeng.

18th cent. C.E. There are fewer Conversos in all of Argentina than in the mining area of Potosí in what is now Bolivia or in colonial Lima. During the century, there are no accounts of Judaizing in Argentina.

18th cent. C.E. By mid-century, most of the major Jewish merchants in London come from the Portuguese community.

1701 C.E. Jews lease a lot on Bevis Marks Street in London and build a synagogue called Kahal Kodesh Sharrei Hashomayim.

1704 C.E. The British capture Gibraltar.

1713 C.E. The Treaty of Utrecht is signed.

1719 C.E. Neve Shalom synagogue constructed in Suriname.

1722–1760 C.E. Judah Monis teaches at Harvard University. He is allowed to write the first Hebrew grammar books published in America, but only after he converts to Christianity. In 1722 he writes *The Truth, the Whole Truth, and Nothing But the Truth*.

1726 C.E. Solomon de Oliveyra creates *Calendario* with three folding tables of the Jewish holidays in Amsterdam.

1727 C.E. Jews are allowed to be naturalized as citizens of the colony of New York.

1728 C.E. Diamonds are discovered in Brazil.

1729 C.E. The British sign a treaty with the Sultan of Morocco permitting the Jewish and Nuevos Cristos subjects to return to Gibraltar.

1730 C.E. Marranos living in Toulouse, Lyon, Montpellier, Nantes, and Rouen are officially recognized as Jews.

1733 C.E. Joseph Salvador, one of the funders of the Dutch East India Company, is president of the Bevis Marks synagogue in London.

1733 C.E. French engraver Bernard Picart illustrates *The Ceremonies and Religious Customs of the Various Nations of the Known World,* with portrayals of Jewish religious rites.

1733 C.E. Dr. Samuel Nunez Ribiero, from Lisbon, arrives in Savannah, Georgia.

1735 C.E. Six hundred Jews live in Jamaica.

1735 C.E. Judah Monis, the Italian Jew of Portuguese descent who converted to Christianity in order to teach at Harvard University, publishes *A Grammar of the Hebrew Tongue.*

1737 C.E. Nathan Levy, the son of Moses Levy, moves from New York to Philadelphia to help start a Jewish community.

1742 C.E. Abraham de Lyon and Isaac Nunes Henriques, originally from Lisbon, leave their plantations and ranches in Savannah, Georgia, when the Spanish threaten them from Florida.

1745–1816 C.E. The life of Gershom Mendes Seixas, minister of Congregation Shearith Israel in New York (the first Jewish congregation in the North American colonies). He becomes known as "Patriot Rabbi" for his support of the Colonies' efforts to rid themselves of British rule.

1746 C.E. Myer Myers, the American colonial silversmith and the first Jewish artist in America, resides in New York City.

1746 C.E. Joseph d'Oliviera represents the King of Portugal in Tuscany.

1749 C.E. Six hundred Jews are living in Gibraltar.

1750–1760 C.E. International trade declines in England, causing social and cultural decline in the Sephardic communities there.

1752 C.E. Aaron Lopez, a Jewish merchant from Lisbon, comes to America.

1766 C.E. Isaac Pinto writes *Prayers for Shabbath, Rosh Hashanah, and Kippur* in New York for Shearith Israel. It is the first Jewish prayer book published in America.

1768 C.E. Aaron Lopez, who was circumcised in America, having been denied the right to practice Judaism in Portugal, establishes the United Company of Spermaceti Chandlers in Newport, Rhode Island, with his father-in-law, Jacob Rodrigues Rivera and members of the Brown family of Providence.

1769 C.E. Eight out of ten Sephardic businesses in London deal in coral and diamonds from Leghorn.

1770 C.E. Five Jewish families are living in Baltimore, Maryland. Between 1790 and 1810, the number will increase to fifteen Jewish families.

1773 C.E. Jews return to England.

1774 C.E. Empress Maria Theresa expels the Jews from Prague. King George III and the British government demand that the order be rescinded.

1775 C.E. The first Jewish school in North America to combine Hebrew and secular studies is formed by Shearith Israel in New York City. It is called the Polonies.

1775–1854 C.E. The life of businessman and noted philanthropist Judah Touro, of Newport, Rhode Island.

1780 C.E. Six Jewish people are living in Richmond, Virginia, including one who was there before the American Revolution.

1781 C.E. An ordinance from the Bishop of Cavaillon, France, gives Jews permission to live outside the Jewish quarter.

1782–1788 C.E. Laws discriminating against Majorcan *Chuetas* are eliminated.

1790 C.E. George Washington writes to the Newport congregation about freedom for all religions.

1791 C.E. Jews gain citizenship and complete freedom in France in September.

1791 C.E. Benjamin Gomez, the first Jewish book dealer in America, opens his business in New York.

1795 C.E. The British take control of Cochin.

1795 C.E. David Sarzedas practices medicine in Charleston, South Carolina.

1795 C.E. Benjamin Gomez publishes *Captain Cook's Third and Last Voyage*.

1799–1822 C.E. Levi Myers serves as Apothecary General of South Carolina.

19th cent. C.E. The British government gives aid to persecuted Jews in foreign lands.

19th cent. C.E. Hebrew printing presses function in Cochin.

19th cent. C.E. Jewish population of Gibraltar is 2,000.

19th cent. C.E. Sephardic families from Baghdad, Bombay, and Cairo establish a Jewish structure in Shanghai.

1800 C.E. The Esnoga Flamenca (Flemish Synagogue) is opened in Gibraltar.

1807 c.e. Napoleon Bonaparte issues a decree in February for a Grand Sanhedrin to take place in France.

1807 c.e. Jews in Carpentras, France, lower their synagogue because by Christian law it may not be taller than the town's church.

1812 c.e. Spanish Cortes suppresses the Inquisition in Spain and the colonies.

1812–1815 c.e. The War of 1812 between the United States and Britain.

1812 c.e. Jacob de la Motta serves as an army surgeon.

1814 c.e. Spanish King Fernando VII reestablishes the Tribunals.

1819 c.e. Daniel L. M. Peixotto receives a degree from the College of Physicians and Surgeons in New York. He will become a pioneer in the field of preventive medicine.

1820 c.e. The Spanish Inquisition is permanently suppressed.

1820 c.e. All of South America (except for Brazil), all of Central America, Mexico, and some of the Caribbean Islands belong to Spain.

1821 c.e. Mexico wins independence from Spain. The Mexican Inquisition is abolished.

1821 c.e. The tiny Inquisition in Argentina is abolished.

1821–1829 c.e. Many Jews lose their lives fighting for the Turks in the Greek war with the Ottoman Empire.

1827 c.e. Uriah Levy purchases Thomas Jefferson's home and restores it.

1833 c.e. The synagogue on St. Thomas is rebuilt.

1833 c.e. The Spanish Inquisition is formally abolished.

1835 c.e. The poems of Penina Moise are published. She is the first Jewish poet to be published in America.

1841–1842 c.e. Juan Lindo, of Jewish roots, is President of El Salvador. In 1841 he founds the University of El Salvador.

1845 c.e. Rabbi Hayyim Pinto, of Portuguese descent, dies in Essaouira, Morocco.

1847–1852 c.e. Juan Lindo is President of Honduras.

1850–1900 c.e. Jewish traders from France and other countries come to the Philippine Islands.

1853 c.e. Solomon Nunes Carvalho, a daguerreotypist, accompanies General John Frémont on his fourth trip across the United States.

1866 c.e. The Kaifeng synagogue is flooded and destroyed.

1870 c.e. The unification of Italy in progress.

1880–1890 c.e. Ashkenazim (Jews from middle Europe) settle in Spanish territories of South and Central America.

1898 C.E. The United States occupies the Philippines.

1900 C.E. By the end of the 19th century, 130,000 Jews live in Brazil.

1906 C.E. The Iranian Revolution allows Jews to become equals in Iranian society.

1910–1920 C.E. Many Jews go from Turkey to Cuba when on their way to the United States, where they are denied entry.

1911 C.E. Fire damages the synagogue Shahar Hashamayim in Gibraltar.

1914 C.E. Havana, Cuba, has one Sephardic synagogue and four Ashkenazic synagogues.

1917 C.E. Samuel Schwartz discovers remnants of Crypto Jews in Belmonte, Portugal.

1918 C.E. The United States enters World War I, which ends in November.

1920–1952 C.E. The Ohel Rachel Synagogue and Jewish School in Shanghai is used by the Sephardic community there.

1922 C.E. China, as a member of the League of Nations, votes for a Jewish homeland.

1922 C.E. Britain begins to reform Iraq into a modern industrial nation.

1925 C.E. Shah Pahlavi of Iran gives Jews opportunities to become economically and socially successful.

1932 C.E. Iraq becomes an independent state.

1933–1945 C.E. Six million Jewish people and six million non-Jews perish as victims of the Third Reich and Hitler's army in Germany during World War II.

1939 C.E. At the beginning of World War II, 77,000 Jews are living in Greece.

1940–1944 C.E. During the Nazi occupation of France, many Jews are deported, mostly to death camps.

1945 C.E. By the end of World War II, 11,000 Jews are living in Greece. 43,800 have been deported from Salonika and killed at Auschwitz and Birkenau.

1948 C.E. Israel becomes a state.

1950 C.E. Thirty-seven thousand Jews emigrate to Israel.

1959 C.E. Fifteen thousand Jews live in Cuba.

1970 C.E. Most of Iraq's Jews have left for Israel or London.

1979 C.E. With the Islamic Revolution in Iran, the Ayatollah Khomeini comes to power and anti-Semitism becomes rampant.

1983 C.E. A community synagogue opens in the Philippines with a Jewish Association of 50 to 100 members.

1985 C.E. The government of Suriname helps to preserve the Neve Shalom synagogue.

1992 C.E. Israel and China establish formal relations in January. The Israel–China Friendship Society is established in March.

1992 C.E. Queen Beatrix of Holland attends a service in the historic Mikvé Israel-Emanuel synagogue on Curaçao.

1993 C.E. Tawfig Sofer is the oldest of the 35 remaining members of the last synagogue in Iraq.

1998 C.E. The Shanghai municipal government provides funds for the renovation of the Ohel Rachel and Ohel Moishe synagogues.

2002 C.E. The Israel–China Friendship Society celebrates its tenth anniversary.

2002 C.E. Kahal Zur Israel synagogue in Recife is reconstructed on the foundations of the original synagogue, and is opened to the public.

2004 C.E. The Greek government on January 27 creates a national day of remembrance for the Jewish-Greek victims of the Holocaust.

2006 C.E. Approximately 5,000 Jews live in Greece; 7,500 Jews live in Morocco; 600,000 Jews live in France; 22,000 Jews live in Turkey; 3,000 Jews live in Peru; 250,000 Jews live in Argentina; 130,000 Jews live in Brazil (most of whom arrived there at the end of the 19th century); 36,000 Jews live in Italy; and 60,000 Jews live in Germany.

Appendix B
Expeditions of Discovery, Conquest, and Colonization from Europe

All dates are in the Common Era (C.E.)

Norse Expeditions

985–986 Bjarni Herjolfsson

1003 Leif Ericsson

1005–1019 Thorvald Ericsson

Spanish and Portuguese Expeditions

1492–1503 Christopher Columbus

1501–1502 Miguel Côrte-Real

1502–1504 Christopher Columbus

1513 Juan Ponce de León

1519–1521 Hernán Cortés destroys Aztecs' Tenochtitlan.

1528–1536 Álvar Núñez Cabeza de Vaca

1539–1540 Francisco de Ulloa

1539–1543 García López de Cárdenas

1542–1543 Juan Rodríguez Cabrillo

1591 Jesuits found first mission in northwestern New Spain.

1598 Juan de Onate helps to establish several hundred colonists in New Mexico.

1602–1603 Sebastián Vizcaíno

1610 Santa Fe founded as the capital of Spanish New Mexico.

1680 Pueblo Indians drive Spaniards from New Mexico into what today is El Paso, Texas.

1690 The first Franciscan ministry to the Caddo Indians of East Texas is unsuccessful.

1691 Jesuit Eusebio Francisco Kino enters what is today southern Arizona.

1692 Spanish colonists under Diego José de Vargas reclaim New Mexico.

1720 Pedro de Villasur's expedition from Santa Fe, New Mexico, is ruined by Plains Indians from eastern Nebraska.

1753 By the Treaty of Paris, France cedes to Spain control over Louisiana west of the Mississippi.

1769 Franciscan friar Junípero Serra establishes San Diego de Alcala mission in present-day California.

1795 By the Nookta Convention, Spain confirms Britain's northwestern trading rights in America.

English Expeditions

1497 John Cabot

1579 Francis Drake sails into Pacific near San Francisco.

1585–1589 John Davis

1610–1611 Henry Hudson

1768–1779 The voyages of James Cook, who sails along the Alaskan coast in search of a northwest passage. He also explores Australia and the Pacific islands, including Hawaii, where he dies.

1783 At the conclusion of the American Revolution and independence from England, the United States extends its territory to the Mississippi River.

French Expeditions

1524 Giovanni da Verrazano

1535–1536 Jacques Cartier

1604–1607 Samuel de Champlain

1608 European settlement and beginning of foundations in America

Russian Expeditions

1799 Alexander Baranov of the Russian-American Company builds a trading post at New Archangel, now Sitka, Alaska.

Appendix C
Literary Comments on the Jewish Plight During the Period of the Inquisition Throughout the World

Even though Jewish people constituted less than one percent of the population in the world, the treatment of them by the Spanish and Portuguese during the time of the Inquisition was often the subject of literary comment by others.

In Nuremburg, Germany, the horrors of the Inquisition's treatment of Jews was described in a publication called *Nuremburg Chronicles*.

The Swedish King wrote a letter to Sephardic Jews who were expelled from Spain, inviting them to come and live in Sweden.

In England, William Shakespeare's *The Merchant of Venice* indirectly concerns the Inquisition's punishment of Jews in its focus on anti-Semitism at the time. The question has often been asked about Shakespeare's feelings in the play: was he sympathetic to the Jews, or was he merely mocking Jews and their traditions and behavior?

The history of the period has been written about by Jews, such as Israeli Prime Minister Benjamin Netanyahu, who wrote *The Origins of the Inquisition in Fifteenth-Century Spain*; and by others, such as Brian Pullan, who wrote *The Jews of Europe and the Inquisition of Venice: 1550–1670*. These are only two examples of thousands of book written on the subject. The subject has been explored in letters, plays, poems, treatises, fiction, and nonfiction, as in *The Mezuzah in the Madonna's Foot: Marranos and Other Secret Jews—A Woman Discovers Her Spiritual Heritage*, by Trudi Alexy.

Other times, simple lists were compiled, such as those of autos da fé in a country, or lists of successful Jews who converted to Christianity but who practiced Judaism secretly at home.

Also, histories such as *Diamonds and Coral*, by Gedalia Yogev, discuss the Marranos' importance as merchants for England, Portugal, and Italy; and *Gente da Nação* (Jews of the Nation), by José Antonio Gonsalves de Mello, who is from a Marrano family himself, is about the Portuguese and Dutch Jews of Brazil.

By Permission of the Honble *ROBERT DINWIDDIE*, Esq; His Majesty's Lieutenant-Governor, and Commander in Chief of the Colony and Dominion of *Virginia*.

By a Company of COMEDIANS, *from* LONDON, At the THEATRE *in* WILLIAMSBURG, On *Friday* next, being the 15th of *September*, will be presented, A PLAY, call'd,

THE
MERCHANT of VENICE.
(Written by *Shakespear*.)

The Part of *ANTONIO* (the MERCHANT) to be perform'd by Mr. CLARKSON.

GRATIANO, by Mr. SINGLETON, *Lorenzo*, (with Songs in Character) by Mr. ADCOCK. The Part of *BASSANIO* to be perform'd by Mr. RIGBY.

Duke, by Mr. Wynell. *Salanio*, by Mr. Herbert. good name The Part of *LAUNCELOT*, by Mr. HALLAM. And the Part of *SHYLOCK*, (the Jew) to be perform'd by Mr. MALONE.

The Part of *NERISSA*, by Mrs. ADCOCK, *Jessica*, by Mrs. Rigby. And the Part of *PORTIA*, to be perform'd by Mrs. HALLAM.

With a new occasional PROLOGUE. To which will be added, a FARCE, call'd,

The ANATOMIST:
OR,
SHAM DOCTOR.

The Part of *Monsieur le Medecin*, by Mr. RIGBY. And the Part of *BEATRICE*, by Mrs. ADCOCK.

** No Person, whatsoever, to be admitted behind the Scenes. BOXES, 7s. 6d. PIT and BALCONIES, 5s. 9d. GALLERY, 3s. 9d. To begin at Six o'Clock.

Vivat Rex.

MERCHANT OF VENICE. The Merchant of Venice, *by William Shakespeare, depicts a Jewish merchant who becomes a moneylender, a job many Jews were forced to do during the Inquisition period in Spain. The play was presented in America in Williamsburg, Virginia, and was so popular it went on to be played in other colonial cities as well.*

However presented, there has always been a rich amount of literature available to be read about the history of the Inquisition. For a detailed list of further reading, see the Bibliography at the back of this book.

Glossary

Adafina A lamb stew.

Alheira A spicy Portuguese sausage.

Anusim, Anousim Those returning to the practice of Judaism after being forced to convert to Christianity in Spain or Portugal or their colonies.

Askenazy, Ashkenazim, Askenazic From the Hebrew word for "Jewish people who came from Germany," these words refer to people who came from Eastern Europe, Russia, Poland, Lithuania, as well as Middle Europe. Ashkenazim do not have Spanish or Portuguese roots.

Assimilate To mix or absorb or adapt. A person of one religion who chooses to mingle with, marry into, or convert to another religion for the sake of becoming a part of that society is said to assimilate.

Auto da fé The public manifestation of the Inquisition as an act of faith, or a ritual blood cleansing, in which those who were judged guilty of not believing in Christianity were burned in flames at the stake in the public square for all citizens to witness.

Baal Mouth.

Banuelos Doughnuts fried in oil.

Baptism The use of water on a person who is becoming a Christian, accepting Jesus Christ as a savior.

Bar Mitzvah The ceremony for a Jewish boy who at the age of thirteen years and twenty-four hours becames a contributing and responsible member of the community. For girls, the ceremony is a Bat Mitzvah, which can be celebrated at the age of twelve years and twenty-four hours.

B.C.E. Before the Christian Era (or Common Era or Current Era), or before the birth of Jesus Christ. Also called B.C.

Bendiganos A traditional Sephardic song.

Bimah The desk in the middle of a Sephardic synagogue sanctuary, from which the Torah is read. An Ashkenazic *bimah* is positioned at the front of the sanctuary.

Blood libel A written or printed statement that maliciously damages a person's reputation, such as a claim that someone was taking blood from a child to use in magic or a spell for religious purposes. Blood libels often resulted in the punishment and death of the accused.

Bolo rei "The cake of kings," a doughnut-shaped pastry.

Bull A letter, document, or statement issued by the Catholic Pope.

C.E. In the Christian Era (or Common Era or Current Era), or after the birth of Jesus Christ. Also called A.D.

Challah Traditional bread made with eggs, to be eaten with meals. Challah in a long shape is eaten on the Sabbath; a round challah is eaten on the New Year.

Cholent A stew cooked by Jews on Friday, which is left to stay warm on the stove, to be eaten on the Saturday Sabbath.

Circumcision An operation to remove the foreskin from the penis of a male. In Jewish tradition, circumcision completes the first covenant with God.

Converso A Spanish or Portuguese Jew who converted outwardly to Christianity during the Inquisition so as to avoid persecution or expulsion but who often continued to practice Judaism in secret.

Cozibo A salt brine in which vegetables are dipped.

Cristos Spanish word for "Christians."

Diaspora Exile of the Jews from their homeland to other lands, as happened following the destruction of their Temple in the sixth century B.C.E., during the Babylonian conquest. The Jews were scattered over the earth at that time and again in 70 C.E., when the Romans burned the Jews' second Temple and carried off the set of religious objects that were so important to the celebration of Jewish religious rites. The Sephardic people consider that they went out to the Diaspora when they were expelled from Spain and Portugal.

Dreidel The top used in the game *pon y saca* during the holiday of Chanukah.

Expulsion The act of sending a person out of a house, society, or country, usually as a punishment for religious, political, or social reasons. The Jewish people were expelled from Spain because of religious and economic reasons.

Fatzedas In folklore, the "Little People."

Fazenda The Portuguese name for a country estate.

Fumo A black ribbon worn by Sephardic Jews during the mourning period.

Ghetto A place where people live because they have been confined to that area by the city, state, or country—such as the ghetto in Venice for Jews.

Grand Inquisitor The person in charge of all the people acting as Inquisitors either civilly or religiously in Spain or Portugal from the 1400s to the beginning of the nineteenth century.

Grand Sanhedrin The Supreme Council for Jews, where laws other than those of the Torah are made, and where the Torah is discussed.

Halel The designated sacred place in a synagogue for the Torah scrolls.

Heresy Having an opinion or doctrine that differs from local established religious orthodoxy, particularly an unorthodox opinion concerning politics, religion, theology, or science. A heretic is someone accused of having unacceptable beliefs or traditions, as the Jews were accused by the Catholic Inquisition.

Holocaust Killing of a people, such as Jews during World War II.

Indigo A shade of blue or purple, a dye of that color, and the plant from which that dye is extracted.

Inquisition An investigation, a rigorous interrogation or scrutiny. Inquisitions were used during the decline of the Roman Empire until the Spanish and Portuguese Inquisition's decline in the early 1800s.

Inquisition origins Shortly before the Albigensian Crusades (1212 C.E.–1220 C.E.), Pope Innocent II sent three monks to Toulouse to take action against people who were thought to be heretics. The monks' actions earned them the title "Inquisitors of the Faith." In time Spain and Portugal became the most active participants in the Inquisition, which lasted for centuries.

Judias, Juderia Street and neighborhood where the Jewish community lived.

Judaism The monotheistic (one God) religion of the Jewish people, having its spiritual and ethical principles embodied chiefly in the Bible (Five Books of Moses), the Talmud, the Zohar, and other accepted Jewish religious explanations.

Kabbalah The mystical writings of Jewish philosophy and teaching, which, if followed, bring one closer to the goodness of God.

Kashrut Jewish dietary laws, including those prohibiting shellfish and pork products.

Kosher Conforming to or prepared in accordance with Jewish dietary laws, such as not eating pork or shellfish, or not mixing milk with meat on the table or in a recipe. Also slaughtering animals in a humane way so that the animal does not suffer.

Malassadas Doughnuts fried in oil such as those that are eaten during Chanukah by Sephardic Jews of Portuguese descent. The word is used in Hawaii for all doughnuts.

Malocchi In folklore, the "Evil Eye."

Marrano The Spanish word for "pig"; Spanish or Portuguese Jews who committed to the outside world to convert to Christianity under duress but without true conviction and who continued to practice Judaism in practice or reality in secret, in their own homes, and with their own families.

Mechitza A cloth that separates men from women in a synagogue, so that they can pray without being distracted by the opposite sex.

Mikveh, mikvah A place for a person to be physically and ritually cleansed.

Mimouna A Moroccan springtime celebration.

Moneylenders People who lend money and then receive the same amount back from the borrower, with more money, called interest.

Mohel A rabbi who performs circumcisions.

Mudajjam Pre-Islamic Moorish people.

Mudejar, mudecha A Moorish or Moslem architectural style used in buildings that are not occupied by Moslems or used for Moslem purposes.

Nuevo Spanish word for "new."

Nuevo Cristo (New Christian) The term given to a Jew who has converted Christianity. Usually Nuevos Cristos were Jews who had been forced to become Christians.

Oracoes Prayers.

Orthodoxy Adhering to an accepted or established doctrine, or relating to the most conservative or traditional forms of a religion, philosophy, or ideology.

Pan de semita Traditional Jewish bread.

Pan sim levadura Bread without leavening, such as the matzah eaten at Passover.

Passover A holiday in celebration of freedom, commemorating the Jews' escape from oppression under Egyptian pharaohs.

Pirinola A game played with a top during Chanukah, like *pon y saca*.

Pon y Saca A Portuguese game with a spinning top.

Pope The Bishop of Rome and leader of the Roman Catholic Church; from the Greek word for father, *"pappas"* or *"peppa."*

Pulpit A stand or high table to hold a book to read in a room.

Rabanada A special bread made in December.

Ruia Portuguese word for "street."

Sanbenito The short shirt or top in yellow with crosses on the front and back worn forcibly by the New Christians who were ordered to do so by the Inquisition.

Sanhedrin Council of Jews to make laws for Jews to follow.

Sema Flat unleavened bread baked for Passover, also called matzah.

Sephardi, Sephardic, Sephardim Jewish descendants of those people who lived in Spain and Portugal, also called the Iberian Peninsula. The words come from the Hebrew word for Spain.

Shabbat, Shabbot The Jewish Sabbath, which lasts from sundown on Friday to Saturday at sundown.

Shochet A Jewish person who kills animals in the ritualistic way which eliminates pain for the animal.

Shomer Shabbat A person who obeys the laws pertaining to the Sabbath (Friday at sundown to Saturday at sundown), by doing no work that one would ordinarily do during the other six days of the week.

Sinagoga Portuguese word for synagogue.

Spermaceti Oil from whales.

Tallis, tallit A garment worn for prayer in a synagogue, traditionally by men.

Talmus The collection of succinct rabbinic writings that form the basis of religious authority or rules of orthodox Jewish practice.

Tevah The reading desk in a synagogue.

Teshuva To return, especially a return to Judaism.

Torah The Five Books of Moses that contain the basic laws of the Jewish tradition.

Yarmulke A skullcap worn by orthodox Jewish men.

Zohar A Jewish mystical and spiritual text that comments on the Torah (Five Books of Moses), the religious doctrine of the Jewish laws and history. From the thirteenth century, the Zohar was first begun in Spain and then in Israel in Safed. The Zohar is the basis for Kabbalistic writings called the Kabbalah. To study the ways of the Torah is to bring a person closer to the goodness of living by God's laws, and therefore closer to God.

Source Notes

References in this section are abbreviated to include author and title. Detailed bibliographical information can be found in the Bibliography.

Part One: The Inquisition and the Marranos

Chapter 1. The Jews in the Iberian Peninsula

Schwartz, Howard. *Tree of Souls: The Mythology of Judaism.* pp. 76–77, 284–286.

Silver, Daniel. *Maimonidean Criticism and the Maimonidean Controversy, 1180–1240.*

Stern, David and Mirsky, Mark Jay, eds. *Rabbinic Fantasies.*

Chapter 2. The Inquisition

Alexy, Trudi. *The Mezuzah in the Madonna's Foot.*

Finkelstein, Norman H. *The Other 1492: Jewish Settlement in the New World.*

The Holy Child of La Guardia

Fita, F. "Edicto de los Reyes Catolicos," pp. 3–134.

Lea, H. C. *Chapters from the Religious History of Spain Connected with the Inquisition.* pp. 203ff.

Lea, Henry C. *A History of the Inquisition of Spain.* pp. 133–135.

Hope, Thomas. *Torquemada, Scourge of the Jews: A Biography.* pp. 153–192.

Chapter 3. The Expulsion of the Jews From Iberia

Edict of the Expulsion of the Jews, 1492

Peters, Edward. "Jewish History and Gentile Memory: The Expulsion of 1492," pp. 9–34.

Chapter 4. The Inquisition in the New World

Liebman, Seymour B. *The Inquisition and the Jews in the New World: Summaries of Procesos 1500–1810.*

Spanish and Portuguese Jews Who Made a Difference

Roth, Cecil. "Marranos," in: JHSET, 12(1931), 92–93

Kayserling, Meyer. in: *Jewish Quarterly Review*

Part Two: Interviews with Descendants of the Marranos

Chapter 5. The Interviews
Phil Pasquini (Pereira)
Pasquini, Philip L. *Indentured Immigrants: A Jewish Family Odyssey from Madeira to the Sandwich Islands.*

Part Three: Sephardic Judaism in the World

Chapter 7. Sephardic Society in the World, Country by Country
Encyclopedia Judaica. "Marrano," "Marrano Diaspora," "New Christians."
Mystica Enclopedia
Wigoder, Geoffrey. *The New Standard Jewish Encyclopedia.*

Africa
Library of Congress. *Country Studies,* February 1989.
Lobban, Richard. "The Next 500 Years."

The Ottoman Empire and Sefed
Ben-Zvi, Itzhak. *Eretz Yisrael under Ottoman rule, 1517–1917.* Volume I, pp. 602–689.

Madeira, The Azores, Bermuda, and Hawaii
Frommer, Harvey and Frommer, Myrna Katz. *The End of the Jews in the Azores.*

Central and South America
Sherman, John W. *The Mexican Right: The End of Revolutionary Reform, 1929–1940.* p. 5.

Caribbean
Ezratty, Harry A. *500 Years in the Jewish Caribbean: The Spanish & Portuguese Jews in the West Indies.*
Adel, David. "Cuba's Jews Take Heart from First New Synagogue Since Revolution."
Arnold, Michael S. "Castro's Jewish Bargaining Chip."
Asis, Dr. Moises. "Judaism in Cuba 1959–1999: A Personal Account."
Bandler, Kenneth. "Jewish Youth Lead the Way in a Long-Isolated Community."
Frank, Ben G. "The Jewish Traveler: Havana."
Anon. "Operation Cigar: A Not-So-Secret Cuban Aliya."

Italy
Avrin, Leila. *Jews in the Arts Magazine.* pp. 51–54.

Holland
Roth, Cecil. *History of the Jews in England.*

England
Yogev, Gedalia. *Diamonds and Coral: Anglo-Dutch Jews and Eighteenth-Century Trade.*

India
Hallegua, Fiona. "The Jewish Community of Cochin: Its Twilight Years."

Iran
Sharshar, Homa, ed., and Sarshar, Houman, translator. *History of Contemporary Iranian Jews.*

Iraq
Singer, David and Grossman, Lawrence, eds. *American Jewish Year Book. 2003.*

The Philippines
The World Jewish Congress

China
The World Jewish Congress
Poy, Vivienne. "The Jews in China."

United States
Sharfman, Harold. *Jews on the Frontier.*
Wirth-Nesher, H., and Kramer, M.P., eds. *Cambridge Companion to Jewish American Literature.*
Kagan, Solomon R., M.D. *Contributions of Early Jews to American Medicine.*
Historical Sketch of Congregation Shearith Israel. The Spanish and Portuguese Synagogue in the City of New York.

Some Portuguese Marranos Who Held Important Posts
American Jewish Heritage Historical Society Publication

Chapter 8. Secret Names of Portuguese and Names of Spanish Jews
Avotaynu. The International Review of Jewish Genealogy. Volume I, Number 1. January 1985.

Part Four: Teshuva, or The Return to Judaism

Chapter 9. Examples of Those Who Continue to Return to Judaism
Romero, Simon. "Hispanics Uncovering Roots as Inquisition's Hidden Jews."

Chapter 10. In Conclusion
All Mexico. The Jewish Journal. 22(4). March 16–22, 2007.
Roden, Claudia. *The Book of Jewish Food: An Odyssey from Samarkand to New York.*
Halapid, Ann de Dola Carpoza. Personal communication. Summer, 1995.

Appendix: Timelines

Spain

Lagasse, Paul, et al., eds. *The Columbia Encyclopedia: Sixth Edition.* "Antonines," "Creed," "Pelayo," "Ferdinand I, Spanish King of Castile and León," "Julius Caesar." "Alfonso VII, Spanish King of Castile and León," "Tomás de Torquemada."

Crow, John A. *Spain: The Root and the Flower: A History of the Civilization of Spain and the Spanish People.* pp. 34, 35, 38, 39.

Netanyahu, B. *The Origins of the Inquisition in Fifteenth-Century Spain.* pp. 24, 29, 33, 35, 36, 38, 39, 50, 52, 59.

Laredo, Victor. *Sephardic Spain.* pp. 27–127.

O'Callaghan, Joseph F. *A History of Medieval Spain.* p. 169.

Ashtor, Eliyahu. *The Jews of Moslem Spain: Volume 1.* pp 7, 8, 15, 283.

Pierson, Peter. *A History of Spain.* p. xiii, 31, 34, 35, 37, 40, 51.

Jones, H. Stuart. *The Roman Empire: B.C. 29–A.D. 476.* p. 108.

Gitlitz, David M. *Secrecy and Deceit: The Religion of the Crypto-Jews.* p. xiv.

Portugal

Lagasse, Paul, et al., eds. *The Columbia Encyclopedia: Sixth Edition.* "Lusitania, Roman Province,"

Livermore, H.V. *A History of Portugal.* pp. 24, 224.

Nowell, Charles E. *A History of Portugal.* p. 58.

Herculeno, Alexandre. *History of the Origin and Establishment of the Inquisition in Portugal (Volume 1, Number 2): History, Economics, and Political Science.*

Heckelman, Joseph. *The First Jews in the New World.*

The World

Lagasse, Paul, et al., eds. *The Columbia Encyclopedia: Sixth Edition.* "Narbonne," "Julius Caesar," "Holy Roman Empire."

Jones, H. Stuart. *The Roman Empire: B.C. 29–A.D. 476.* p. 108.

Glick, Leonard B. *Abraham's Heirs: Jews and Christians in Medieval Europe.* pp. 27, 33, 34.

Macdonald, Kevin. *Separation and Discontent: Toward an Evolutionary Theory of Anti-Semitism.* p. 116.

Baer, Yitzhak. *A History of the Jews in Christian Spain: Volume I, From the Age of Reconquest to the Fourteenth Century.*

Cohen, Martin A. and Peck, Abraham J., eds. *Sephardim in the Americas: Studies in Culture and History.* p. 210, 215, 216, 220, 221, 223.

Lockhart, James and Schwartz, Stuart B. *Early Latin America: A History of Colonial Spanish America and Brazil.* p. 226.

Constable, Olivia, ed. *Medieval Iberia: Readings from Christian, Moslem and Jewish Sources.*

Bibliography

Adel, David. "Cuba's Jews Take Heart from First New Synagogue Since Revolution." The Jews of Cuba, http://www.jewishcuba.org/camajuey.html, 1998.

Alexy, Trudi. *The Mezuzah in the Madonna's Foot: Marranos and Other Secret Jews—A Woman Discovers Her Spiritual Heritage.* San Francisco: HarperSanFrancisco, 1994.

Angel, Marc D. *Remnant of Israel: A Portrait of America's First Jewish Congregation, Shearith Israel.* New York: Riverside Book Company, 2004.

Anon. *Abarbanel Haggadah.* Spain. Owned by Sandra and Kenneth Malamed.

Anon. "All Mexico," in *The Jewish Journal.* 22(4). March 16–22, 2007.

Anon. *The Barcelona Haggadah.* Owned by Sanda and Kenneth Malamed.

Anon. *The Bloodletting Inquisition Records of the Child de la Guardia in Madrid and Toledo, 1683, with Torquemada in Counsel.* Owned by Sandra and Kenneth Malamed.

Anon. *Denuncuacoes e Confissoes de Pernambuco 1593–1595.* Pernambuco, Brazil: Colecao Pernambucana, Vol XIV. 2nd Fase.

Anon. *Granada Focus.* Granada, Spain: The Alhambra Historico.

Anon. "Jews of Modern Day Portugal," "Marranos Living in Portugal," in *Avotaynu, The International Review of Jewish Genealogy.* Volume I, Number 1. January 1985, pp. 1–14.

Anon. "Operation Cigar: A Not-So-Secret Cuban Aliya." Jewish Agency for Israel. http://www.jewishagency.org/jewishagency/english, October 14, 1999.

Anon. *Orden de Ros Asanah Y Kypur.* Amsterdam, 1663. Owned by Sandra and Kenneth Malamed.

Anon. *Sefer Zevach Pesach.* Venice: 1545. Owned by Sandra and Kenneth Malamed.

Anon. "The Sephardim: The Origin of Their Liturgical Customs," in *American Jewish Historical Society Quarterly Publication.* Volume LXXII, Number 2, p. 172.

Arbell, Mordecai. *Spanish and Portuguese Jews in the Caribbean and the Guianas: A Bibliography.* Providence, R.I.: John Carter Brown Library, 1999.

Arlego, Edvaldo. *Os Holandes No Nordeste.* Brazil: Edificantes, 1993.

Arnold, Michael S. "Castro's Jewish Bargaining Chip." *Jerusalem Post,* October 19, 1999.

Ashtor, Eliyahu. *The Jews of Moslem Spain: Volume 1.* Philadelphia, PA: Jewish Publication Society, 1992.

Asis, Dr. Moises. "Judaism in Cuba 1959–1999: A Personal Account." The Jews of Cuba, http://www.jewishcuba.org/asis.html, 1998.

Avrin, Leila. *Jews in the Arts Magazine*, November, 1989, pp. 51–54.

Baer, Yitzhak. *A History of the Jews in Christian Spain: Volume I, From the Age of Reconquest to the Fourteenth Century.* Philadelphia, PA: Jewish Publication Society, 1993.

Bandler, Kenneth. "Jewish Youth Lead the Way in a Long-Isolated Community." The Jews of Cuba, http://www.jewishcuba.org/bndlr1.html, 1998.

Benjamin of Tudela. *Travels of Rabbi Benjamin of Tudela.* London, 1783. Owned by Sandra and Kenneth Malamed.

Ben-Zvi, Itzhak. *Eretz Yisrael under Ottoman Rule, 1517–1917.* New York: Harper, 1960.

Blady, Ken. *Jewish Communities in Exotic Places.* New York: Jason Aronson, 2000.

Carroll, James. *Constantine's Sword: The Church and the Jews—a History.* New York: Houghton Mifflin Company, 2001.

Cohen, Martin A. and Peck, Abraham J., eds. *Sephardim in the Americas: Studies in Culture and History.* Tuscaloosa, AL: University of Alabama Press, 2003.

Constable, Olivia, ed. *Medieval Iberia: Readings from Christian, Moslem and Jewish Sources.* Philadelphia, PA: University of Pennsylvania Press, 1997.

Crow, John A. *Spain: The Root and the Flower, A History of the Civilization of Spain and the Spanish People.* New York: Harper & Row, 1975.

Ezratty, Harry A. *500 Years in the Jewish Caribbean: The Spanish & Portuguese Jews in the West Indies.* Baltimore, MD: Omni Arts, March 1997.

Finkelstein, Norman H. *The Other 1492: Jewish Settlement in the New World.* New York: Charles Scribner's Sons, 1989.

Fita, F. "Edicto de los Reyes Catolicos," in *Boletin de al Aademia de la Historia, Madrid. II (1887),* pp. 3–134.

Folberg, Neil. *And I Shall Dwell Among Them: Historic Synagogues of the World.* New York: Aperture Books, 1995.

Franco, Bartolini. *Como Nascosta.* Rome: Editoriale, 2007.

Frank, Ben G. "The Jewish Traveler: Havana." *Hadassah Magazine,* January 2005.

Freitas, J.F. *Hawaiian Memories.* Honolulu, Hawaii: Portuguese Geneaogical Society, 1930.

Frommer, Harvey and Frommer, Myrna Katz. "The End of the Jews in the Azores." January 2009.

Gitlitz, David M. *Secrecy and Deceit: The Religion of the Crypto-Jews.* Philadelphia, PA: Jewish Publication Society, 1996.

Glick, Leonard B. *Abraham's Heirs: Jews and Christians in Medieval Europe.* Syracuse, NY: Syracuse University Press, 1999.

Goldstein, Joyce. *Savoring Spain and Portugal.* New York: Time-Life Books, 2003.

Hallegua, Fiona. "The Jewish Community of Cochin: Its Twilight Years." Master's thesis, California State University, 1984.

Heckelman, Joseph. *The First Jews in the New World.* New York: Jay Street Publishing, 2004.

Herculeno, Alexandre. *History of the Origin and Establishment of the Inquisition in Portugal (Volume 1, Number 2): History, Economics, and Political Science.* Stanford, California: Stanford University Press, 1926.

Hope, Thomas. *Torquemada, Scourge of the Jews: A Biography.* London: G. Allen & Unwin, 1939.

Jones, H. Stuart. *The Roman Empire: B.C. 29–A.D. 476.* New York: G.P. Putnam's Sons, 1908.

Kagan, Solomon R., M.D. *Contributions of Early Jews to American Medicine.* Boston: Boston Medical Publishing Co., 1934.

Katz, Jacob. *Out of the Ghetto: The Social Background of Jewish Emancipation, 1770–1870.* Syracuse, NY: Syracuse University Press, 1998.

Kaufman, Tania Neumann. *Passos Perdidos, Historia Recuperada: A Presenca Judaica em Pernambuco.* Recife, Brazil: Editora Bagaco, 2000.

Kayserling, Meyer. "Christopher Columbus and the Participation of the Jews in the Spanish and Portuguese Discoveries," in *Jewish Quarterly Review*, 12 (1900), pp.708–717.

Lagasse, Paul, et al., eds. *The Columbia Encyclopedia: Sixth Edition.* New York: Columbia University Press, 2000.

Laredo, Victor. *Sephardic Spain.* Spain: Editorial Mensaje, 1978.

Lea, H.C. *Chapters from the Religious History of Spain Connected with the Inquisition.* Philadelphia: Lea Brothers and Co., 1890.

Lea, Henry C. *A History of the Inquisition of Spain.* New York: Macmillan, 1906.

Liebman, Seymour B. *The Inquisition and the Jews in the New World: Summaries of Procesos 1500–1810.* Miami, FL: University of Miami, 1973.

_____. *The Jews in New Spain: Faith, Flame, and the Inquisition.* Miami, FL: University of Miami, 1970.

Livermore, H.V. *A History of Portugal.* Cambridge, U.K.: Cambridge University Press, 1947.

Lobban, Richard. "The Next 500 Years." Saudades in http://www.saudades.org, February 11, 1996.

Lockhart, James and Schwartz, Stuart B. *Early Latin America: A History of Colonial Spanish America and Brazil.* Cambridge, U.K.: Cambridge University Press, 1983.

Macdonald, Kevin. *Separation and Discontent: Toward an Evolutionary Theory of Anti-Semitism.* Westport, CT: Praeger Publishers, 1998.

Maimonides, Rabbi. *Ha'Hogayon/Shel Hachacham.* First Edition. Owned by Sandra and Kenneth Malamed.

Mello, José Antonio Gonsalves de. *Gente da Nação: Cristaos-Novos e Judeus em Pernambuco, 1542–1654.* Recife, Brazil: Fundacao Joaquim Nabuco, 1989.

Mudd, Patricia Marirea. *Portuguese Bermudians: Early History and Reference Guide 1849–1949.* Louisville, KY: Historical Research Publishers, 1991.

Netanyahu, B. *The Origins of the Inquisition in Fifteenth-Century Spain.* 2nd ed. New York: New York Review Books, 2001.

Nowell, Charles E. *A History of Portugal.* New York: Van Nostrand Publishers, 1962.

O'Callaghan, Joseph F. *A History of Medieval Spain.* Ithaca, NY: Cornell University Press, 1983.

Pasquini, Philip L. *Indentured Immigrants: A Jewish Family Odyssey from Madeira to the Sandwich Islands.* Flypaper Press, 1999.

Peters, Edward. "Jewish History and Gentile Memory: The Expulsion of 1492," in *Jewish History*, 9 (1995), pp. 9–34.

Pierson, Peter. *A History of Spain.* Westport, CT: Greenwood Press, 1999.

Pietzschke, F. *Novo Michaelis Dicionario Ilustrado: Ingles Portugues.* Lisbon: Melhoramentos, 1984.

Poy, Vivienne. "The Jews in China." Speech given to Soloway Jewish Community Center, Ottawa, Ontario, http://sen.parl.gc.ca/vpoy/english/Special_Interests/speeches/jews_in_china_021002.htm. 2002.

Pullan, Brian. *The Jews of Europe and the Inquisition of Venice: 1550–1670.* London: I.B. Tauris, 1998.

Rembrandt van Rijn. *Dutch and Flemish Etchings; Engravings* (two books). Amsterdam: Vangendt & Co., 1967. Owned by Sandra and Kenneth Malamed.

Ribemboim, José Alexandre. *Senhores de Engenho: Judeus em Pernambuco Colonial 1542–1654.* Recife, Brazil: Comuniçao e Editora, 1995.

Roden, Claudia. *The Book of Jewish Food: An Odyssey from Samarkand to New York.* New York: Knopf, 1996.

Roland, Joan G. *Jews in British India: Identity in a Colonial Era.* Boston: Brandeis, 1989.

Romero, Simon. "Hispanics Uncovering Roots as Inquisition's Hidden Jews," in *The New York Times,* October 29, 2005.

Roth, Cecil. *History of the Jews in England.* New York: Oxford University Press, 1978.

———. "Marranos," in *Jewish Historical Society of England Transactions,* Volume XXVI, pp. 92–93.

Schwartz, Howard. *Tree of Souls: The Mythology of Judaism.* New York: Oxford University Press, 2007.

Shakespeare, William. *William Shakespeare's Plays and Sonnets.*

Sharfman, Harold. *Jews on the Frontier.* Chicago: Henry Regnery Co., 1977.

Sharshar, Homa, ed., and Sarshar, Houman, translator. *History of Contemporary Iranian Jews.* Los Angeles: Center for Iranian Jewish Oral History, pp. 97, 99.

Sherman, John W. *The Mexican Right: The End of Revolutionary Reform, 1929–1940.* Westport, CT: Praeger, 1997.

Silver, Daniel. *Maimonidean Criticism and the Maimonidean Controversy, 1180–1240.* Boston: E.J. Brill, 1965.

Singer, David and Grossman, Lawrence, eds. *American Jewish Year Book. 2003.* New York: American Jewish Committee, 2003.

Skolnik, Fred, ed. *Encyclopedia Judaica.* New York: Gale Cenage/Macmillan Reference U.S.A.

Solsten, Eric, and Meditz, Sandra W., eds. *Spain: A Country Study*. Washington: GPO for the Library of Congress, 1988.

Stern, David and Mirsky, Mark Jay, eds. *Rabbinic Fantasies*. New Haven, CT: Yale University Press, 1998.

Suarez-Fernandez, Luis, ed. *Documentos acera de la expulsion de los Judios*. Valladolid, Spain: S.S.I.C, 1964.

Wheatcroft, Andrew. *Infidels: A History of the Conflict Between Christendom and Islam*. New York: Random House, 2005.

White, William Charles. *Chinese Jews*. Toronto: University of Toronto Press, 1942.

Wigoder, Geoffrey. *The New Standard Jewish Encyclopedia*. New York: Facts on File, 1992.

Wirth-Nesher, H., and Kramer, M.P., eds. *Cambridge Companion to Jewish American Literature*. New York: Cambridge University Press, 2003.

Yerushalmi, Yosef Hayim. *From Spanish Court to Italian Ghetto: Isaac Cardoso: A Study in Seventeenth-Century Marranism and Jewish Apologetics*. New York: Columbia University Press, 1971.

Yogev, Gedalia. *Diamonds and Coral: Anglo-Dutch Jews and Eighteenth-Century Trade*. Teaneck, N.J.: Holmes & Meier, 1978.

Index of Interviewees

Index of Places

Index does not reference names in the Appendixes, Glossary, Source Notes, or Bibliography.

Index of People

Index does not reference names in the Appendixes, Glossary, Source Notes, or Bibliography.

Illustration Credits

All images were photographed from their original sources by Laird M. Malamed.

PAGE 1. **The Dominicans Predict...** Contained in a 1890 book on Lago di Como. From the collection of Sandra and Kenneth Malamed.

PAGE 6. **The Iberian Peninsula.** Courtesy of Justin D. Silverman.

PAGE 7. **Moses ben Maimonides.** Courtesy of the Spanish Embassy and the Historical Society of Cordoba, Spain.

PAGE 7. **Maimonides's *Logica*.** From the collection of Sandra and Kenneth Malamed.

PAGE 8. **Jews at the Court of Prince Henry.** Contained in *The Jewish Encyclopedia of the Spanish Inquisition,* published in Toledo, Spain, ca. 1780. From the collection of Sandra and Kenneth Malamed.

PAGE 9. **Man From the Kabbalah.** From the collection of Sandra and Kenneth Malamed.

PAGE 9. **The Barcelona Haggadah.** From the collection of Sandra and Kenneth Malamed.

PAGE 10. **Zacuto's Astrological Chart.** Courtesy of the Visitors' Center of Evora, Portugal.

PAGE 11. **Grand Inquisitor Torquemada.** Contained in *The Jewish Encyclopedia of the Spanish Inquisition.* From the collection of Sandra and Kenneth Malamed.

PAGE 14. **The Inquisition Logo.** Contained in *The Jewish Encyclopedia of the Spanish Inquisition.* From the collection of Sandra and Kenneth Malamed.

PAGE 14. **Tortures of the Inquisition.** Courtesy of the Department of Special Collections, University of Notre Dame.

PAGE 15. **An Inquisition Court in Spain.** Engraving by Bernard Picart, 1722. Courtesy of the Jewish Historical Society, Amsterdam, Holland.

PAGE 15. **The Inquisition in Lisbon.** Engraving by Bernard Picart. Courtesy of the Jewish Historical Society, Amsterdam, Holland.

PAGE 16. **Sausages Over the Fireplace.** Photograph by Kenneth Malamed.

PAGE 17. **Jews with Sanbenito Hats.** Drawing by Bernard Picart. From the collection of Sandra and Kenneth Malamed.

PAGE 18. **La Guardia, Spain.** Contained in a Blood Libel volume. From the collection of Sandra and Kenneth Malamed.

PAGE 19. **Martyr's Death Frontispiece.** Contained in a Blood Libel volume. From the collection of Sandra and Kenneth Malamed.

PAGE 21. **Nuremberg Chronicle Account of Persecution.** From the collection of Sandra and Kenneth Malamed.

PAGE 25. **Queen Isabella of Spain.** Panel of 1490, courtesy of Museo del Prado.

PAGE 26. **The Alhambra, Granada, Spain.** Photograph by Kenneth Malamed.

PAGE 27. **The Edict of Expulsion.** Contained in *The Jewish Encyclopedia of the Spanish Inquisition.* From the collection of Sandra and Kenneth Malamed.

PAGE 28. **A Friar Borrowing Money from a Jew After the Expulsion.** Contained in *The Jewish Encyclopedia of the Spanish Inquisition.* From the collection of Sandra and Kenneth Malamed.

PAGE 28. **The Expulsion of the Jews.** From the collection of Sandra and Kenneth Malamed.

PAGE 31. **Inquisition Procession in Goa.** Contained in *The Jewish Encyclopedia of the Spanish Inquisition.* From the collection of Sandra and Kenneth Malamed.

PAGE 35. **Inquisition Palace in Mexico City.** Photo courtesy of the Embassy of Mexico, Washington, D.C.